Nonprofits and Their Networks

Nonprofits and Their Networks

Cleaning the Waters along
Mexico's Northern Border

Daniel M. Sabet

The University of Arizona Press   Tucson

The University of Arizona Press
© 2008 The Arizona Board of Regents

www.uapress.arizona.edu

Library of Congress Cataloging-in-Publication Data
Sabet, Daniel M., 1976–
  Nonprofits and their networks : cleaning the waters
along Mexico's northern border / Daniel M. Sabet.
     p. cm.
  Includes bibliographical references and index.
  ISBN 978-0-8165-2618-5 (hardcover : alk. paper)
   1. Water — Pollution — Government policy — Mexico,
North — Case studies. 2. Nongovernmental
organizations — Mexico, North — Case studies. I. Title.
HC137.N6S33 2008
363.739′4609711 — dc22   2008018874

Publication of this book is made possible in part by the
proceeds of a permanent endowment created with the
assistance of a Challenge Grant from the National Endowment
for the Humanities, a federal agency.

Manufactured in the United States of America on acid-free,
archival-quality paper containing a minimum of 30% post-
consumer waste and processed chlorine free.

13   12   11   10   09   08   6   5   4   3   2   1

To the public entrepreneur

Contents

Illustrations

Tables

Acknowledgments

This work would not have been possible without the help of countless people. First and foremost, I would like to thank Elinor Ostrom, Kenneth Bickers, Kirsten Grønbjerg, and Amber Levanon-Seligson, as well as my anonymous reviewers, for providing invaluable comments and advice. My heartfelt thanks to Laura Silvan, Erik Lee, Víctor Álvarez, María Josefina Guerrero, Alma Cota de Yánez, Verónica Leyva, Gonzalo Bravo, Gustavo Córdova Bojórquez, Luciano Fernández, Irasema Coronado, José Luis Flores, Ricardo Rodríguez Aguilar, Carlos Rincón, Zetl de la Cruz García, David Negrete, Arnulfo Tejada Lara, Víctor Oliveros, Michael Layton, and Jeffrey Lockridge.

I wish to acknowledge and thank La Comisión México–Estados Unidos para el Intercambio Educativo y Cultural (COMEXUS) for the Fulbright-García Robles fellowship that funded the field research for this project; the Center for Latin American and Caribbean Studies at Indiana University; the Tinker Foundation; the Colegio de la Frontera Norte; and the Center for U.S.–Mexican Studies at the University of California, San Diego, for providing essential institutional support during the research stage of this project.

Throughout, I have been able to count on the support of my dearest Shanna, my family, colleagues, and friends.

Thank you all!

Abbreviations

AC, A.C.	*asociación civil* (civil association)
ACOPO	Asociación de Colonias Populares (Association of Popular Colonias)
APSA	Asociación de Profesionales en Seguridad Ambiental, A.C. (Environmental Security Professionals Association)
ARAN	Asociación de Reforestación en Ambos Nogales (Ambos Nogales Revegetation Partnership)
BECC	Border Environment Cooperation Commission (Comisión de Cooperación Ecológica Fronteriza)
CANACINTRA	Cámara Nacional de la Industria de Transformación (National Chamber of the Manufacturing Industry)
CBC	Christian-based community
CCC	Consejo Coordinador Ciudadano (Citizen Coordinating Council)
CDP	Comité de Defensa Popular (Popular Defense Committee)
CEC	Commission for Environmental Cooperation (Comisión de Cooperación Ambiental)
CEMEFI	Centro Mexicano para la Filantropía (Mexican Center for Philanthropy)
CERM	Center for Environmental Resource Management
CIERB	Centro Internacional de Estudios del Río Bravo (Río Bravo International Studies Center)
CIGA	Centro Industrial de Gestión Ambiental (Industrial Center for Environmental Management)
CILA	Comisión Internacional de Límites y Aguas (International Boundary and Water Commission)
CINL	Consejo de Instituciones de Nuevo Laredo (Nuevo Laredo Council of Institutions)
CISO	Centro de Investigación y Solidaridad Obrera (Center for Labor Research and Solidarity)

COAPAES	Comisión de Agua Potable y Alcantarillado del Estado (State Commission for Potable Water and Sewer)
COLEF	Colegio de la Frontera Norte (College of the Northern Border)
CONAGUA	Comisión Nacional de Agua (National Water Commission)
COPLADEM	Comisión de Planeación del Desarrollo Municipal (Municipal Commission for Planning and Development)
COREVA	Comité Regional de Vigilancia y Protección al Medio Ambiente (Regional Committee for the Monitoring and Protection of the Environment)
CRAP	Citizens Revolting against Pollution
CTM	Confederación de Trabajadores de México (Confederation of Mexican Workers)
DA	*donataría autorizada* (authorized donee)
EECC	Environmental Education Council for the Californias (Consejo de Educación Ambiental de las Californias)
EHC	Environmental Health Coalition
EPA	Environmental Protection Agency
FECHAC	Fundación del Empresariado Chihuahuense A.C. (Chihuahuan Business Foundation)
FEMAP	Federación Mexicana de Asociaciones Privadas (Mexican Federation of Private Associations)
FESAC	Fundación del Empresariado Sonorense A.C. (Sonoran Business Foundation)
FIC	Fundación Internacional de la Comunidad, A.C. (Tijuana)
GNEB	Good Neighbor Environmental Board
GPPRB	Grupo Promotor Parque Río Bravo (Rio Grande Park Promoter Group)
GUAC	Groundwater Users' Advisory Council
IAP	*institución de asistencia privada* (private assistance institution)
IBWC	International Boundary and Water Commission (Comisión Internacional de Límites y Aguas)
ICF	International Community Foundation (San Diego)
IFAI	Instituto Federal de Acceso a la Información Pública (Federal Institute for Access to Information)
IMIP	Instituto Municipal de Investigación y Planeación (Municipal Institute for Research and Planning [Ciudad Juárez])
IMPLAN	Instituto Municipal de Planeación (Municipal Insitute for Planning [Tijuana])
INEGI	Instituto Nacional de Estadística Geografía e Informática (National Institute of Statistics, Geography, and Information)

IRSC	Institute for Regional Studies of the Californias
JAP	Junta de Asistencia Privada (Private Assistance Board)
NAALC	North American Agreement on Labor Cooperation (El Acuerdo de Cooperación Laboral de América del Norte)
MNC	multinational corporation
NADB	North American Development Bank (Banco de Desarrollo de América del Norte)
NAFEC	North American Fund for Environmental Cooperation (Fondo de América del Norte para la Cooperación Ambiental)
NAFTA	North American Free Trade Agreement (Tratado de Libre Comercio de América del Norte)
OPI	Organización Popular Independiente (Popular Independent Organization)
PAN	Partido Acción Nacional (National Action Party)
PFEA	Proyecto Fronterizo de Educación Ambiental, A.C. (Border Environmental Education Project)
PRD	Partido de la Revolución Democrática (Democratic Revolution Party)
PRI	Partido Revolucionario Institucional (Institutional Revolutionary Party)
PROFEPA	Procuraduría Federal de Protección al Ambiente (Federal Attorney General's Office for Environmental Protection)
PRONASOL	Programa Nacional de Solidaridad (National Solidarity Program)
RETC	Registro de Emisiones y Transferencia de Contaminantes (Pollutant Release Transfer Registry)
SADEC	Salud y Desarrollo Comunitario de Ciudad Juárez (Health and Community Development of Ciudad Juárez)
SAT	Servicio de Administración Tributaria (Tax Administration Service)
SDSU	San Diego State University
SEMARNAT	Secretaría de Medio Ambiente y Recursos Naturales (Secretariat for the Environment and Natural Resources)
SISI	Sistema de Solicitudes de Información
SIUE	Secretaría de Infraestructura Urbana y Ecología (Secretariat of Urban Infrastructure and Ecology)
TCPS	Texas Center for Policy Studies
TRNERR	Tijuana River National Estuarine Research Reserve

I The Emergence of Civil Society Organizations

1 A New Choice

Civil Society Organizations

Introduction

In the late 1970s, Rudolfo Cota Martínez was beginning a career in politics in the northeastern Mexican border town of Nuevo Laredo. At a young age, his exemplary work on a political campaign earned him the job of personal secretary to the city's newly elected mayor. Later he was given responsibility for coordinating the implementation of the 1980 census in the region. Cota also gained experience working in the housing construction business. Through these diverse opportunities, he came to know the problems of his region and developed a great number of personal and professional contacts.

Cota Martínez observed that one of region's most salient concerns was the absence of a viable legal housing market for low-income residents. Builders had to make their way through an inefficient and at times corrupt bureaucracy, and buyers had no access to credit to help pay for housing. The result was a market that low-income residents could not afford to enter. When government policy failed to address this problem, society's most marginalized members took to invading land and building unregulated communities. However natural a response, land invasions created serious problems. Communities settled through invasion were unplanned and lacked public goods and services such as paved roads, water services, sewer lines, and electricity.

Cota argues that people like him had two options at that time. They could fight the government and, through social mobilization, protest, and contentious politics, demand better housing policy and the introduction of infrastructure such as for water and sewer services. Or they could work within the political system controlled by the Partido Revolucionario Institucional (PRI; Institutional Revolutionary Party) to achieve the same objectives. Cota opted for the latter. Using his contacts in the community and in government, Cota established the Asociación de Colonias Populares (ACOPO; Association of Popular Colonias) to serve as what he calls an "interlocutor between citizens and government." The organization grew quickly, soon becoming a political presence no administration could afford to ignore.

Cota counts it as one of the early successes of ACOPO's intermediation that the city mayor began to visit a different neighborhood, or *colonia*, every week to meet with the community, learn of its problems, and then help develop solutions. Even though many ACOPO neighborhoods lacked land rights, the government began to invest in much-needed public goods and services. Water infrastructure was the top priority in many communities. During the summer months, daily temperature highs averaged over 100 degrees. Communities without water services had to rely on water supplied by trucks and stored in large barrels. As a result, water was expensive, often in short supply, and of suspect quality. Even if originally purified, it was frequently contaminated in storage.

Cota argues that ACOPO democratized governmental decision making. Whereas previous administrations could ignore the needs of the city's low-income residents, the party and the government had to take ACOPO into account. But the organization's access to government and public goods such as water and sewer infrastructure came at a price. To serve the needs of its low-income constituents, ACOPO had to serve the needs of the party as well: it was responsible for organizing local party meetings, enrolling new members, promoting PRI candidates, and mobilizing voters on election day in the neighborhoods where it operated. Like many associational efforts in Mexico, it chose to pursue its objectives through clientelism, or the surrendering of autonomy for the promise of material benefits.

ACOPO continues to serve as a broker between low-income residents and government officials, but sacrificing its political autonomy has come at a cost. In 2002, ACOPO was forced to back down from supporting the candidate it favored for municipal president and to put the PRI's interests over those of its own constituents. The organization was further undermined when a competing organization, United Leaders (Lideres Unidos), emerged to support a rival aspirant. Even though ACOPO has lost much of its bargaining power, it loyally continues to mobilize support for the party to which it is inextricably bound.

A contrasting story can be found in Ciudad Juárez, Chihuahua. In the mid- to late 1980s, colonia residents, university students, and community activists confronted many of the same problems Cota faced before founding ACOPO. Many were working as community organizers and leaders in the liberation theology movement, a leftist movement within the Catholic Church that stressed the Church's responsibility to attend to the material and social as well as spiritual needs of its flock. Like Cota, they observed the problems created by failed housing markets, the lack of urban planning, and the absence of water and sewer services. They, too, established an organization to address these concerns; they, too, had to choose: should they fight against the PRI government or become a client within the political system?

Unlike ACOPO, however, this group of concerned citizens chose to fight. They established an organization called the "Organización Popular Independiente" (OPI; Independent Popular Organization) and, as their name suggests, declared their independence from partisan politics (and from the Church as well). They worked with communities in the western section of Ciudad Juárez and advocated for the introduction of water and sewer services in communities that were suffering in the hot Chihuahuan Desert. OPI rejected the role of intermediator that ACOPO had chosen and marched on the city hall, demanding services. Even as they confronted the government, they challenged traditional organizations and community leaders who had gained their access to power through mobilizing votes.

More important, OPI's evolutionary path differed greatly from ACOPO's. In the 1990s, as political opportunities expanded, OPI began to professionalize, hire full-time employees, develop programmatic activities, seek grant funding, and enter into formal agreements with universities, other nonprofit organizations, U.S. groups, and even government agencies. The organization continues to address community needs for basic water and sewer services, but it has more options to select from than merely mobilizing votes or marching on city call. For example, in the 1990s, OPI joined an initiative developed by the Center for Environmental Resource Management at the University of Texas at El Paso. Through a program called "Drinking Water" (Agua para Beber), OPI's health promoters went door to door in communities without water services. They delivered free water storage containers, educational materials, and water treatment kits. Health workers made regular visits, evaluated water practices and knowledge of disease transmission, described the connection between poor water storage and gastrointestinal illness, explained how to treat and properly store water, and tested chlorine levels in drinking water (for a detailed account of Agua para Beber, see Hill 2000).

Partnership with other organizations led to additional opportunities. OPI was invited to participate in a program to promote composting latrines in communities without sewer infrastructure. Perhaps most important, in 1999, OPI and several other organizations, funded by the Paso del Norte Health Foundation as part of the $1.7 million program When Water Works for Health, worked autonomously with government agencies and residents to extend water and sewer services.

Over the years, OPI's focus has evolved with the needs of the communities it serves. For many of the colonias in western Ciudad Juárez, the need for water services has given way to other needs. Thus OPI responded to the need for green spaces and recreational activities for youth by becoming a core participant in a citizen initiative to renovate a portion of a green corridor that one day may stretch the length of the Rio Grande in the Ciudad Juárez urban area. Under the umbrella of "Grupo Promotor Parque Río Bravo" (Rio Grande Park Promoter Group), it joined in a coalition with other nonprofit organizations, government agencies, construction companies, and private citizens working to that end. OPI is also involved in a number of other community-related activities, such as running preschools and participating in public security programs.

The histories of the two organizations highlight three important ways the path taken by OPI differed from ACOPO's. First, OPI managed to go beyond the choice between clientelism and contentious politics to professionalism, autonomy, and citizenship. Second, OPI's actions directly address public problems rather than lobbying for a governmental response. Instead of waiting for water and sewer services to be extended, OPI became involved in education efforts, public health campaigns, and even the construction of composting latrines in the absence of sewer services.

Third, OPI's efforts involve autonomous non-clientelistic partnership with other nonprofits, organizations on the opposite side of the border, business leaders, and even government.

The different paths taken by ACOPO and OPI are not specific to these two organizations or to Nuevo Laredo and Ciudad Juárez. Throughout Mexico's long history of social mobilization, activists have faced the choice between co-option by political patrons and radicalization against a state-held monopoly over the public sphere. Studies of social mobilization in Mexico have thoroughly documented both paths. Thus, on the one hand, Francisco Lara Valencia and Roberto Sánchez (1994; see also Cornelius 1975; Holzner 2004) have documented how associations in a few fortunate neighborhoods of Nogales, Sonora, used political ties to obtain free water infrastructure in lieu of the low-cost programs created by the water utility. And, on the other hand, Vivienne Bennett (1995; see also Eckstein 1990; Lau and Quintana Silveyra 1991) has documented how, in response to a severe crisis in the water supply, the women and neighborhood associations of Monterrey, Nuevo León, blocked streets, washed clothes in the fountains outside of city hall, and even took trucks and drivers from the water utility hostage.

Missing from the list of tactical options, however, were citizen efforts to independently engage public officials, monitor and hold government accountable, and form autonomous nonprofit organizations to address policy problems. These were simply not seen as effective. Bennett (1995) views contentious politics as a natural response by Monterrey's citizens to government foot-dragging. Faced with two unsatisfactory choices, however, many citizens became skeptical about the ability of individuals to solve public problems and cynical about the motives of those who tried.

As Mexico moves from a one-party form of government toward liberal democracy, many Mexicans have turned away from the clientelism, radicalism, and skepticism of the past in favor of autonomous collective action. There has been a dramatic growth in the number of what I refer to as "civil society organizations," such as OPI. Nonetheless, clientelistic groups such as ACOPO continue to operate much as they did under one-party rule, and many citizens remain far removed from the public realm.

A primary motivation for examining associational life is its potential for finding solutions to public problems. In the border region, there are few policy challenges as acute as those related to water. Border cities face an uncertain future water supply, low-income communities often lack water and sewer services altogether, and water contamination endangers the health of both humans and the environment itself. Governmental responses to these concerns, encumbered by cross-border political and jurisdictional divisions, have been insufficient. Economic development has also failed to bring about solutions; in many cases, industrial growth has actually exacerbated water-related problems.

The limitations of both government and the market and the challenge created by binational divisions raise the potential of what has been called the "third sector." Organizations such as OPI can bring human and financial resources to bear on public problems, advocate for better public policy, monitor and hold government officials accountable, cross political boundaries, and promote engagement in the public realm. In short, autonomous associational life can improve the functioning of democratic government not only in Mexico but also in many other developing countries whose political history has restricted the development of such groups.

To understand how autonomous nonprofit organizations emerged and developed in northern Mexico to address water-related problems along the U.S.–Mexico border, this study compares the experiences of civil society organizations in four Mexican cities: Tijuana, Baja California; Nogales, Sonora; Ciudad Juárez, Chihuahua; and Nuevo Laredo, Tamaulipas. It analyzes data from over 260 interviews with members of these organizations and with public officials, from surveys of neighborhood association leaders, and from observation of public meetings, drawing as well on extensive secondary sources.

The Nonprofit Sector and Civil Society Organizations

Many scholars have wrestled with defining a sector that is extremely diverse and complex, and some have simply concluded, "we know what civil society organizations are when we see them" (Gaberman 2003, 2; see also Olvera Rivera 2004; Verduzco 2003; and Zabin 1997). Research on nonprofit nongovernmental organizations has described this sector variously as the "nonprofit" or "independent sector," as the "voluntary," "third," or "charitable sector" or more broadly as "civil society." The

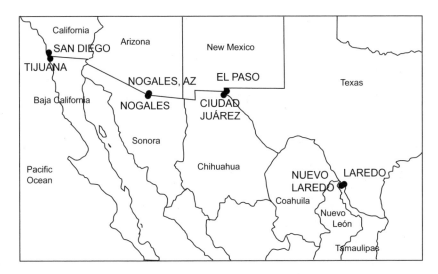

Figure 1.1.   The Mexico–U.S. border region and the four research sites

most commonly used term, "nonprofit sector," is merely a statement of what the sector is *not*, rather than what it is. Criticizing the term, Roger Lohmann (2001) asks rhetorically whether "lettuce" should be referred to as a "nonanimal."

The nonprofit sector, broadly understood to include neighborhood associations, social clubs, professional organizations, unions, churches, and private schools, has a long history in Mexico (Forment 2003). Data from 1996 revealed that private education accounted for over 40 percent of the sector's employment (Verduzco, List, and Salamon 1999). Professional associations and trade unions accounted for an additional 30.5 percent. What is newer to Mexico's nonprofit sector, however, are organizations such as OPI that are neither political nor parochial, which is to say, organizations that are independent from government, not guided by political ambition, and primarily concerned with solving public rather than private problems. I refer to these groups as "civil society organizations."

The term "civil society" speaks to both a much larger and a more specific concept than the term "nonprofit sector." The notion of civil society attempts to capture the tension between individualism and the interdependencies that connect private citizens to one another to create what John

Dewey (1927) calls "the public." It is in the space termed "civil society" that individuals interact with one another to address these interdependencies. The existence of a civil society attests to the fact that solutions to problems produced by such interdependencies are not necessarily the sole jurisdiction of governments or the invisible hand of self-interest. Instead, they also depend on the human agency of concerned citizens, working together and operating on the basis of enlightened self-interest, or what Alexis de Tocqueville termed "self-interest properly understood." Civil society thus includes not only formal associations and organizations but also more loosely formed social movements and concerned citizens engaged in the public arena (Olvera Rivera 2004).

In this analysis, I follow the use of the term "civil society" in much of the current literature on democratic transitions (for an excellent review of the many different approaches to and conceptualizations of civil society generally, see Hodgkinson and Foley 2003; on civil society within the Mexican context, see Olvera Rivera 2004). Revolutionaries and intellectuals in Eastern Europe such as Adam Michnik and Vaclav Havel, building on the Gramscian notion of civil society, viewed it as an arena where they could challenge the hegemony of the political order. Scholars of democratic transitions have observed that, in locations as diverse as South Korea, Taiwan, Chile, Poland, Czechoslovakia, South Africa, Nigeria, Benin, Brazil, and Mexico, civil society has played a major role in leading a transition from authoritarian to democratic regimes (Diamond 1999). From this perspective, the actors of civil society are normatively viewed as democratic actors, challenging the hegemony and checking the power of the state.

Larry Diamond (1999) distinguishes civil society from economic, political, and parochial society. Like the term "nonprofit sector," Diamond's use of "civil society" excludes endeavors that have a profit-making objective—what Diamond calls "economic society." It also excludes governmental agencies and bodies and what Diamond calls "political society." His interpretation of political society, whose goal he sees as winning control of the state or some part of it, is actually much broader than government alone. It also includes political parties and clientelistic organizations co-opted by the state or subordinate to political patrons. Therefore, in Diamond's and my view, civil society excludes organizations and individuals that use nonprofit organizations as a vehicle to win elections or gain an appointed position. The exclusion of political society, broadly understood, is of primary importance in the Mexican context, where societal forms of organization have traditionally been controlled by the state and have overlapped with the political sphere.[1] This overlap persists at least to some extent, and many citizens remain distrustful of the motives of nonprofit organizations. This distrust represents a major threat to the sector's development, for it is civil society's lack of political and economic ambition that provides it with credibility before the broader public.

Diamond also separates civil society from what he terms "parochial society," which includes the family, many social clubs, religious institutions, and business associations that are not primarily concerned with public affairs.[2] Professional associations, for example, exist to improve the economic performance of their members in the marketplace. Many social clubs, such as the famous example of bird-watching groups, exist for the pleasure of their members and, for the most part, address no public concerns. Religious institutions are frequently more focused on the spiritual realm than public issues. It is not that these organizations are unimportant to developing a more democratic society. Robert Putnam (1993) provides evidence that such groups bring people together in what Tocqueville called the "art of association," producing norms of trust and reciprocity that strengthen not only democracy but also economic development. Because, however, they have only an indirect impact on policy matters and often exemplify only parochial rather than public concerns, these groups are not the focus of Diamond's or this study. Nonetheless, if a business association becomes nervous about the availability of water in the city, a bird-watching group grows concerned about the effects of pollution on bird habitat, or a religious institution begins to worry about the physical needs of its congregation, then all of these groups might choose to participate in civil, rather than parochial, society.

Accordingly, I use the terms "nonprofit" and "third sector" to refer to a broad and diverse set of associational life that is nongovernmental and does not seek to earn a profit. Although this study will examine a number of different nonprofit organizations, including professional associations, clientelistic groups, the church, and universities, it is particularly concerned with the emergence and development of a specific subset of the nonprofit sector, civil society organizations, which are decidedly independent of the political realm and focused on the resolution of public problems.

Water Problems along the Border and the Importance of Civil Society Organizations

The U.S.–Mexico border stretches 2,000 miles from the Tijuana–San Diego region in the west to the Matamoros-Brownsville region in the east. The international border is shared by 6 Mexican and 4 U.S. states, including 38 Mexican municipalities and 25 U.S. counties.[3] The border region's most salient feature is its dramatic industrial and population growth, particularly along the Mexican side. Economic integration of the U.S. and Mexican economies and the international division of labor have converted the region into a center of industrial production. Industry is dominated by maquiladoras, manufacturing plants on the Mexican side of the border that take advantage of geographical proximity, favorable tax and business laws, and lower labor costs to produce goods for the U.S. market. The creation of the maquiladora industry began in 1965 with the Border Industrialization Program (Programa de Industrialización Fronteriza) and was accelerated by the North American Free Trade Agreement (NAFTA), which went into effect in 1994. The growth of the industry has produced an inflow of migrants from the interior of the country in search of work. At the industry's peak in 2000, there were 3,590 maquiladoras operating throughout Mexico, employing around 1.02 million maquiladora workers in the six Mexican border states (Clement 2002).

Border cities also serve as a stopping point for migrants traveling to the United States. Although the number of people crossing into the United States from Mexico without proper documentation is unknown because many border crossers are arrested more than once, the U.S. Border Patrol reports that it made approximately 1.3 million apprehensions during 2006. As a result of internal migration and external emigration to the United States, the population along the border has grown considerably. Tijuana's population grew from a mere 165,000 in 1960 to more than 1.4 million by 2005. Although population growth along the border has slowed somewhat, Mexico's National Institute of Statistics, Geography, and Data Processing shows that, from 2000 to 2005, the four Mexican border communities examined in this study grew at more than twice the rate of Mexico generally (2.7 versus 1.2 percent).

The economic boom in the border region has been at best a mixed blessing. Urban users must vie with the agricultural sector and the environment for the region's already over-allocated water resources. Moreover, population and industrial growth has produced an increase in human and industrial waste, which threatens to contaminate existing water resources and damage the fragile desert ecosystem. Although, in theory, the region's economic growth should have generated sufficient wealth to address the negative consequences of industrial growth, in practice, this has not been the case.

In light of these problems, governmental responses such as planning, zoning, protection of aquifer recharge points, preservation of crucial habitat areas, efficient water and sewer infrastructure extension, water conservation programs, water metering, and industry regulation could all facilitate the sustainable development of the region. Despite their attempts to address these issues, however, agencies and officials in the border region have for a variety of reasons been unable to respond sufficiently to the negative side effects of growth. As a result, land invasions still occur; strategic plans are not fully followed; the extension of water, sewer, and wastewater treatment infrastructure lags behind growth; existing infrastructure is not properly maintained; crucial habitat and aquifer recharge areas are not sufficiently protected, nor are environmental regulations adequately enforced.

Given the inability of either markets or government to effectively address these problems, attention has turned to the third sector generally (Douglas 1983; Hansmann 1987; Weisbrod 1988). Civil society organizations in the nonprofit sector offer a means to overcome such failures through two routes. First, such organizations can directly confront public problems neglected by the market and government. Second, they can advocate for improved public policy and promote accountability in both the private and public sector through monitoring and oversight.

As nongovernmental, nonprofit entities, civil society organizations have attributes that both government and the market lack. James Douglas (1983) lays out several constraints that prevent the state from effectively addressing many of society's problems. He argues that elected, Western-style government (1) implements policy in a uniform and universal fashion, (2) responds to the majority, (3) operates with a short, electoral time horizon, (4) lacks sufficient local knowledge, (5) and utilizes a large unwieldy bureaucracy. On the other hand, Douglas (1983) contends that third sector organizations do not face these constraints: because they are private, do not depend on majority approval, are able to leverage funds from different sources, possess specialized knowledge, and are small and flexible, nongovernmental nonprofits can produce goods and services that government is unable to deliver.

In Tijuana, for example, economic and population growth has created problems for the city's coastal area. Wastewater production in Tijuana exceeds its treatment capacity, and despite evidence of toxicity in the wastewater, untreated sewage is introduced into the environment with only chlorine injections. Large amounts of trash also harm the beach environment and devalue coastal property. Although the municipal government offers garbage collection services, trash is visible all along the beaches and surrounding properties. Industrial and population growth and user fees for services have failed to generate sufficient revenues to address these problems. Moreover, government efforts are also hindered by the behavior of the many residents, beachgoers, and migrants who contribute to the contamination problem.

Recognizing the failure of government to provide adequate services and of citizens to take collective action, several individuals and organizations have sought to develop solutions on their own. A coalition of local nonprofits and concerned citizens formed JaJan, meaning "good water" in the Pai Pai indigenous language. The group monitors the quality of ocean water and makes the information available to the public. More important, the organization seeks to get young people and adults involved in the water monitoring process as a means to teach about the importance of water quality and a clean environment. In addition, several times a year the Proyecto Fronterizo de Educación Ambiental (PFEA; Border Environmental Education Project) organizes members of the community (particularly students) in massive trash cleanup campaigns. The organization not only picks up the trash but it also documents all that is collected and how much it weighs as a means to make the overwhelming quantities of garbage known to the community.

Through their work, the individual members of JaJan and PFEA are not only responding to problems that the market and the government have failed to address, they are also educating citizens about environmental concerns and promoting citizen participation in their own self-governance. As a result of their activities, the beaches in Tijuana are cleaner, and citizens are more aware of the problems of pollution and environmental degradation.

Accountability exists when public officials face consequences for acting outside the law or for failing to perform their entrusted duties. Many scholars have noted the role played by civil society organizations both in promoting better public policy and in holding government officials accountable (Clark, Fox, and Treakle 2003; Scholte 2004; and Siddiquee 2005). In a study of global governance, Jan Scholte (2004) finds that civil society increases public transparency, monitors and reviews public policy, seeks redress for mistakes made by government officials, and advances the creation of accountability mechanisms. Nonprofit and civil society organizations use citizen oversight and monitoring (e.g., requesting and analyzing public information) as well as citizen voices and participation (e.g., at protests, in letters to elected officials; at complaint proceedings, judicial venues, public meetings) to pressure officials and hold them to account when they fail to address public problems.

In Tijuana, for example, the PFEA worked with government officials and other members of civil society to develop the city's municipal environmental regulations (*reglamento municipal para la protección del medio ambiente*). In addition, PFEA and others have played an important role in promoting right-to-know, or transparency, legislation in Mexico (Kelly 2002).

One of the most notable efforts to hold government and private sector accountable to Mexico's environmental laws is the fight against Metales y Derivados, a U.S.–based company in Tijuana's Mesa de Otay industrial park that extracted lead, copper, and phosphorous from batteries and scrap metal from 1972 to 1994. Rather than properly dispose of the waste produced in the extraction process, the plant illegally stockpiled it on the premises (CEC 2002). Carried through the air and rain runoff to the densely populated community below the Otay Mesa, the toxic waste put local children at risk for lead poisoning and other ailments. In response to the pollution, the Comité Ciudadano Pro-Restauración del Cañón del Padre (Padre Canyon Restoration Citizen Committee) with the support of the San Diego–based Environmental Health Coalition (EHC) led protests against the plant. Under considerable public pressure, Mexican authorities finally shut down the operation in 1994.

Nonetheless, the Metales y Derivados problem was far from resolved: the pollutants, estimated at 6,000 metric tons, remained at the site. Continuing their strategy of public pressure, the committee and EHC also filed a complaint in 1998 with the Commission for Environmental Cooperation (CEC), a trinational commission established under the side agreements to the NAFTA. The CEC's Citizen Submissions on Enforcement Matters process allows citizens an opportunity to report instances of a NAFTA member country's failure to observe its own environmental laws. Following a lengthy investigation period, in 2004, the CEC issued its factual findings, which supported the claims made by the committee and EHC (CEC 2002; see also Yang 2004).

Nevertheless, there was still resistance to the expensive cleanup effort and disagreement over who should foot the bill. The committee and the EHC, now joined by the voice of a new organization called the Colectivo Chilpancingo (Chilpancingo Collective), maintained the pressure on government officials. Finally, in 2004, with joint Mexican and U.S. funding, an initial cleanup effort was undertaken. The final stage of the $900,000 remediation project is slated for completion in 2008. Although resolution of the Metales y Derivados problem has been slow in coming and some contamination still remains, the case highlights the important role of civil society organizations in demanding action and accountability on the part of public officials. Had these organizations not insisted, it is doubtful that environmental laws would ever have been enforced.

Addressing Binational Policy Problems

Civil society organizations play an even more important role in addressing binational water-related policy concerns. Although governments everywhere face constraints, these constraints increase dramatically in border regions. And water-related policy problems along the U.S.–Mexico border are typically binational. Contamination or use of water resources on one side affects the quality or availability of water resources on the other. Thus neither the Mexican nor the U.S. government is able unilaterally to address most water-related concerns. The governments of the two countries can and often do collaborate, but cooperation is frequently frustrated by competing interests, asymmetric financial resources, and cultural and communication barriers. As Helen Ingram, Nancy Laney, and David Gillilan (1995, 5) explain, "What should be optimally treated as a unified whole is managed instead through different and often conflicting regimes. Boundaries fragment legal and political power, with the result that there is no single jurisdiction with the power to make and enforce decisions."

Even though both governments' legal jurisdictions stop at the political boundary, border residents have to confront the binational nature of life in the region. However better equipped their representatives are to deal with purely domestic issues, these residents have a strong interest in ensuring that binational problems are also resolved. To that end, citizen initiatives are leading efforts to resolve binational problems all along the border.

Perhaps the biggest challenge in the region is limited water supply amid high demand. During the drought years of the late 1990s and early 2000s, binational disputes over water supply in the Rio Grande and Colorado River basins became major sources of contention between the two countries (Sánchez Munguía 2004; TCPS 2002). In the Paso del Norte region, Ciudad Juárez and El Paso, Texas, both draw water from the Hueco Bolson, a large underground aquifer. No binational agreement exists over the use of the aquifer, which is consequently being exploited at an unsustainable rate. Because overexploitation threatens to produce a tragedy of the commons, university professors, nonprofit organizations, and large water users have formed a binational coalition to address the region's water supply problem. The subsequent Paso del Norte Water Task Force followed on the heels of a previous task force that had successfully improved air quality in the region and led to the creation of a binational citizen advisory committee. Many of this initial group's protagonists hoped to build on their success by tackling the even more complicated challenge of water supply.

With foundation funding, the water task force has held a series of conferences and meetings where water users and experts in the region have together analyzed the possibility of creating common water markets for agricultural and urban water users, studied water-saving mechanisms, facilitated the transfer of technology between the El Paso and Ciudad Juárez water utilities, and standardized the flow of information between the United States and Mexico, which use different criteria for measuring water use. In an interview, one of the promoters of the effort argued that, as a citizen initiative, the task force allows key stakeholders the opportunity to speak openly and think creatively in a way they never could within the confines of an official binational meeting. Understanding the role of efforts such as the Paso del Norte Water Task Force in addressing the challenges of binational water resource management is important not only for the U.S.–Mexico border: Ingram, Laney, and Gillilan (1995) note that almost 40 percent of the world's people live in river basins shared by more than one nation.

In summary, civil society organizations have the potential to effectively address public problems, promote behavioral change among citizens, develop improved public policies, transcend political borders, and hold government officials and for-profit sector actors accountable to the law and standards of good governance. Despite its own limitations, the nonprofit sector offers advantages that can be found in neither the state nor the for-profit sector. Unlike the government, nonprofits have the flexibility of corporations in the marketplace. And, unlike corporations, civil society organizations do not operate for pecuniary gain and seek public rather than parochial benefits. As the above examples illustrate, through participation in a civil society organization, citizens need to wait neither for a mysterious market mechanism nor for an unresponsive government agency: they can engage in their own self-governance. Speaking to these sentiments, Carlos Forment (2003, 211) quotes a Mexican editorialist from 1846:

> Our citizens know best how to administer their own professional affairs, artisan workshops and farms, and so by consulting and seeking assistance from each other, relying mainly on associative ties rather than government intervention to get ahead. Citizens have a direct, immediate interest in their affairs. . . . The 400,000 sovereign citizens [male electors] in this country must not lose sight of the power they have to create associations and use them to limit the state.

Further Potential and Limitations

Although the primary focus in this book is the pragmatic resolution of public problems, another body of literature, concerned with deepening democracy and constructing social capital and descended from Tocqueville's *Democracy in America*, is worthy of mention. This literature also relates civil society to the functioning of democracy, but in a less direct, albeit more fundamental way. Gabriel Almond and Sidney Verba (1963) argue that participation in associational life helps create a civic culture and that participation in nonprofits correlates with support for democracy, trust in others and government, and willingness to participate in civic life. Putnam (1993) and the growing literature on social capital argue that, through collective participation, individuals develop the norms of trust and reciprocity necessary for democracy. Associational life that crosses society's ethnic, geographical, and ideological divisions produces what Putnam (2000, 23) calls "bridging social capital," or "sociological WD-40."

Tocqueville (1969, 517) was referring to such impacts when he said, "Among laws controlling human societies there is one more precise and clearer, it seems to me, than all the others. If men are to remain civilized or to become civilized, the art of association must develop and improve among them at the same speed as equality of conditions." He further argued that participation in associational life creates the "habits of the heart" that facilitate cooperation and create a culture supportive of democratic governance.

Notwithstanding the clear benefits of an organized civil society, one cannot assume that civil society organizations all share the same understanding of public problems or that they prefer the same responses. As several authors have asked, how can one view nonprofits as agents of the public interest when they disagree over the definition of that interest? (Carothers and Barndt 2000; Foley and Edwards 1996). As a reflection of the broader public, civil society is characterized by the same inequalities, divisions, and diversity of interests that can be found in society itself (Foley and Hodgkinson 2003). Thus Carothers and Barndt (2000, 21) argue: "Struggles over the public interest are not between civil society on the one hand and bad guys on the other but within civil society itself."

For all that, the nonprofit sector has the potential to enrich democratic governance and to produce the norms of trust and reciprocity necessary to reduce conflict and produce cooperation. If we conclude that civil society organizations and the nonprofit sector are important, then we must ask how they emerge and develop.

The Emergence of Civil Society Organizations in Mexico

Civil society organizations emerge when autonomous citizens, concerned about the public problems that affect their lives and those of their families, friends, and neighbors, step forward to effect change. These citizens can be seen as public or social entrepreneurs. Like their counterparts in the for-profit sector, they bear the initial costs of collective action, but, unlike business entrepreneurs, they do so with the hope of producing a public, rather than a solely private, benefit (for a discussion of the public entrepreneur, see Oakerson and Parks 1988; Ostrom 1965; Schumpeter 1942).

The transformation from concerned citizen to public entrepreneur is by no means a simple process. No action can be expected from citizens who believe they have no power to effect change; active efforts to address public problems require an investment of time and energy that must compete with a host of other work, family, and leisure commitments. Furthermore, participating in associational life is only one of several tactical routes available to concerned citizens: individuals motivated to action might select clientelistic strategies rather than public entrepreneurship. Finally, there are the collective action problems inherent in associational efforts.

All of these factors are affected by concerned citizens' institutional environment. "Institutions are the rules of the game in a society or, more formally, are the humanly devised constraints that shape human interaction" (North 1990, 3). Rules can be formal — such as established constitutions, laws, regulations, and procedures — or they can be informal such as norms, conventions, customs, and standards. They define what actions are required, prohibited or permitted, and they delineate (although at times informally) appropriate sanctions for breaking rules (Crawford and Ostrom 1995). Individual rules can be nested within one another, support one another, or contradict one another. The rules of the game in a given country or community can either favor or disfavor public entrepreneurship. Unfortunately, Mexico's political history and the informal rules that supported a one-party political system have traditionally discouraged the founding of civil society organizations.

One-Party Rule and Political Opportunity

Charles Tilly (1978, 98) argues that collective action cannot occur unless there is "the opportunity to act together." As the experiences of ACOPO and OPI and the academic literature attest (e.g., Stokes 1995), potential public entrepreneurs in closed political systems have historically had to choose between co-option and radicalization. For both groups, autonomous citizenship strategies were not perceived as an effective option. Scholars consistently blame the absence of autonomous nonprofits during almost all of the twentieth century squarely on state efforts to control societal forms of organization (Cook, Middlebrook, and Molinar Horcasitas 1994; Hernández and Fox 1995; Olvera Rivera 2004; Teichman 1988; Verduzco 2003).

It could even be argued that Mexico has lacked the opportunity to engage in the form of self-governance represented by civil society organizations until quite recently. According to Rico Valero (2002), associational life was dominated through the first half of the nineteenth century by the Catholic Church, which was the primary beneficiary of philanthropic contributions from Mexico's elite.[4] In 1899, reluctant to surrender too much control to private and religious initiatives, the government of Porfirio Díaz created the *instituciones de asistencia privada* (IAPs; institutions of private assistance; Rico Valero 2002), which allowed for the existence of a philanthropic sector while maintaining strict governmental control (Carillo Gamboa 1997). Díaz laid the foundation, but it was the rise of the Institutional Revolutionary Party (PRI) that cemented the state's dominance over private initiatives in the public realm.

A great deal has been written on the corporatist and clientelistic nature of the Mexican state throughout most of the twentieth century (Chalmers and Piester 1995; Cornelius 1975; Fehrenbach 1995; Hernández and Fox 1995; Krauze 1998; Spalding 1981; Wiarda 1973; Verduzco 2003). Briefly, in the two decades after the Mexican Revolution, a diverse set of societal actors were incorporated into one political party, which would eventually become known as the "Partido Revolucionario Institucional" (PRI; Institutional Revolutionary Party). The party succeeded in managing the conflict between factions in Mexican politics by incorporating a broad spectrum of social actors under its umbrella. Formal organizations were created to speak for different social groups within the party — and consequently the government. Even the business community's access to government was channeled through mandatory business chambers, frequently dominated by the government, the party, or powerful political figures. As Evelyn Stevens (1974, 94) writes, "the regime's success in limiting, discouraging and manipulating [citizen] input is the system's most distinguishing characteristic." Thus, even though societal organizations formally existed during the semi-authoritarian era, they were heavily dependent on the political machine.

Unfortunately, the informal rules of Mexican politics during one-party rule did not offer political opportunities for autonomous problem-solving citizenship. The statist philosophy underlying the PRI regime gave the state, rather than self-governing citizens, the responsibility for the public realm. The Mexican government became a "benefactor state" or, as Octavio Paz (1979) famously put it, the "philanthropic ogre," responsible for the well-being of all its citizens. Ann Craig and Wayne Cornelius (1980, 355) assert that "Mexicans seem to have assessed the utility of participation in such limited 'democratic' institutions as are available to them, and to have concluded that their interests are best served by abstention or participation through brokers." Gustavo Verduzco (2003) contends that *priista* hegemony pervaded all aspects of public life even as late as the 1990s.

Nonetheless, Howard Wiarda (1973; Wiarda and Guajardo 1988) points out that the PRI's model was unsustainable. He contends that the system required an ever-expanding economic pie to keep passing out slices to new clients without denying old ones theirs. Once that pie stopped expanding, the system began to fall apart. The Mexican political and economic system was in fact in decline in the 1970s, but political leaders were able to financially prop it up using high oil revenues and unsustainable state spending (Rubio and Newell 1984). When oil prices declined sharply in 1982, the economy collapsed. As a result, the incoming administration of Miguel de la Madrid Hurtado (1982–1988) was forced to undertake major economic reforms and to sacrifice the state's dominant position in the economy. The government began to sell off state-owned enterprises and to reduce subsidies for public goods. As the Mexican state surrendered its control over the economy, it was no longer able to subsidize its political bases, which dramatically reduced patronage to client groups (Bizberg 2003).

Electoral changes also altered the relationship between state and society. Conventional wisdom traces the opening of the political system to the 1968 massacre of student protestors at Tlatelolco in Mexico City. The murder of between 200 and 300 protestors and the subsequent cover-up of the incident produced calls for political change. To pacify the regime's critics, the Mexican state gradually began to implement political reforms. For example, in 1977, a partial proportional representation voting system was incorporated into the method to determine seats in the Chamber of Deputies. This reform allowed opposition parties greater representation in the legislature. After additional reforms in 1986, 200 of 500 seats in the chamber were determined by proportional representation. By 1987, the PRI had lost enough seats in the legislature that it could no longer unilaterally amend the constitution. That same year, the PRI witnessed a large-scale defection, and in the 1988 elections the party barely maintained control of the presidency amid allegations of fraud.

For a variety of reasons, including his own administration's lack of democratic legitimacy, the new president Carlos Salinas de Gortari (1988–1994) was forced to recognize the first opposition party victory of a state governorship in 1989 (in Baja California). Political change accelerated under the administration of Ernesto Zedillo Ponce de León (1994–2000). In 1996, for example, the body responsible for overseeing elections, the Federal Electoral Institute, became independent of the executive branch. On the heels of opposition victories for governors, deputies, senators, and municipal presidents, Vicente Fox Quesada of the Partido Acción Nacional (PAN; National Action Party) won the presidency in 2000. With the advent of electoral competition and the ascent of opposition parties to power, membership in the PRI structure no longer guaranteed access to government resources, effectively ending monopoly dependence on the PRI.

Electoral and economic changes also favored administrative reforms that decentralized public administration and opened it to public participation and scrutiny. Decentralization is often celebrated as bringing the policy process closer to citizens (Peterson 1997). If the locus of power is at city hall, rather than the state or national capital, it lowers the transaction costs that citizens must absorb to participate in public affairs. In fact, Presidents de la Madrid and Salinas marketed their decentralization reforms with the phrase "decentralizar es democratizar" (to decentralize is to democratize) (Rodríguez 1997; on the mixed relationship between democratization and decentralization, see Rodríguez 1997; Selee 2006; Ward and Rodríguez 1999). There have been particularly strong calls for decentralization along the border. Practitioners and scholars involved in addressing water-related problems there have viewed federal jurisdiction and formal binational negotiations to be a major obstacle to the timely resolution of regional water problems (Herzog 1990; Lara 1999; Mumme and Brown 2002). Under a centralized system, it is argued that those who have the greatest stake in finding solutions are essentially locked out of the process.

Major decentralization began in 1984 following reforms to Article 115 of the Mexican constitution. Despite the democratic rhetoric, evidence suggests that the administrations of de la Madrid and Salinas viewed decentralization as a political tool (Cornelius, Craig, and Fox 1994). As Victoria Rodríguez (1997, 57) writes, "Broadly speaking, the decentralization policy of both de la Madrid and Salinas pursued the general premise that, by strengthening government (and the party) at the lower levels, the stability of the system could be preserved." During his first week in the presidency, Salinas instituted the Programa Nacional de Solaridad (PRONASOL; National Solidarity Program), a public spending program that involved local committees in spending decisions. Despite the impressive social spending achieved under PRONASOL, research shows that the program's investments were targeted at key electoral areas and sought to regain PRI support among voters (Cornelius, Craig, and Fox 1994).[5] Peter Ward and Victoria Rodríguez (1999) argue that, by the time Ernesto Zedillo took office amid a new economic crisis in 1995, however, he was forced to implement the reformist rhetoric of his predecessors.

Thus economic decline, which dried up government patronage, and the rise of electoral competition, which ended dependence on the PRI, threatened the informal rules that held together the corporatist-clientelistic system and created new opportunities for the emergence of autonomous nonprofit organizations. This process was facilitated by decentralization reforms that brought government closer to the people and lowered the transaction costs of civil society participation in the policy process. As the state receded and decentralized, the rationale for clientelistic dependence on political patrons and the party diminished as well.[6] Potential public entrepreneurs today have an unprecedented opportunity to act autonomously. Stated in the economic terms of an entrepreneur, the probability of receiving a return on an investment of time and energy in autonomous organization has increased significantly.

Indeed, in response to these changes, the nonprofit sector has grown considerably. The exact number of Mexican nonprofit organizations is not known because such organizations exist both formally and informally and under several different legal auspices (Layton 2004). Nonetheless, Consuelo Castro Salinas (2001) finds that the number of Mexico's authorized donees, considered by the taxing authority to be tax exempt and thus able to offer tax-deductible receipts, grew at an average annual rate of 34 percent between the years 1995 to 1999, from 1,426 to 4,594. By 2005, this number had increased to 5,447 and in fact would have been considerably larger were it not for changes in regulatory policies.

Persistent Informal Rules

Although, by most accounts, today's Mexico is a democratic nation with a growing civil society, there are compelling reasons for only restrained optimism. Douglass North (1990, 6) notes that, after a revolution and a changing of the formal political system, informal rules often continue unaltered: "Although formal rules may change overnight as the result of political or judicial decisions, informal constraints embodied in customs, traditions, and codes of conduct are much more impervious to deliberate policies. These cultural constraints not only connect the past with the present and future but also provide us with a key to explaining the path of historical change." Thus, he argues, revolutions produce change, but path-dependent change. Path dependency, according to North (1990), occurs when choices made in the past affect the range of options available in the future.

A political opportunity approach to institutions assumes that citizens and potential public entrepreneurs are merely waiting for the chance to abandon clientelism and dependency and throw off cynicism and feelings of powerlessness in favor of forming nonprofit organizations and taking personal responsibility for public problems. However, electoral political opportunities make up only one part of the institutional environment. Even after a transition to democracy, one cannot assume that the diverse mix of informal rules that grew to support the PRI regime over the course of over seventy years will disappear. For example, an article written by the Centro Mexicano para la Filantropía (CEMEFI; Mexican Center for Philanthropy) in 1996 argued that the dominance of the state and Church throughout Mexican history has produced a "deeply rooted paternalistic and state culture in which most individuals expect the government to do everything for them" (CEMEFI 1996, 188). Such a culture would certainly suppress the emergence of public entrepreneurs and their ability to attract support. In fact, the end of one-party rule might only result in an associational life with loyalties divided among diverse political parties, as has occurred in other countries (Gay 1994; Weyland 1996). Unfortunately, the continuation of partisan organizations such as ACOPO and recent academic literature (CEMEFI 1996; Fox 1994; Holzner 2004) suggest that informal rules of clientelism do persist in some areas of the Mexican political landscape.

Although some citizens might maintain what Almond and Verba (1963) have called a "subjective political culture" friendly to clientelism, survey data suggest that a more dominant informal constraint is skepticism and cynicism. Despite the changes in Mexican democracy, if people feel that the rules of politics continue much as before, then they can be expected to respond to the perceived choice between co-option and radicalism with simple nonengagement and even cynical resignation. National surveys such as the 2003 National Survey on Political Culture and Citizenship Practices (ENCUP) consistently offer negative evaluations of the state of Mexican democracy (Secretaría de Gobernación 2003). Despite (or perhaps because of) high commitment to the idea of democracy, when asked whether Mexico was a democracy, only 37.2 percent of survey respondents said that it was. Over 50 percent felt that the government was more authoritarian than democratic and that it made choices on its own without consulting citizens. When asked how much citizens could influence the decisions of government, 43.1 percent said a little and 13.3 percent said not at all.

These attitudes of skepticism and cynicism are not just directed at the government. In the 1999–2000 World Values Survey, over 1,500 Mexicans were asked, "Generally speaking, would you say that most people can be trusted or that you need to be very careful in dealing with people?" In response, 78.2 percent said that you needed to be very careful. When asked, "Do you think most people would try to take advantage of you if they got a chance, or would they try to be fair?" 62.6 percent said that they would take advantage. Although interpersonal distrust in Mexico is comparable to that in other Latin American countries, it is far higher than in advanced industrial democracies (Moreno 2002).

This distrust carries over into the nonprofit sector as well. The 2005 National Survey on Philanthropy and Civil Society (Encuesta Nacional sobre Filantropía y Sociedad Civil, or ENAFI) found that, although Mexicans donated time and money to nonprofit organizations, a significant number only appeared to do so through their church (Proyecto sobre Filantropía y Sociedad Civil 2005). When asked whether they preferred to give directly to a needy person or through an institution or organization, 79 percent said they preferred to give directly, whereas only 13 percent said through an institution or organization. When asked to what extent people distrusted organizations that asked for donations, 45 percent reported some or a lot. These negative attitudes toward the nonprofit sector are significant because one of the hallmarks of the sector is the trust that people are supposed to have in its noneconomic and nonpolitical motives (Weisbrod 1988).

These prominent surveys suggest that the informal constraints of distrust, cynicism, and skepticism are widespread. If there is an expectation that emerging public entrepreneurs cannot be trusted to fulfill their promises, then people will be reluctant to join those pledging to make a difference. The persistence of such a political culture can be expected to undermine the growth of civil society organizations. Public entrepreneurs have to convince not only themselves but others as well that the creation of a nonprofit organization is an effective means to address public problems.

Returning to the economic metaphor, the initial investment of the entre-preneur must attract additional investors in order to acquire the social capital necessary to confront such problems.

These informal constraints (referred to interchangeably as "informal rules," "social norms," or "cultural constraints") persist for a number of different reasons. At the most basic level, social norms, like all rules, reduce uncertainty and simplify life. As North (1990, 83) explains, "They allow people to go about the everyday process of making exchanges with-out having to think out exactly the terms of an exchange at each point and in each instance." If asked for a donation to a charitable cause on the street, the informal constraint of distrust allows a passerby to reject the offer without having to learn the details of the organization or to decide whether a contribution is warranted. In a related vein, individuals follow social norms because they are perceived to work (Axelrod 1986). When residents in a community without water and sewer services hear that their neighbor wasted the whole day downtown trying to speak to a representa-tive from the water utility, it reinforces the rule that you need to "know someone" to gain access to government.

However, it is not the functional nature of norms that has caught the attention of scholars; rather, it is the mechanisms through which they are enforced by other members of society (Heckathorn 1988; Ellickson 1998). In some neighborhoods, for example, individuals might be ex-pected to devote some of their free time to voluntary endeavors in the neighborhood or community. Those who do not, or who reject invitations to do so, might be looked down upon or excluded from social circles. Enforcement occurs through a variety of means, including through power-ful actors that benefit from their existence (Axelrod 1986). For example, patrons who maintain their positions of power through the loyalty of their clients can be expected to resist efforts to reduce clientelism or their access to patronage resources.

Informal rules might also be supported or undermined by formal rules (Finnemore and Sikkink 1998). A law stipulating a fine for daily watering of lawns and gardens would support a norm of conservation, whereas a rule highly subsidizing the cost of water would undermine conservation. Finally, norms might be self-enforced through internalization. A person with internalized environmental norms, for example, will not throw trash on the ground even if no one is around to witness.

As a result of their heuristic and functional nature, enforcement, and internalization, changing or introducing new norms is a complicated process. Martha Finnemore and Kathryn Sikkink (1998, 897) write that, "new norms never enter a normative vacuum but instead emerge in a highly contested normative space where they must compete with other norms and perceptions of interest." Consequently, norms of clientelism, co-option, and cynicism can be expected to be resilient. In fact, chapter 3 of this volume explores in detail the resilience of norms unfriendly to associational life in the eastern Mexican border town of Nuevo Laredo. The topic is revisited in chapter 7, which explores change and continuity in the relationship between the nonprofit sector and government.

Nonetheless, scholars agree that social norms are not deterministic (Eckstein 1988; Jackman and Miller 2004). Despite the challenges, norms do change. As Finnemore and Sikkink (1998) point out, the norms that once supported slavery, dueling, piracy, and torture no longer exist. Norm change is promoted by those whom Cass Sunstein (1996) calls "norm entrepreneurs." Like public entrepreneurs, who invest in associational life to address a public problem (and their counterparts in the for-profit sector), norm entrepreneurs seek to introduce new norms. "Norms do not appear out of thin air; they are actively built by agents having strong notions about appropriate or desirable behavior in their community" (Finnemore and Sikkink 1998, 896).

Unfortunately, this places a double burden on public entrepreneurs in Mexico. Whereas forming a civil society organization is commonplace, accepted, and even encouraged on the U.S. side of the border, it must be justified on the Mexican side. More so than their northern counterparts, Mexican public entrepreneurs must work to convince cynics and skeptics that they can be effective; they must provide evidence they are not clientelistic or acting out of their own narrow self-interest. Therefore, almost by default in countries with a historically weak civil society, public entrepreneurs have the double job of norm entrepreneurs.

However, there is more to norm change than human agency. Scholars agree that norms are also not entirely constant across a polity (Thompson,

Ellis and Wildavsky 1990). Mark Granovetter (1985) proposes that the impact of norms varies based on the social networks in which individuals are embedded. Because network members interact with one another regularly and have good information about one another's actions, they have incentives to comply with the norms of the network (Coleman 1988). Because there are numerous different networks across a society, one would expect the enforcement and explanatory power of different informal constraints to vary across these networks. It follows that some social networks may be burdened by cynicism, others by clientelism, and still others may be supportive of public entrepreneurship.

The importance of networks is not just necessary for understanding variation in informal rules, however. Networks also help explain how new norms can be created. Although it is difficult to imagine norm entrepreneurs changing the informal rules of a whole community, it is much easier to imagine their changing norms within a small social network. A public entrepreneur cannot create a massive membership organization overnight, but he or she could convince a close network of friends and neighbors of the desirability of forming an association. With time, informal rules might develop within this group to ensure its preservation. For example, members might express disapproval if a fellow associate fails to show up for a meeting.

In addition, networks also provide a tool to understand how norms become diffused. Because social networks overlap one another, norms fostered in one network can be promoted in another. Pamela Popielarz and J. Miller McPherson (1995) document, for example, how volunteers are drawn into organizations through their social networks. Michael Layton (2006) finds a similar phenomenon in the Mexican context.

Social networks thus have a threefold purpose. First, they serve to help members understand norms and informal rules, which can be expected to vary within any given network. Second, they serve as breeding grounds for new norms. And finally, through their ties with other networks, they serve to diffuse new rules throughout society. Chapter 4 explores in depth this process of norm change in Ciudad Juárez, Chihuahua, where norm entrepreneurs have introduced new informal rules friendly to autonomous associational life. Although these norms are not constant throughout Juárez society, chapter 6 explores efforts to spread these norms into the networks of the border business community.

Social networks are also of primary importance for an entirely different reason. In addition to political opportunity and informal rules friendly to associational life, the emergence and development of civil society organizations also requires resources, such as knowledge and organizational skills, financial assets, and access to information. As the following section will discuss, networks serve an important role in linking public entrepreneurs with these necessary resources.

Resources Broadly Understood

Tilly (1978) views political opportunity as a necessary but insufficient condition for collective action. He contends that such action also requires the mobilization of resources to exploit political opportunities. Indeed, many scholars writing in the distinct but related social movements literature have focused exclusively on access to resources to explain collective action (McCarthy and Zald 1973; 1977; Oberschall 1973). The nonprofit literature in the United States has also found a relationship between human and financial resources and the number of nonprofit agencies (Ben-Ner and Van Hoomissen 1992; Corbin 1999; Grønbjerg and Paarlberg 2001; Marsh 1995; Zakour and Gillespie 1998).

Nonetheless, it would be a mistake to reduce the resource mobilization argument to financial resources alone: the creation of an organization entails a wide range of costs. Information, human resources, new ideas, organizational skills, and the ability to manage collective action problems and interdependencies are essential inputs into any collective action effort. Although individuals might possess a considerable supply of such resources, public entrepreneurs are more readily able to obtain these resources and address interdependencies through their networks (Burt 1992; Cook 1977; Granovetter 1973). For example, an environmental activist might possess considerable organizational skill but lack popular support or political influence. Alternatively, a community organizer might garner support from the organizer's constituency but lack financial resources to sustain organizational efforts. Thus Joseph Galaskiewicz (1979) found that successful organizations in a U.S. city were more often the ones best able to mobilize resources through their networks, rather than the ones already having the most resources.

In the U.S. literature on nonprofit organizations, the business community, including both for-profit corporations and the men and women who manage them, has been an important source of financial and human resources for the third sector. Business leaders commonly sit on boards of directors for civil society organization, help confront interdependencies exogenous to the organizations, and provide funding (Hall 1975; Middleton 1987; Pfeffer and Salancik 1978; O'Connell 2000; Zald 1969). Moreover, foundation endowments, an important source of nonprofit revenue, traditionally have been created by wealthy business leaders (Hall 2001). Businesses themselves also play an important role participating in civil society organization activities, providing in-kind services, and donating funds (Fry, Keim, and Meiners 1982; Sinclair and Galaskiewicz 1997; Useem 1987). Although one would expect the public entrepreneurs of Mexico also to seek human and financial resources in the business community, the literature on the third sector in Mexico (and Latin America more generally) provides evidence to the contrary. Studies of nonprofit organizations in Mexico frequently cite the lack of philanthropy in the country as a major obstacle to the sector's development (Castro Salinas 2001; CEMEFI 1996; Layton 2004; Verduzco 2003), and this concern holds true for the border region as well (Bejarano 2002; Kelly 2002). In a comparative study, Gustavo Verduzco, Regina List, and Lester Salamon (1999) found that the nonprofit sector in Mexico drew only 6.3 percent of its funding from private philanthropy, versus 85.2 percent from fees. Mexican public entrepreneurs will thus have to look to alternative resource bases to foster and incubate collective action efforts.

In the distinct but related study of social movements, Aldon Morris (1981) documented the role of churches and universities in supporting collective action. "Pre-existing social structures provide the resources and organization that are crucial to the initiation and spread of collective action" (Morris 1981, 746). In the border region, churches, universities, foreign nonprofit organizations, and preexisting civil society organizations offer a potential alternate means to obtain resources necessary to overcome the barriers to successful organization. Public entrepreneurs can, for example, gain access to a large network of potential donors and volunteers through their ties within a church community. A church might provide an incipient organization in-kind services such as a place to meet, support staff, access to phones and computers, and office supplies until it can stand on its own. Affiliation with a respected social institution can also provide important credibility in front of other members of society. Indeed, Verduzco (2003) argues that the guiding thread uniting non-co-opted social organizations throughout the twentieth century in Mexico was affiliation with the Catholic Church.[7]

As a type of "social infrastructure," groups such as churches provide incubating support to collective action,[8] such support can also be found outside of the religious community. Universities and university students in Mexico have a long history of social action (Mabry 1982). Indeed, the student movement of 1968 is considered to be the first widespread manifestation of discontent with the PRI-dominated regime. Susan Eckstein (1990) documented the role of student groups in assisting and supporting colonia residents after Mexico's devastating 1985 earthquake. Ruben Lau and Victor Quintana Silveyra (1991) described the role of students and professors from the Universidad Autónoma de Chihuahua in creating and strengthening the Comité de Defensa Popular (CDP; Popular Defense Committee) to advocate for the rights of Chihuahua's low-income residents. Although these more famous examples of collective action in Mexico are social movements, universities can also incubate nonprofit organizations. Like the Church, universities are a potential source of human and financial capital, technical knowledge, and in-kind services. In fact, many Mexican universities require their students to put in a set number of hours of volunteer social service before they can graduate.

The prevalence of foreign funding for nonprofit organizations in the developing world has been well documented (see, for example, Bailey 1999). Verduzco (2003) reports the presence of foreign-based philanthropy in Mexico even during the nineteenth century. Moreover, studies have recorded the important role of U.S. nonprofit organizations and foundations in supporting civil society organizational efforts specifically along the border (Alfie Cohen 2002; Bandy 2004; Verduzco Chávez 2001; Zabin 1997).

It is also possible that network ties within preexisting civil society or social movement networks can provide the resources necessary for mobilization. Organizations such as foundations often have as their stated objective to support the development of other civil society initiatives. Not only do foundations provide funding but many also offer technical and legal support. Gaberman (2003, 1) has argued that efforts to promote foundations "are building the global infrastructure of philanthropy in order to be able to more effectively support the institutions of civil society in their important activities." In the United States, "infrastructure organizations" that exist solely to support the development and effectiveness of nonprofit organizations have become a cottage industry (Abramson and McCarthy 2002).

Forming an organization to address a public problem or autonomously pushing government to do so is no small undertaking. A potential public entrepreneur faces a wide variety of questions: What is the nature of the public problem and what can an independent organization do to address it? What is the legal process to establish an organization? What other people would be interested in joining such an effort? How will the organization be funded? How could a citizen initiative address dependencies on the government or on industry? How does an organization undertake planning, arrive at decisions, manage a budget, and address a host of other logistical concerns? Although few individuals readily know the answers to most of these questions, it is not necessary to reinvent the wheel every time an organization is founded. The answers to many questions can be found within preexisting forms of social organization. I argue that churches, universities, the foreign nonprofit community, and preexisting civil society networks, can help public entrepreneurs bear the start-up costs of organization, provide financial and human resources, offer in-kind services, recommend new ideas, provide information, and help address interdependencies. I argue further that the transformation from concerned citizen to public entrepreneur is more likely to occur given network ties to these already existing forms of social infrastructure.

Conclusion

Chapter 1 has laid out the essence of the arguments that will run throughout this book. Political change is a necessary precondition to the establishment of an independent third sector. Under one-party government, the informal rules of Mexican politics pointed those who wanted to address public problems down two paths. Citizens could take the path of co-option or the path of radicalization. The middle road of autonomous citizenship and civil society organization was obscured and not seen as effective. Although, with the emergence of divided and competitive government, such a route is now a possibility, the path is neither fully cleared nor delineated, and persistent informal rules may continue to obscure it. Potential public entrepreneurs must therefore use network ties to social infrastructure along this alternative route to provide direction (e.g., information), supplies (e.g., financial resources and in-kind services), and lodging (e.g., a place to meet).

Unfortunately, perhaps the greatest legacy of one-party rule is the simple withdrawal of many citizens from public affairs. Even as new routes begin to emerge, many individuals continue to distrust available political opportunities and those who ask for their time and resources. Because such skepticism, however warranted, runs the risk of becoming a self-fulfilling prophecy, public entrepreneurs must also serve as norm entrepreneurs, tasked with writing new informal rules of engagement, participation, association, and autonomy.

2 Cities, Policy Problems, and Nonprofits

Introduction

Recognizing the important role that civil society organizations play in solving public problems, promoting better public policy, holding government accountable, transcending borders, and promoting norms supportive of self-governance, this study seeks to understand how these organizations have emerged and developed in four Mexican border communities. To do so, it focuses on how three key variables affect the presence of civil society organizations: (1) the political opportunities available to potential public entrepreneurs; (2) the informal rules that impact the relationship between potential entrepreneurs, the state, and the public arena; and (3) the network ties and preexisting social infrastructure available to these entrepreneurs.

The study analyzes these variables through three levels: city, policy arena, and organizational. At its most basic level, it is a comparative case study of civil society organizations across four cities. At the next level, it compares different policy arenas within each city, exploring a number of different water-related issues: extending water and sewer services, obtaining sufficient water resources to meet urban needs, urban planning, wastewater treatment, protecting natural resources, addressing industrial contamination, preventing public health problems, and educating people about water resources and the environment. Finally, at the organizational level, it examines seventy-two nonprofit organizations operating in the four cities, a sample of neighborhood associations, and numerous members of civil society who create and sustain organizational efforts. Analyzing the selected research question at the city, policy arena, and organizational levels helps mitigate a common methodological problem of comparative studies: too many variables and too few cases.

A City Level of Analysis: The Four Research Sites

The four Mexican cities of Tijuana, Baja California; Nogales, Sonora; Ciudad Juárez, Chihuahua; and Nuevo Laredo, Tamaulipas, border the four U.S. cities of San Diego, California; Nogales, Arizona; El Paso, Texas; and Laredo, Texas. All four research sites have experienced high population and industrial growth rates. For example, according to Mexico's statistics and information agency, INEGI (Instituto Nacional de Estadística Geografía e Informática), Ciudad Juárez grew at an average annual rate of 4.4 percent between 1950 and 2005 from 122,000 residents to over 1.3 million. Similarly, at its peak in 2000, the city's maquiladora industry had grown to 312 plants employing 255,740 workers (Turner, Hamlyn, and Ibáñez Hernández 2003). Not only has this growth increased pressure on natural resources but it has also impacted the social fabric of border communities. It is not unusual to hear longtime residents of the region complain of more recent arrivals, who are frequently blamed for everything from litter on the streets to increases in crime.

Partly as a result of growth, all of the cities suffer from acute water-related policy problems. All four lack sufficient wastewater treatment capacity, face uncertain water supplies for the future, have residents without access to water and sewer services, and risk losing valuable natural resources to contamination and development. Despite their similarities, however, the four cities differ in two important respects: their political environments and the amount of social infrastructure available to potential public entrepreneurs.[1] Although Mexico has transitioned to democracy at the national level, there is considerable variation in local political environments. In Nuevo Laredo and the state of Tamaulipas, the PRI has been in power for decades and continues to win both municipal and state elections by large margins. In the 2004 elections, for example (as in past elections), the PRI candidate for municipal president won by a margin of over 22 percent (see table 2.1). At the other extreme, Ciudad Juárez and the state of Chihuahua have been governed by both PRI and PAN administrations in an environment of very close and competitive elections. In the middle of this continuum are Nogales and Tijuana. At the time of research in Nogales, the PRI still maintained control of the municipal government but under very competitive elections. In Tijuana, the PAN (Partido Acción

Table 2.1   Electoral competition at the time of research

City	PAN votes	PRI votes	Other party votes	Margin of victory
Tijuana (2001)	46.80%	37.57%	13.33%	9.23%[a]
Nogales (2003)	30.77%	34.49%	27.05%	3.72%
Ciudad Juárez (2002)	46.92%	46.17%	3.67%	0.75%
Nuevo Laredo (2002)	37.02%	59.66%	3.24%	22.64%

Source: Data on Tijuana are from Instituto Estatal Electoral de Baja California; data on Nogales from Consejo Estatal Electoral del Estado de Sonora; data on Ciudad Juárez from Instituto Estatal Electoral de Chihuahua; and data on Nuevo Laredo from Instituto Estatal Electoral de Tamaulipas.
[a]In Mexico, because the percentages of votes are given in terms of total numbers of votes cast, rather than total numbers of valid votes, official percentages do not add up to 100.

Nacional; National Action Party) dominated both municipal and state politics for a period of fifteen years following the defeat of the PRI in 1989.[2] As the continuation of one-party rule is expected to limit the opportunities available to potential public entrepreneurs, one would expect to find less political opportunities in Nuevo Laredo than in the other three cites, particularly in Ciudad Juárez.

The four cities also differ in terms of social infrastructure, defined as preexisting forms of organization that offer a potential source of information and human and financial resources, and which this study operationalizes by focusing on the U.S. nonprofit community, churches, universities, and preexisting civil society and social movement networks. The two larger cities of Tijuana and Ciudad Juárez fare much better in availability of social infrastructure. Although all the cities are close to potential mobilizing elements in the form of U.S. nonprofit organizations, there is a much greater supply across the border from Tijuana. Ciudad Juárez's Catholic Church has a history of an activism inspired by liberation theology and guided by internationally known bishops. Furthermore, Tijuana and Ciudad Juárez have more universities, intermediary organizations (such as foundations), and strong preexisting civil society networks. Tijuana and Ciudad Juárez's greater social infrastructure can be expected to facilitate the emergence of new civil society organizations. To elucidate both the common and the unique elements of the four research sites, a brief introduction to each is in order.

Tijuana

Tijuana is the principal city in Baja California, accounting for almost half of the state's population. According to INEGI, of the city's over 1.4 million residents, only 40 percent were born in the state of Baja California. Perhaps even more so than other border cities, Tijuana's population growth has been dramatic. Tijuana only had 165,000 inhabitants in 1960, and Baja California did not even become a state until 1953.

Made up of hills, canyons, and mesas, Tijuana is bordered by the greater San Diego area and located within the binational Tijuana River watershed. The region has few water resources and relies almost entirely on water imported from the Colorado River and northern California. Economically, Tijuana has one of the border's largest maquiladora sectors, traditionally known for the production of televisions.

Baja California was the first Mexican state to elect an opposition governor since the consolidation of the PRI in the early twentieth century. In 1989, the PAN candidate, Ernesto Ruffo Appel, won the gubernatorial election by a margin of nearly 10 percent. More important, his victory was accepted by the administration of President Carlos Salinas de Gortari. In subsequent years, the state developed as a stronghold for the PAN and became known for a number of political innovations, preceding the federal government in the creation of its own registry of voters and electoral credentials and of an autonomous electoral agency (Selee 2006). In the early 2000s, the PAN and its coalition came to control four of Baja California's five municipalities, the governorship, and the state legislature.[3] Tijuana itself was governed by PAN administrations from 1989 to 2004.

Although all four research sites are located opposite U.S. cities, Tijuana sits across from the greater San Diego metropolitan area, which has a sizable nonprofit community, and is itself home to several universities including the Colegio de la Frontera Norte (College of the Northern Border), the Universidad Autónoma de Baja California, and private universities such as the Universidad Iberoamericana. Potential public entrepre-

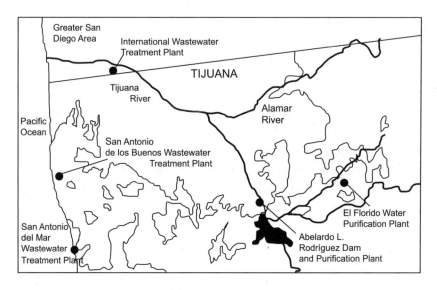

Figure 2.1.   Tijuana, Baja California

neurs in Tijuana also benefit from the city's history of environmental activism. The end of one-party priista rule in Tijuana and a large supply of social infrastructure can be expected to support the emergence of an autonomous nonprofit sector with diverse social networks.

Nogales

The smallest city in the study, Nogales, Sonora, had a population of just under 200,000 in 2005 by official count, although conventional wisdom in the city put the number closer to 350,000. Population statistics are contested all along the border but particularly in Nogales. In 1995, for example, the city's water utility estimated the population to be 215,000, or 15,000 more than the official 2005 figure (SIUE 1995). On the one hand, many border residents argue that the federal government undercalculates the size of the population to reduce federal budget obligations to wealthier border cities on the country's periphery. On the other hand, skeptics counter that local officials overreport population numbers to excuse failures in public administration.

It is estimated that almost half (47 percent) of Mexican produce bound

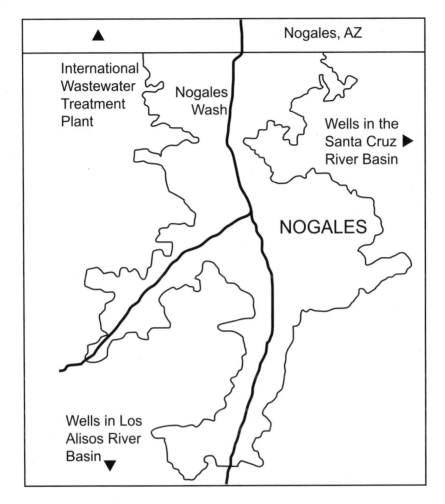

Figure 2.2. Nogales, Sonora

for the United States passes through the Nogales port of entry (Nogales–
Santa Cruz County Chamber of Commerce 2002). The city's economic
development and urban planning have been hampered, however, by its
location in a narrow valley along the Nogales Wash (part of the larger
Santa Cruz watershed), upstream from its sister city on the U.S. side of the
border, Nogales, Arizona. Perhaps even more than Tijuana and San Diego, Nogales's historic development is strongly tied to its U.S. neighbor, a
fact reflected in the name "Ambos Nogales" (Both Nogaleses).

At the time of research, the PRI continued its uninterrupted hold on city hall, although within the context of growing electoral competition. In the 2000 presidential elections, a majority of Nogales's citizens voted for the PAN presidential candidate, Vicente Fox, and the PAN won electoral victories in nearby municipalities. In 2003, the PRI narrowly won the municipal election in a close, three-way race with less than 35 percent of the vote.[4]

Although growing electoral competition can be expected to disrupt the PRI monopoly that limited political opportunities for autonomous association, Nogales has very little social infrastructure with which to take advantage of these opportunities; Nogales, Arizona, is even smaller than its southern neighbor and has few nonprofit organizations. The universities of Nogales, Sonora, are primarily two-year colleges oriented toward technical education and focused on feeding the maquiladora industry. The city has neither a long history of associational life outside of professional organizations and social clubs nor long-standing foundations or other intermediary organizations. All of these factors are expected to constrain the ability of potential public entrepreneurs to develop diverse networks and overcome the informal rules that support clientelism or cynicism.

Ciudad Juárez

Ciudad Juárez, Chihuahua, sits opposite El Paso, Texas, where the Rio Grande (or Río Bravo as it is called in Mexico) turns toward the southeast to form the border between the United States and Mexico. The two cities make up part of the Paso del Norte region, which extends up to Las Cruces, New Mexico. Ciudad Juárez, named for Mexico's national hero Benito Juárez, is slightly smaller than Tijuana, with a population of over 1.3 million residents in 2005. Although the city has become infamous as the site of hundreds of unsolved murders of young women, Ciudad Juárez is best known for its vibrant automotive parts and electronics industries.

Ciudad Juárez and the state of Chihuahua played a key role in Mexico's democratic transition. In 1983, the city was one of the first major Mexican cities to elect an opposition party mayor, businessman Francisco Barrio Terrazas, on the PAN ticket. Barrio ran for the governorship in 1986 but was denied the post amid widely accepted allegations of electoral fraud (Chand 2001). Barrio's campaign had been supported by a growing num-

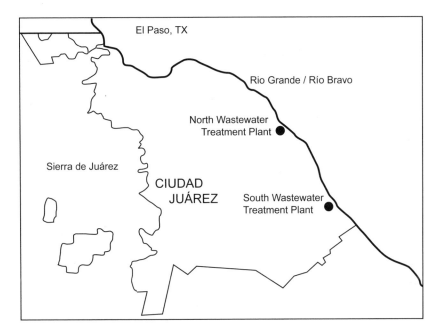

Figure 2.3.   Ciudad Juárez, Chihuahua

ber of people disillusioned with the PRI's monopoly on power, a movement that only grew stronger following the disputed elections (Chand 2001). The former businessman and Ciudad Juárez mayor would finally win the state executive office in the free and fair elections of 1992. Prior to the democratic movement of the 1980s, the city had also had a thriving liberation theology movement, led by former bishop Manuel Talamás Camandari. Its strong history of collective action can be expected to facilitate the development of civil society organizations.

Nuevo Laredo

Nuevo Laredo sits along the lower Rio Grande 200 miles upstream from the Gulf of Mexico. With a population of over 350,000, it shares a common history, evolution, and name with its neighbor Laredo, Texas, or as the two cities are known, Los Dos Laredos. Nuevo Laredo was founded in 1848 by residents of Laredo wanting to remain Mexican when south Texas

became part of the United States with the signing of the Treaty of Guada-
lupe-Hidalgo. The two closely connected cities even shared a binational
baseball team, Los Tecolotes, which used to play in the Mexican baseball
league. Like Nogales, Nuevo Laredo is a major port of entry for trade
between the United States and Mexico. Some 9,000 commercial trucks
cross the border at Los Dos Laredos every day, accounting for a major
portion of Mexico's trade (R. Ayuntamiento de Nuevo Laredo 2006).

During the years of PRI domination, Nuevo Laredo and the state of
Tamaulipas typified the corporatist system of clientelism and political
control (Garza and Pariente Fregosa 2000). The city's politics were controlled for decades by the local leader of the Confederación de Trabajadores de México (CTM; Confederation of Mexican Workers), Pedro
Pérez Ibarra, until he fled to the United States following an uprising in
1992. The city and state still remain strongholds for the PRI, thus limiting
political opportunity. Like Nogales, Nuevo Laredo has very limited social
infrastructure: it is the only city in the study without a local foundation, its
university community is small, and its strongest social movements have
been dominated by the PRI and the corporatist CTM labor union.

Water-Related Policy Problems

A comparison of the existing nonprofit sector across the four research
sites offers a window on the emergence and development of civil society
organizations. However, it is also possible to compare these organizations
across different public problems related to the policy topic of this book:
water. One of the methodological advantages of studying water-related
public problems is that water flows its way into a number of different
policy arenas: water and sewer service provision, obtaining water resources for urban areas, urban planning, wastewater treatment, protecting natural resources, industrial contamination, environmental education, and water-related public health, to name the most notable. A brief
summary of each of these policy arenas appears below, along with the
public problems it generates and the limits of government efforts to address them, highlighting the need for greater direct citizen action and
greater oversight of public officials.

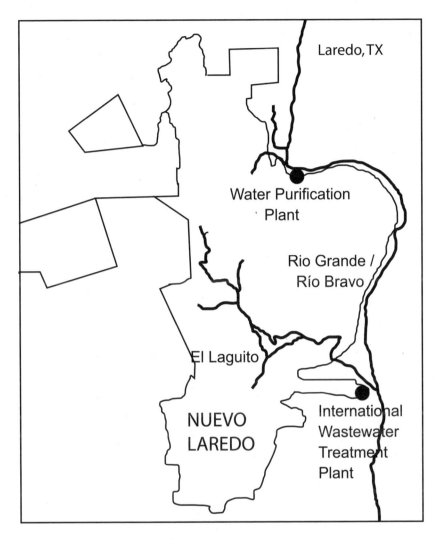

Figure 2.4.   Nuevo Laredo, Tamaulipas

Water and Sewer Service Provision

All along the border, local water utilities have had to contend with a number of obstacles to providing quality service and keeping pace with rapid population growth. At the time of research, between 5 percent and 15 percent of households in the four cities lacked water services and be-

Table 2.2   Infrastructure coverage at the time of research

	Reported water coverage (%)	Reported sewer coverage (%)
Tijuana	94.6	79
Nogales	85	75
Ciudad Juárez	91	80
Nuevo Laredo	92	87.5

Source: Data on Tijuana are from Camp Dresser & McKee Inc. 2003; data on Nogales from the Municipality of Nogales Web site, http://www.nogalesmunicipio .org (accessed April 2005); data on Ciudad Juárez from IMPLAN 2002; and data on Nuevo Laredo from Parsons Engineering 2002.

tween 12 percent and 25 percent lacked sewer infrastructure (see table 2.2). While all of the cities face similar challenges, Nogales has more acute water and sewer problems, with less coverage and an inability to provide 24-hour service to all but a minority of its population.

Historically responsible for water and sewer services, the federal government relinquished this responsibility to the states in 1980; in 1983, it was constitutionally devolved to the municipalities (Ozuna and Gómez 1998). Despite this constitutional reform, many of the water utilities remain under the control of the state government for financial, political, or administrative reasons. At the time of the research, service was still provided by agencies of the state government in Tijuana, Nogales, and Ciudad Juárez.[5]

Regardless of state or municipal auspices, service provision has been complicated by poorly planned urban growth, and utilities are often asked to introduce services after houses and communities have already been constructed. With limited resources, maintenance budgets are often the first to be cut, causing existing water and sewer lines to deteriorate rapidly and resulting in water and sewer leaks (Ingram, Laney, and Gillilan 1995, 72). Even Tijuana's relatively well run water and sewer utility is estimated to lose almost 25 percent of its water and almost 15 percent of its sewage to leaks in infrastructure (Camp Dress & McGee Inc. 2003, chap. 2, p. 36). Theoretically, water utilities should be able to generate sufficient resources through user fees to sustain their maintenance and operations. Because, however, water is viewed as a constitutionally guaranteed right in Mexico, its delivery has been highly subsidized. With little emphasis placed on bill collection, users have traditionally been able to avoid payment. As a result of these factors, utilities have become highly dependent on federal funding not just to expand services but even to maintain existing infrastructure. Water utility reforms calling for dramatically higher user fees and increased use of metering have been hampered by what Vivien Foster (1996) calls a "financing dilemma": service providers cannot justify rate increases because of the poor quality of service, and they cannot improve services because of the lack of revenue. Nogales, Sonora, in particular has been caught in this dilemma: few users have functioning water meters and the commercial department of the water utility estimates that only half (50–54 percent) of them pay their bills on time, if at all.

Despite the clear need, there are obstacles to professionalizing the provision of water service. Water utilities have frequently served as the "caja chica," or a source of petty cash, for the administration in power; water subsidies, debt forgiveness, and service extension have often been used as patronage resources to gain political support (Ward 1986). Furthermore, although many water utilities have undergone technocratic reforms, employment and promotions are often granted for reasons other than merit. With such patronage at its disposal, it is not uncommon for the position of utility director to serve as a jumping-off point for elected office.[6] Deficiencies in the provision of water service and evidence of political manipulation have increased the demand for greater citizen participation and oversight.

Water Supply

Supplying water to urban areas is one of the crucial issues throughout the arid border region. According to the U.S. Census Bureau, annual precipitation ranges from just under 9 inches in Ciudad Juárez–El Paso and just under 10 inches in the Tijuana–San Diego (true deserts are commonly understood to receive less than 10 inches per year) to just under 19 inches in Ambos Nogales and just over 21 inches in Los Dos Laredos. The region contains several vast aquifers, but the arid climate and geological factors combine to keep recharge rates low. Two very large river basins in the region, those of the Colorado River and the Rio Grande, are fed by snowfall in the Rocky Mountains of the United States and the Sierra Madre of

Mexico; their waters are retained in reservoirs throughout the region. A number of stakeholders, both along the border and in the interior of the two countries, compete for access to this water. The competition has become all the more pitched due to accelerated urban growth in the larger region since the 1960s and to less than average rainfall through most of the 1990s and the early 2000s

Tijuana is almost entirely dependent on an insufficient supply of water imported 120 miles over the Otay Mountains from the Colorado River. Its Abelardo L. Rodríguez Dam, located within the city limits, is frequently without water. Nogales draws more than half of its water from the over-exploited Santa Cruz River basin east of the city, which it shares with Nogales, Arizona. Like Nogales, Ciudad Juárez relies on groundwater resources. The city's supply comes from the overexploited Hueco Bolson, which is also used by El Paso, Texas. The full extent of the aquifer is not known, but even liberal annual recharge estimates of 35 million cubic meters (28,375 acre-feet) pale in comparison with extraction rates. Ciudad Juárez alone extracted more than four times as much, 150 million cubic meters (121,600 acre-feet), in 1999 (Turner, Hamlyn, and Ibáñez Hernández 2003). Impounded by the Amistad Dam, the Rio Grande provides the water supply for Nuevo Laredo and other urban and agricultural users. Although the city's climate is less arid than the rest of the border, the lower Rio Grande basin is drought prone and relies on occasional hurricanes from the Gulf of Mexico to fill the region's dams. According to the International Boundary and Water Commission (IBWC), at its lowest point in 2004, the water retained at the Amistad Dam had dropped to 13 percent of capacity (Claudio 2004).

These descriptions illustrate the considerable challenges and binational interdependence surrounding the issue of water supply. While Mexico's Comisión Nacional de Agua (CONAGUA; National Water Commission) has primary jurisdiction over the nation's water resources, the United States and Mexico address binational water issues through the International Boundary and Water Commission (IBWC)/ Comisión Internacional de Límites y Aguas International (CILA). The IBWC, which traces its history back to 1889, is made up of a U.S. and a Mexican section organized under the auspices of the U.S. State Department and the Mexican Secretariat of Foreign Affairs, respectively. The two sections are responsible for binational negotiations on water issues, monitoring the enforcement of existing treaties and agreements, and operating certain water-related infrastructure in the region.

A 1944 treaty negotiated through the IBWC established allocation rules governing surface water in the Rio Grande and Colorado River basins. While the treaty has a number of critics, it has governed surface water allocations for over a half century. By contrast, no agreement has been reached to govern groundwater resources despite recognition of its urgency (GNEB 2005; Ingram 2000). Consequently, there is insufficient information regarding the size of aquifers, rates of extraction, and recharge rates for seventeen shared aquifers along the border (for a summary description of the aquifers, see Mumme 2000b). As U.S. and Mexican users consume water at what appear to be clearly unsustainable rates, groundwater resources along the border risk suffering a "tragedy of the commons."

City Planning

All four of the cities are defined by a common history of unplanned, disorderly growth through land invasions, a problem encountered throughout Mexico (Bennett 1995; Ward 1986). Bypassing the legal housing market, invading families take over land and quickly establish provisional housing. Tito Alegría and Gerardo Ordóñez (2002) estimate that 57 percent of the houses in Tijuana at one time lacked legal title. Unregulated growth has complicated the provision of water and sewer service, caused erosion, and accelerated degradation of the environment. The rugged terrain of Tijuana and parts of Nogales and Ciudad Juárez has further complicated planning and exacerbated the negative consequences of unplanned growth. For example, a community established without legal title along Tijuana's Alamar River floodplain could not obtain water infrastructure and suffered severe flood damage during the rainy months. The government relocated the community in 2005, but to still dangerous, erosion-prone slopes along Tijuana's Los Laureles Canyon.

The fundamental problem is not the absence of planning (whether for land use, environmental protection, or infrastructure extension) but the failure to adhere to plans from one administration to the next. As one of the unfortunate aspects of politics in Mexico, each administration seeks to clearly distinguish itself from its predecessor, even when the predecessor is from the same party (Guillén López 1996, 23).[7] New administrations typically reappoint all top and middle management positions throughout the bureaucracy and do not honor agreements made by previous administrations. Because municipal terms last only three years, there is constant turnover and change. A common quip is that municipal officials spend one year learning the job, one year working, and one year preparing for what they will do at the end of the administration.

There have been governmental efforts to overcome this continuity problem. In Tijuana, Ciudad Juárez, and Nuevo Laredo, the binational Border Environment Cooperation Commission and the U.S. Environmental Protection Agency have supported long-term technical planning efforts for water supply, service line extension and rehabilitation, and wastewater treatment. In Tijuana, Ciudad Juárez, and Nuevo Laredo, municipal planning institutes have been created with a number of attributes designed to protect them from the capriciousness of shortsighted administrations.[8] Nevertheless, in all three cities, these planning agencies have become isolated and undermined. In Nuevo Laredo, for example, the municipal government created the Instituto Municipal de Planeación (IMPLAN; Municipal Planning Institute) in 2000, making this eastern border city one of the first Mexican municipalities to create a planning institute. Unfortunately, however, the institute was never recognized by the state government; even though the city contracted with the Colegio de la Frontera Norte (COLEF; College of the Northern Border) to undertake a technical planning study, the resulting plan was legally subordinated to a less thorough state initiative.

Wastewater Treatment

Although industrial and population growth has yielded a corresponding increase in the wastewater generated by each city, before the 1990s, only a low percentage of the wastewater received any treatment whatsoever. Ciudad Juárez, for example, had no treatment facilities until 2002. Currently, however, all four cities treat the vast majority of their wastewater, a large portion of it through binationally constructed treatment plants, which may be one of the greatest policy successes in the region. Despite considerable advances, however, problems remain at each of the research sites.

During the 1990s, an international wastewater treatment plant was constructed in San Diego County to treat a portion of Tijuana's sewage. Unfortunately, the effluent from the new plant is not in compliance with the U.S. Clean Water Act or an international agreement between the two countries (International Boundary and Water Commission Minute 283); the combined treatment capacity of the international plant and Tijuana's own plant is insufficient to treat all of the city's sewage. Consequently, a portion of the wastewater that arrives at the southern plant is introduced into the environment with only chlorine injections.

Wastewater from Nogales, Sonora, is also treated at an international plant, along with sewage from Nogales, Arizona, 9 miles north of the two cities. Unfortunately, the plant does not have sufficient capacity to handle increased flow during rainy periods, and recent changes in U.S. regulations have brought the facility out of compliance with the U.S. Clean Water Act. Litigation and subsequent court rulings have demanded a resolution to the plant's problems, but renegotiation of the agreement between the United States and Mexico is hindered by U.S. government complaints that it pays too high a proportion of the operation and maintenance costs of the plant and Mexican concerns that it is de facto surrendering water rights over its effluent (a precious resource that feeds a wide riparian habitat in the Santa Cruz River basin on the U.S. side of the border).

In Ciudad Juárez, two sewage treatment plants were recently constructed with certification from the Border Environment Cooperation Commission (BECC; Comisión de Cooperación Ecológica Fronteriza) and financing from the North American Development Bank (NADB), NAFTA institutions created to encourage development of infrastructure for water, sewer, wastewater treatment, and solid waste disposal along the border. At about the same time, however, communities were built in the southeastern part of the city whose sewer systems were not connected to the new plants. In addition, because the southern treatment plant is over capacity, untreated wastewater is discharged from the plant along with the treated effluent. These sources of contamination are combined with river and well water and used for irrigation in the nearby Valle de Juárez, potentially impacting human health in the valley. The southern plant's sludge (a by-product of wastewater treatment) has also been a source of contention: methane gas emitted from the sludge in the desert heat has caught fire spontaneously on several occasions.

In Nuevo Laredo, wastewater is treated at a plant completed in 1996 with partial U.S. support. Although the plant is in good condition, crushed sewer lines in the city center and recent growth south of the city resulted in the introduction of 4.2 million gallons a day of sewage into the Rio Grande (Parsons Engineering 2002). In 2004, the city initiated a multiyear sewer line rehabilitation project certified by the BECC to partially address the problem. Thus, despite the successful introduction of binational wastewater treatment plants in Mexico's border cities, there still remain gaps in these cities' services that endanger both public health and the environment.

Protecting Natural Resources

Among the environmental hazards posed by the diversion of water resources for human use and the rapid expansion of urban and industrialized areas, the growth of Tijuana and its eastern neighbor Tecate has put at risk a number of endemic species of plants and animals in the Tijuana River watershed (for more information on the watershed, see the Tijuana River Watershed Web site, http://trw.sdsu.edu/; Wakida and Riveles 1997). By the time the Tijuana River reaches its estuary at the Pacific Ocean, it contains high levels of contaminants, suspended solids, and heavy metals. Of particular danger to the estuary (one of only twenty-six National Estuarine Research Reserves in the United States) is massive sediment flow provoked by poorly planned urban development in the canyons that feed into the estuary on the Tijuana side of the border. Similar problems occur at the other research sites. In Nogales, Sonora, the Nogales Wash serves as a conduit for water losses and sanitary sewer overflows. In the Ciudad Juárez area, insufficient flow in the Rio Grande River deprives the environment of needed water and subjects it to higher concentrations of urban contamination.

Fortunately, Mexico has adopted strong environmental legislation to help confront these problems. For example, the 2004 reform to the National Waters Law actually recognizes the environment as a water user with its own water rights, a provision absent from the environmental laws of the United States and many other developed countries.[9] That said, the problem is not so much one of laws as of applying those laws. Without enforcement, legal efforts to protect the environment can even backfire. For example, all waterways in Mexico fall under the jurisdiction of the federal government and remain outside of the regulatory power of state or municipal officials. As an unintended consequence of this arrangement, waterways and floodplains are frequently the target of land invasions. In Tijuana, for example, a group of families hired heavy machinery in 2004 to rechannel the river in Los Laureles Canyon and create a new community, the colonia Divina de Providencia. With dirt and rocks excavated from the canyon walls, they created a level surface for settlement along the canyon floor. Their actions exacerbated erosion, increased trash and untreated sewage in the canyon, and created a flood and safety risk.

Environmental problems along the border take on a different dimension due to their binational nature. The border has long been an environmental hotspot, and binational agreements before and after the NAFTA have sought to address environmental concerns. Table 2.3 lays out important agreements and dates in the binational governance of water and environmental resources along the U.S.–Mexico border. In 1983, Presidents Miguel de la Madrid and Ronald Reagan signed the La Paz Agreement, which brought the two nations' federal environmental authorities together for the first time through technical working groups. Although it was criticized as hollow, the Integrated Border Environmental Plan (IBEP), developed in 1991, laid out objectives for cross-border government collaboration. In 1993, member governments signed what became known as the side agreements to the NAFTA. In addition to the infrastructure-focused BECC–NADB arrangement mentioned above, the side agreements also created the tri-national Commission on Environmental Cooperation, which receives and investigates allegations that a member country to the agreement has failed to enforce its environmental laws (for a detailed account of these cross-border agreements, see Livermore et al. 1999). Since the NAFTA went into effect on January 1, 1994, the U.S. Environmental Protection Agency (EPA) and its counterpart the Secretaría de Medio Ambiente y Recursos Naturales (SEMARNAT; Secretariat of the Environment and Natural Resources) have collaborated on the Border XXI (1995–2000) and Border 2012 (2002–2012) programs, which have created arenas for

Table 2.3 Important agreements and dates in the binational governance of water and environmental resources

Year	Event	Objective(s)
1848	Treaty of Guadalupe Hidalgo	Define the U.S.–Mexico Border
1889	Convention creating the International Boundary and Water Commission (IBWC)	Establish institution to demarcate border and oversee border and water treaties
1944	Treaty for the "Utilization of Waters of the Colorado and Tijuana Rivers and of the Rio Grande"	Determine distribution of surface water resources between United States and Mexico
1983	Agreement for the Protection and Improvement of the Environment in the Border Area (La Paz Agreement)	Establish governmental working groups to address transborder environmental concerns.
1992	Release of the Integrated Environmental Plan for the U.S.–Mexico Border Area (IBEP)	Strengthen enforcement of environmental law, reduce pollution, and increase binational cooperation
1993	Creation of the Border Environment Cooperation Commission (BECC) and the North American Development Bank (NADB)	Establish institutions to promote the development of environmental infrastructure in the border region.
1993	Creation of the Commission for Environmental Cooperation (CEC)	Establish tri-national institution to help prevent potential conflicts between trade and protection of environment and to promote the effective enforcement of environmental law.
1996	Release of the Border XXI Program (1996–2000)	Create nine work groups to address different border-wide environmental topics.
2003	Release of the Border 2012 Program (2003–2012)	Continue topical work groups and create regional work groups with local task forces to encourage greater local involvement in addressing binational environmental problems.

Sources: Brown et al. 2003; Liverman et al. 1999.

binational collaboration among all three levels of government and civil society. Although these agreements have helped reduce the problems associated with poorly regulated growth, they have not been able to reverse the tide of environmental degradation that has become synonymous with border development.

Industrial Contamination

Opponents of the NAFTA feared that the treaty would create a pollution haven in the border region by attracting manufacturers seeking to escape tough environmental regulations in the United States (Barkin 1998). In point of fact, cases of industrial contamination can be found all along the border (Peña 1997). In Tijuana, the most pressing industrial contamination issue is the Metales y Derivados case described in chapter 1. A lupus and cancer cluster was officially recognized across the border from Nogales, Sonora, in Nogales, Arizona, in 1994, provoking concerns about industry in the region.[10] Ciudad Juárez has been the home to several industrial contamination controversies. The Condados Presto plant, a lock-manufacturing facility, was closed down in 1994 for failing to properly dispose of its hazardous waste. Residents still complain that (like the Metales y Derivados case in Tijuana) the contamination at the site has not been sufficiently addressed. Although Nuevo Laredo lacks high-profile cases of industrial pollution, a binational water quality study of the Rio Grande in and around the city found the presence of contaminants of "major concern" (IBWC 2002).[11] Enforcement of emissions regulations is divided across federal, state, and municipal jurisdictions. The federal environmental enforcement agency, the Procuraduría Federal de Protección al Ambiente (PROFEPA; Federal Attorney General's Office for Environmental Protection), created in 1992, is responsible for control of heavy metal, explosive, toxic, inflammable, biologically infective, and reactive pollutants. Control of other pollutants is divided among state and municipal environmental authorities, who typically react in response to *denuncias*, or official complaints of pollution, which initiate a process of investigation. In addition, some water utilities along the border conduct regular water quality testing, and many have programs to promote the pretreatment of industrial discharge before it enters municipal sewer systems. However, such efforts remain understaffed, underbudgeted, and are frequently criticized as ineffective. Recognizing the limits of the government's enforcement power, Mexico has relied heavily on voluntary programs to reduce industrial pollution (Barkin 1999).

The current extent of contamination along the border is unknown. On the one hand, many government officials who participated in this study argue that the maquiladora sector is highly regulated and that industrial contamination is limited to individual incidents that are often prosecuted. This view appears to be supported by recent binational monitoring efforts in Baja California (Villacorta and Martínez 2005). On the other hand, several respondents in civil society and academia worry that the maquiladora sector is able to avoid prosecution and that industrial contamination persists (see, for example, García and Simpson 2004, by two environmental activists). What is clear is that major pollution events occurred at least up through the 1990s (CEC 2002). Moreover, there are high concentrations of hazardous waste being produced in the heavily industrialized border region (Kopinak and Barajas 2002; Sánchez 1990). In addition, the regulatory capacity of government agencies in Mexico appears to vary widely. Tijuana has established an exemplary program to verify the quality of effluent from industry, benefiting from an estimated $1.1 million in support and technical assistance from San Diego and California (Villacorta and Martínez 2005). Other Mexican border cities have neither received such support nor developed the same regulatory capacity. Furthermore, in the view of most study participants, many small businesses operating outside the realm of government regulation, such as local mechanics shops, are an often neglected source of pollution.

Water-Related Public Health

As noted above, between 5 percent and 15 percent of households in the four cities lack water services and between 12 percent and 25 percent lack sewer infrastructure (see table 2.2). While the lower ends of these ranges make up a relatively small percentage of the total population, 5 percent of, say, Tijuana's inhabitants represents a sizable number of people: 70,000. Households that lack water services must store water delivered by trucks in large drums, risking contamination both in the course of delivery and storage. In the worst-case scenario, families use discarded barrels from the maquiladora industry to store water, a practice that appears to have declined dramatically but still continues. Additionally, neighborhoods without sewer services, a larger percent of the subject population, face health risks from improper disposal of human waste.

Children under the age of five are most susceptible to the effects of giardia and cryptosporidium, common infections from contaminated water. Fortunately, the efforts of officials in the four states' health secretariats have decreased the incidence of and mortality from gastrointestinal illness. Through programs such as free medical attention for children under five with gastrointestinal illnesses, health promotion campaigns, free rehydration mixes, daily cholera monitoring, and regular water quality monitoring, the worst dangers of gastrointestinal illness have been greatly reduced. Nonetheless, even the small city of Nogales reported 6,267 cases of gastrointestinal illness in 2003. Prevention initiatives typically only occur in response to an outbreak and are constrained by limited staff and the broad expanse of health topics that officials must address.

Environmental Education

Insufficient environmental education is a concern at all of the four sites and throughout Mexico. In the personal opinion of one high-level PROFEPA official, the lack of environmental education and a poor environmental culture is the root of at least 65 percent of the country's environmental problems. Although everyone agrees that environmental education is a major concern, in practice, it is constantly under-prioritized. In 1996, President Ernesto Zedillo made environmental education a mandatory part of the school curriculum, but experts report that the vast majority of teachers along the border have received no training on how to provide such education. Working in conjunction with the schools, the local water utility at all four research sites runs water-related environmental education programs, typically centered on conserving limited water resources. In some cases, such as Nogales, these efforts are well funded and heavily prioritized, but in most locations they are limited in scope. Some environmental agencies at the municipal, state, and federal levels also manage environmental education programs, but, with the exception of Nuevo Laredo, these efforts are also very limited.

This discussion illustrates the limitations of government efforts to resolve the numerous water-related public problems that exist along the border. Civil society organizations have an important role to play in addressing these problems directly or in pushing for an accountable government response; in fact, they have responded to all of these problems in one form or another.

— In the absence of sewer services, organizations in Tijuana, Nogales, and Ciudad Juárez have acted to help residents build or finance latrines. In Ciudad Juárez, a network of groups, including the Centro de Mujeres Tonantzin (Women's Center Tonantzin), has assisted in the construction of *eco-baños*, or bathrooms that do not require connections to sewer or water infrastructure.

— In the face of insecure water supply in Ciudad Juárez, the Paso del Norte Water Task Force, promoted by researchers at universities in Ciudad Juárez, Las Cruces, and El Paso, has advanced binational and tri-state information sharing and water planning.

— In response to a lack of continuity and direction, civic and business leaders in Ciudad Juárez have created the highly inclusive and transparent Plan Estratégico de Juárez (Strategic Plan of Juárez) to consensually arrive at a desirable image for the future of the city and a plan for how to make that image a reality.

— In Tijuana, the Colegio de la Frontera Norte (COLEF; College of the Northern Border) in cooperation with the local water utility runs a small-scale wastewater treatment plant called "Ecoparque," which treats a small section of the city's wastewater and uses the effluent to irrigate one of Tijuana's many hillsides.

— In response to environmental degradation, the binational, multi-sector coalition Asociación de Reforestación en Ambos Nogales (ARAN; Nogales Revegetation Partnership) has emerged to revegetate the urban area and protect the city's hillsides from erosive winds and rains.

— At the site of the former Condados Presto plant in Ciudad Juárez, the Centro de Investigación y Solidaridad Obrera (CISO; Center for Labor

Research and Solidarity) has hired a doctor to conduct epidemiological tests and attend to the medical needs of colonia residents who might be affected by contamination.

— Eight public health and community development organizations in Tijuana have joined in the coalition Promoción y Acción Social (PAS; Promotion and Social Action) to build a network of health promoters in low-income communities. Several of the PAS organizations have incorporated a clean drinking water program into their health promotion efforts.

— Also in Tijuana, a group of environmental organizations and teachers have formed the Proyecto Bio-Regional de Educación Ambiental (PROBEA; Bio-Regional Environmental Education Project) to develop curricula and train Baja California teachers in environmental education.

Because water-related public problems touch a number of policy arenas and involve a diverse set of associational efforts, this study is able to compare the development of civil society organization not only across the four cities but also across these different policy arenas. Multiple arenas allow this research to overcome some of the methodological problems found in a comparative case study.

Organizations

In examining seventy-two nonprofit organizations and a sample of smaller neighborhood level associations, this study draws two important distinctions. The first is between those organizations which exist for public benefit, such as environmental groups, community development organizations, and city improvement associations, and those which seek a narrower parochial benefit, such as social clubs, professional associations, and business groups. This distinction is not to suggest that public benefit organizations are purely altruistic or that parochial organizations cannot yield public benefits. Although these categories are probably best represented by a continuum, for the sake of simplicity, they are presented as two discrete categories in table 2.4.

Organizations that operate for public benefit in Mexico are incorporated primarily as institutions of private assistance (IAPs) or civil associa-

Table 2.4 Typology of nonprofit organizations

Type	Autonomous with respect to political society	Nonautonomous
Public benefit	Civil society organizations, including many environmental groups, community development organizations, public health groups, service organizations, and city improvement associations	Many neighborhood associations dependent on political patrons and political parties themselves
Parochial benefit	Social clubs, professional associations, many business chambers, and interest groups	Mandatory business chambers that existed during one-party rule and labor unions tied to political parties

tions (*asociaciones civiles*, or ACs). IAPs are automatically tax exempt and able to offer tax incentives for contributions; however, they are highly regulated by the Junta de Asistencia Privada (JAP; Private Assistance Board) made up of both members of civil society and governmental officials. ACs are much more common and barely regulated at all, but they are not able to offer tax incentives for contributions. Civil associations wishing to do so must file to become "donatarias autorizadas" (authorized donees). Business and professional organizations that operate for the benefit of their members typically incorporate as chambers, colleges, societies, and associations. There also exist a number of other less common legal auspices, and of course many associational efforts are not formally and legally constituted.

The study makes a second important distinction, between those organizations which are dependent on government and political society and those which are not. Organizations connected to political parties are typically clientelistic neighborhood associations that mobilize their neighbors to support political candidates in exchange for the promise of material benefits. Dependence is determined by examining organizational networks and interview responses. Groups that have exclusive ties to partisan actors and no links to other organizations are likely to suffer from overdependence. These two distinctions create four categories in a two-by-two typology of organizations within Mexico's nonprofit sector, illustrated in table 2.3.

This study focuses on organizations that address water-related public problems beyond the level of the individual neighborhood, or colonia, as identified through a number of sources, including the Internet database *The Border Environmental Education Resource Guide*, directories compiled by local foundations in Tijuana, Nogales, and Ciudad Juárez, and a municipal directory of organizations in Tijuana (Environmental Education Exchange 2000; International Community Foundation 2003; Desarrollo Social Municipal 2003; FESAC 2003; FECHAC 2000). In a method known as a "non-fixed snowball sampling method," the identified organizations were asked about other groups they interact with. In total, the study found 72 nonprofit organizations operating in water-related policy arenas (Tijuana, 23; Nogales, 11; Ciudad Juárez, 27; and Nuevo Laredo, 11), all presented in the appendix.[12]

In addition, the study conducted interviews with and surveys of a sample of formal and informal associations that operated at the neighborhood level in Nuevo Laredo, Ciudad Juárez, and Tijuana (these are enumerated in the appendix). Because there were hundreds of such associations in each city (some 470 in Ciudad Juárez alone), a study of all neighborhood-level associations was not practical. Consequently, a smaller sample of neighborhood associations was examined in three of the four research sites, namely, Tijuana, 24; Ciudad Juarez, 25; and Nuevo Laredo: 11.[13]

In total, 63 interviews were conducted with representatives from municipal, state, and federal government agencies that operate in water-related policy arenas (listed in the appendix) in the four cities (Tijuana, 15; Nogales, 14; Ciudad Juárez, 20; and Nuevo Laredo, 14).[14]

In addition, this study conducted interviews with a total of 43 U.S. nonprofit organizations involved in binational water issues, as identified through *The Border Environmental Education Resource Guide*, Guidestar .com (an Internet database of U.S. charitable organizations), and a snowball sampling method (San Diego area, 15; Santa Cruz and Pima Counties, Arizona, 9; El Paso, Texas, and Las Cruces, New Mexico, 15; and Laredo, Texas, 4; see the appendix).[15]

Beyond interviews, research activities also included archival study of organization documents and Web sites. Furthermore, observation and informal discussions at organization, coalition, and public meetings made up an important part of the study. In total, I attended forty-six meetings during the research period.

3 Nuevo Laredo

Persistent Informal Rules

Introduction

This chapter is about nonprofit organizations, political opportunities, and informal rules in the city of Nuevo Laredo, Tamaulipas, which is distinct from the study's other research sites in three important respects. First, there are fewer, less-institutionalized organizations operating at a lower level of intensity in Nuevo Laredo than in the other three cities (even accounting for differences in population). Second, the organizations that do exist are more often engaged in the activities of parochial or political society than in the search for solutions to public problems. Third, the opportunities for citizen participation in public affairs are more likely to be politically manipulated and taken advantage of by citizens with political ambitions.

The chapter first identifies the government and market failure to solve water-related policy problems in Nuevo Laredo and the need for a civil society response to that failure. It then documents the relative weakness of Nuevo Laredo's nonprofit community and the political manipulation of opportunities to participate in the public affairs. To explain these findings, the chapter focuses on the continuation of one-party rule in Nuevo Laredo and the state of Tamaulipas and the persistence of informal rules that governed state-society relations during much of the twentieth century. Moreover, it finds little social infrastructure capable of challenging these norms operating in associational life, offering alternative proposals, or supporting the autonomous solution of policy problems.

The Need for Civil Society Organizations

Like the other three cities in this study, Nuevo Laredo struggles with a number of water-related policy problems. A diagnostic report prepared for the city by Parsons Engineering (2002) found that 8 percent of the population did not have running water and 12.5 percent were not connected to the sewer system. The city's water comes entirely from the Rio Grande, and public concern generates headlines when water stored in the nearby Amistad Dam drops to low levels.

Wastewater from the city is treated at a plant whose construction in the late 1990s was partly funded by the U.S. government. Even though the facility is in excellent condition and even operates below capacity, a significant portion of the city's wastewater never actually makes it to the plant. Sewer infrastructure in Nuevo Laredo's center was not properly maintained for decades; many of the sewer lines, now over 30 or 40 years old, collapsed. Rather than rehabilitate them or devote more resources to maintenance, government authorities found it cheaper to channel the backed-up, untreated sewage into the city's pluvial drainage system (Parsons Engineering 2002) and let it flow directly into the Rio Grande. In recent years, new communities have sprung up to the south of the city and downstream from the wastewater treatment plant. While city authorities debate whether to pump sewage north to the existing plant or build a second plant, additional wastewater from these new communities also flows into the river.

Despite efforts by city and state officials to address water-related policy problems, the response has been insufficient and controversial. In the early 2000s, the city's water utility, the Comisión Municipal de Agua Potable y Alcantarillado (COMAPA; Municipal Commission for Potable Water and Sewer), made plans to rehabilitate the city's water and sewer infrastructure. To fund the project, the city calculated that it would have to increase water and sewer fees by at least 30 percent. Members of the nonprofit community, though clearly recognizing the need for such a project, expressed their doubts that the water utility could turn a 30 percent fee increase into an effectively functioning water and sewer system. Some recalled the fate of a poorly designed water cistern, which failed in 2002 after only a few days in operation (*El Mañana* 2004). This widely known failure and problems with current service were enough to make most citizens skeptical. At a meeting on the subject, the former president of the Council of Institutions of Nuevo Laredo, a coalition of primarily professional and business associations, declared: "We will be the first to support the project if we know that it is being managed well." However, given that the utility had wasted public monies in the past, it seemed likely it would do so again. Or, as another person at the meeting remarked: "They don't manage their current resources well, so how are we going to trust them and give them more money?"

As discussed in chapter 2, political manipulation of public utilities in Mexico is not new. Service is sometimes extended to communities that lack infrastructure (often low-income communities settled by invasion) to gain votes. Prices are reduced or outstanding debts waived in exchange for political support or to silence criticism. Jobs within the utility are also offered as political favors, and building contracts awarded to preferred companies. Finally, because the utility generates a large amount of revenue, it can be exploited as a source of petty cash for the government. Obviously, all of these actions reduce the efficiency and effectiveness of government's response to water-related policy problems.

Although the actual extent of such mismanagement in Nuevo Laredo's water utility is beyond the scope of this study, in interviews, several members of the city's nonprofit sector agreed that these concerns are all too real. In this context, greater citizen oversight and transparency could help reduce political manipulation of public resources and ensure adequate hiring and contracting procedures. Moreover, the advantage of the nonprofit sector is that it does not have to wait for governmental action: it can look for solutions on its own. All along the border, civil society initiatives are leading the search for policy solutions. In Ciudad Juárez, organizations are helping residents construct and finance dry toilets that do not require a connection to the sewer system. Citizen initiatives are also leading government actors and large water users toward a tristate (Chihuahua, New Mexico, and Texas) and binational solution to overexploited groundwater reserves. In Tijuana, organizations are educating citizens about the dangers of untreated water, and a civil society initiative has created a small-scale wastewater treatment plant that recycles wastewater to irrigate an ecological park. Unfortunately, however, as the following section illustrates, Nuevo Laredo lacks a nonprofit sector that can play such a leadership role in the policy arena.

Evidence That the Nonprofit Sector Is Weaker in Nuevo Laredo

Of the 72 nonprofit organizations in water-related policy arenas identified by this study, 23 operate in Tijuana, 11 in Nogales, 27 in Ciudad Juárez, and 11 in Nuevo Laredo (see table 3.1). Within this border nonprofit community, there is considerable variation. Only some of these organizations can be considered "civil society organizations," independent of political society and concerned with finding solutions to public problems. Although some are highly institutionalized, with a full-time staff, offices, an active board of directors, and reliable funding sources, others rarely meet, have no staff, and are centered on one or two concerned citizens. Some nonprofits are not formally incorporated, others are incorporated as civil associations (*asociaciones civiles*), and still others are considered authorized donees (*donatarias autorizadas*), able to offer tax deductions for donations. The degree of institutionalization corresponds to the extent of organizational activities. Many nonprofits have a number of ongoing programs that mobilize a large number of people, whereas others have little or no programmatic activity.

Because of such variation in the nonprofit sector, the number of organizations participating in a given policy arena at a given location tells us very little by itself. Thus, although Nogales and Nuevo Laredo, the two smaller cities in the study, both have more organizations per capita than the larger cities of Ciudad Juárez and Tijuana, even a shallow qualitative analysis of the four cities would reveal the much greater capacity of organizations in the two larger cities. It is therefore necessary to develop a measure that captures not only the number of organizations participating but also the degree of institutionalization and intensity of activity. Fortunately, such measurement is possible because of the qualitative and systematic research methodology employed here.

To compare the four cities, the simple measure "civil society organization presence" takes into account not only the number of nonprofit organizations but also the percentage that are civil society organizations (autonomous organizations seeking solutions to public problems), have paid employees, have obtained authorized donee status, and implement programmatic activities. Table 3.1 summarizes these factors across the four cities. As the table illustrates, Ciudad Juárez is considered to have a high

Table 3.1 Civil society organization presence

	Number of nonprofits	Population	Nonprofits with authorized donee status		Nonprofits with paid employee(s)		Nonprofits with programmatic activities		Autonomous nonparochial nonprofits		Civil society organizational presence
			No.	Percent	No.	Percent	No.	Percent	No.	Percent	
Tijuana	23	1,410,687	4	17.4	16	69.6	18	78.3	18	78.3	Medium–High
Nogales	11	193,517	1	9.1	6	54.5	5	45.5	8	72.7	Medium
Ciudad Juárez	27	1,313,338	7	25.9	19	70.4	19	70.4	24	88.9	High
Nuevo Laredo	11	355,827	0	0.00	3	27.3	2	18.2	2	18.2	Low

Source: Population data are from *INEGI 2005*; all other data were collected by author in 2003 and 2004.

civil society organization presence because of the large percentage of associations that score well across these criteria. Tijuana is regarded as having a medium-high presence because it has slightly fewer organizations than Ciudad Juárez despite a high level of institutionalization. Nogales is deemed to have a medium civil society organization presence: even though it has a higher number of organizations per capita than either Tijuana or Ciudad Juárez, they are less institutionalized and have far fewer and more limited programmatic activities. Nuevo Laredo ranks the lowest of the four cities. As the table shows, only two of Nuevo Laredo's associations (active in the policy arena) are actually civil society organizations, none are authorized donees, and few have paid employees or take action to directly address public problems.

A closer examination of civil society organizations in Nuevo Laredo offers even greater cause for concern. Of the eleven organizations in Nuevo Laredo involved with water-related public problems, three have their roots in political parties. Lideres Unidos (United Leaders) and Asociación de Colonias Populares (ACOPO; Association of Popular Colonias) serve as both community organizations and mobilizing agents for the PRI. The Frente Unido Nacional (the National United Front) has close ties to the Partido de la Revolución Democrática (PRD; Democratic Revolution Party). Two additional organizations, the Consejo Coordinador Ciudadano (Citizen Coordinating Council) and the Comité Regional de Vigilancia y Protección al Medio Ambiente (the Regional Committee for Environmental Monitoring and Protection), were created by government. In other words, of the mere eleven organizations operating in the policy arena, five — almost half — owe their creation to government and the political sphere.

Of the remaining six organizations, four are business or professional organizations and one is a coalition of primarily business organizations, service organizations (e.g., Rotary Club) and social clubs. All of these organizations operate at a very low level of intensity in the policy arena and have few programmatic activities. Indeed, only one of the organizations identified in the study, the Centro Internacional de Estudios del Río Bravo (CIERB; Río Bravo International Studies Center) actually has a strong programmatic focus in the policy arena. For the other ten organizations in Nuevo Laredo, participation in the policy arena occurs either through involvement in government created committees or through efforts to pressure government officials.

As such, Nuevo Laredo contrasts sharply with Ciudad Juárez and Tijuana, where the vast majority of organizations have programs that directly address water-related public problems. For example, Tijuana is home to organizations such as Proyecto Fronterizo de Educación Ambiental (PFEA: Border Environmental Education Project). Having spent more than fifteen years developing environmental education programs and working to hold government officials accountable, the staff and young volunteers of PFEA have mobilized national and international resources to protect the environment, lead beach cleanups, help write environmental legislation, and conduct workshops on transparency and institutional development. PFEA has hosted border-wide meetings of the border environmental community, participated actively in a coalition to train local teachers in environmental education, and served as a clearinghouse of information on environmental issues in the region. Unfortunately, there are no comparable organizations present in Nuevo Laredo. This raises the question that is the focus of this chapter: Why is Nuevo Laredo's nonprofit sector different from that of Ciudad Juárez and Tijuana? For answers, let us turn to the political opportunities, informal rules, and existing social infrastructure in Nuevo Laredo.

Political Opportunity and Informal Rules

One of the main reasons why Nuevo Laredo's nonprofit sector is more dependent on the political arena and less solution-oriented is the city's political environment. Simply put, the continuation of one-party rule has allowed for the perpetuation of informal rules inimical to the formation of autonomous, solution-oriented nonprofit organizations.

As Mexico has transitioned from a one-party, semi-authoritarian government to a competitive electoral democracy, the local political environment has changed dramatically in Tijuana, Ciudad Juárez, and, to a lesser extent, Nogales. In Tijuana and Ciudad Juárez, the PAN opposition party was swept into power as early as the 1980s. In Nogales, although the PRI still maintained control of the local administration during the research period, electoral competition increased dramatically. By contrast, local politics in Nuevo Laredo and the state of Tamaulipas have remained essentially unchanged from thirty years ago. In the 2004 municipal election, for example, the PRI candidate (like his predecessors) beat his closest challenger by over 20 percent. This continued political monopoly allows the informal rules that developed under one-party rule to continue unchallenged.

A look at Nuevo Laredo's recent political history reveals a highly clientelistic, closed political environment. Throughout the twentieth century, Nuevo Laredo and the state of Tamaulipas came to typify the mixture of corporatism and clientelism fostered under the PRI political system (Garza and Pariente Fregosa 2000; Herrera 1999).

> Another aspect of the multi-polar political character of Tamaulipas during the second half of the twentieth century was the corporatist consolidation of the main part of the labor sector through confederations of workers created by the state party. . . . This created bureaucratic labor and agrarian structures that produced large power blocks in the distinct cities and regions of the state. This type of political organization was fed by clientelistic mechanisms and patronage, which controlled the urban and rural proletariat and was entrusted to recruit loyal representative to occupy positions of the public administration that by quota corresponded to them. (Herrera 1999, 229)

In the decades following the Mexican Revolution, from 1925 to 1947, the state of Tamaulipas was de facto governed by Emilio Portes Gil, who also served two years as Mexico's interim president (Herrera 1999). Portes Gil and his followers were eventually marginalized in 1947 when President Miguel Alemán Valdés used an economic and security crisis to dissolve the state government, allowing for greater control by Mexico City and the growth of corporatist organizations (Herrera 1999). As the state began to urbanize in the early 1960s, the Confederación de Trabajadores de México (CTM; Confederation of Mexican Workers) began to consolidate its control over city and state politics (Herrera 1999). In each of Tamaulipas's major cities, powerful labor leaders emerged.

Nuevo Laredo's politics were controlled for decades by the local cacique Pedro Pérez Ibarra.[1] Although he was never elected municipal president, Pérez Ibarra led the CTM in Nuevo Laredo from 1956 to 1992 and used his position to dominate local politics. Even an unabashedly favorable historian of the CTM in Nuevo Laredo is forced to admit, "It should remain clear that the CTM has always been a determining factor in the economic, political, and union life of Nuevo Laredo" (López González 1998, 286).[2] Critics, however, were less subtle in their assessment of Pérez Ibarra's power. One editorialist stated, "Conventional wisdom suggests that nobody can open a business, build a house, or make a political decision in this city without consulting the head of the union and most importantly without soliciting the services of some of his numerous businesses grown under the protection of his union power" (*El Diario* 1984b).

A general strike by Nuevo Laredo's CTM members in February 1984 illustrated both the power of Pérez Ibarra and the growing frustrations with his leadership. In that year, the city's mayor attempted to assert his independence from the union by seeking to contract independently with sixty-four workers to tend the city's gardens and parks (Duenas 1984). In response, Pérez Ibarra and the CTM brought the city to its knees with a massive general strike of unionized workers, including the entire transportation sector. The strike produced antiunion counterprotests, championed, rumor had it, by angry business interests in nearby Monterrey, the industrial capital of northern Mexico. Although the massive strike demonstrated Pérez Ibarra's power, the counterprotests turned so violent that the union leader's house was actually burned down, and it seemed they might usher in a new era in local politics.

As Pérez Ibarra stated after the incident, however, "They have destroyed my house and my properties, but they have not destroyed me or my conscience" (*El Diario* 1984a). The union leader would continue to dominate local politics until the event that has become known as the "aduanazo." In 1992, Pérez Ibarra led a march to protest new rules restricting the amount of goods that could be transported across the border. When Nuevo Laredo's customs office (*aduana*) was burned down, however, a warrant was issued for his arrest. Although sympathizers claim that Pérez Ibarra was set up, he was forced to flee to the United States (López González 1998, 286).

Such events are both evidence and a symptom of the city's closed political environment. The CTM, in fact, still remains an important force in local politics, and the man who emerged to replace and repudiate Pérez

Ibarra, José María Morales, continues to lead the organization sixteen years later. Daniel Peña, a union leader who helped orchestrate Morales's succession was elected mayor in 2004. Peña won the PRI nomination for mayor as a "unity candidate," which despite the euphemism signifies that the nomination was determined behind closed doors by powerbrokers within the party. That same year, the party's candidate for governor, Eugenio Hernández Flores, also emerged as a "unity candidate." Because of the lack of viable opposition parties in both the state and the municipality, nomination by the party ensured election. In fact, both candidates won their offices by a margin of over 20 percent of the vote.

As a result of a closed nomination process and continued one-party dominance, Nuevo Laredo's party elite still hold a monopoly on power. Not forced to share power by elections, it is unlikely that political leaders will surrender it to civil society. Consequently, today's potential public entrepreneurs face the same dilemma that Rudolfo Cota Martínez faced in 1983 when he founded ACOPO. The informal rules of Nuevo Laredo politics severely limit the options of potential public entrepreneurs, who can seek the favor of political patrons within the PRI system, engage in contentious politics, or avoid public affairs entirely. The following subsections examine three prevailing informal rules that continue to govern state-society relations in Nuevo Laredo: clientelism, co-option, and cynicism.

Informal Rules: Clientelism

Three of Nuevo Laredo's eleven organizations concerned with water-related policy issues are clientelistic organizations that have their roots in political parties. ACOPO, Lideres Unidos, and Frente Unido Nacional all double as both community organizations and mobilizing agents for political parties in low-income communities throughout the city. Because water and sewer services and the costs of these are so important to low-income residents, all three of the organizations are very active in the policy arena.

Over twenty years since its founding, the Association of Popular Colonias (ACOPO) loyally continues to mobilize votes for the PRI, gambling that its usefulness at the polls will result in patronage and policy benefits for its constituents. Although many ACOPO communities have received important material benefits for their party loyalty, the exchange is inherently clientelistic, and as discussed in chapter 1, ACOPO leaders have had to put the needs of the party before the needs of their neighborhoods.

ACOPO is actually a coalition of neighborhood associations. When new colonias are established, the ACOPO leadership helps establish a neighborhood chapter. ACOPO committees are governed by a president and a board of directors and hold regular meetings. Neighborhood presidents then represent the community in periodic citywide meetings. For small concerns, committee presidents tend to work directly with government agencies; for large infrastructure needs, committee requests are channeled through ACOPO's leadership.

Some ACOPO neighborhood associations adopted formal names such as "Comité Pro-Mejoramiento Berta del Avellano" (Berta del Avellano Improvement Committee) and "Comité de Desarrollo Social de la Colonia Arnulfo Tejeda Lara" (Colonia Anulfo Tejeda Lara Social Development Committee). Others did not, and at least two of the respondents simply considered themselves to be presidents of their neighborhoods (despite their partisan affiliation).

Interviews with ten neighborhood committee presidents under the ACOPO umbrella illustrate both the accomplishments and clientelistic limitations of ACOPO. Interviewees felt that they were performing an important service for their neighborhoods and attributed the introduction of numerous public services to their hard work. In point of fact, some of the committees had obtained water, sewer, electricity, and pavement for their neighborhoods at no cost to the residents.

All of the respondents openly admitted to actively supporting the PRI party. One answered flatly, "Yes, it's part of the job." Interviewees generally viewed participation in political society to be effective. One committee president answered, "Yes, we enter into politics. This is how we can accomplish things." Respondents brushed off concerns about backing the wrong political candidate with statements such as "We usually pick the right horse," or "We have never lost," although at least one interviewee was less optimistic. Although this president proudly considered himself to be priista and had campaigned hard for the city's mayor, his community had not benefited from his loyal efforts. As a PRI candidate, the mayor had promised to introduce sewer services into the neighborhood; as the mayor's administration drew to a close, however, he had not made good on his promise and, the association president admitted, he was unlikely to.

Interviewees also received personal benefits for their community activism. Once elected, party candidates typically pays the committee leaders who supported their candidacies. Another committee president reported that she pays a discounted rate for water and sewer services because of her work with the water utility. Respondents did not see anything wrong with these benefits; they were merely appropriate remuneration for services rendered. However, the informality of the benefits has fostered the image of corruption, an image further encouraged by the role of the associations in handling community funds. Unlike in Tijuana and Ciudad Juárez, neighborhood committees in Nuevo Laredo are actually tasked with collecting money from residents for the introduction of water and sewer services. Although there have been efforts to improve the transparency of these collections, respondents themselves reported two cases of neighborhood leaders stealing from community funds.

According to one of its members, Lideres Unidos was formed around 2000 as a mobilizing agent for the PRI by some 70 neighborhood leaders who felt that ACOPO personnel were using their positions for their own benefit: for example, to obtain jobs in the municipal government. In the member's words, Lideres Unidos was composed of leaders who "truly wanted to benefit the community" (ACOPO members of course contest this claim). The organization emerged as an important force in Nuevo Laredo politics when ACOPO supported the losing candidate for the PRI nomination for municipal president. By backing the man who emerged as the winner, Lideres Unidos was able to fill the gap between the nominee and party bases in low-income communities. What is astonishing is that, despite its stated differences with ACOPO, Lideres Unidos has pursued the very same clientelistic strategy.

In addition, the founders of the Frente Unido Nacional (FUN; United National Front), which emerged in 1997, also could not resist the temptation to tie partisan objectives to citizen concerns about the provision of basic water and sewer services (among others). Despite its name, the organization is locally based in Nuevo Laredo with activity in other northern Tamaulipas cities. Although the organization's leadership claims that the

Figure 3.1. Water and sewer policy network in Nuevo Laredo. Squares represent nonprofits; triangles, professional organizations; and diamonds, government agencies.

group is an independent organization seeking improved public services for its members, FUN is a strong supporter for the Democratic Revolutionary Party (PRD). In fact, the organization's president earned a seat on the city council on the PRD ticket in the 2004 elections.

Thus the tradition of tying community organizations to political parties is not just a vestige of the past. On the contrary, new organizations are being formed in the twenty-first century using the same clientelistic strategies. The social networks that have formed in Nuevo Laredo to address water and sewer issues are represented in figure 3.1. In contrast, rather than forming links with one another or with other organizations, ACOPO, Lideres Unidos, and FUN are instead entirely dependent on their links with government actors, including the water utility, the city, and the city's social development agency. Without access to alternative opportunities, there is little hope that such organizations will pursue new, autonomous strategies. Indeed, beholden as they are to the partisan political arena, such organizations may find themselves acting contrary to the interests of their constituents.

Informal Rules: Co-option

The presence of informal rules that join nonprofit organizations to political society in Nuevo Laredo is not specific to low-income residents desperate for public goods and services. In 1999, the municipal administration created the Consejo Coordinador Ciudadano (CCC; Citizen Coordinating Council) to offer the city's associational life access to the policy process. At first glance, this government-established citizen organization appears to be an innovative mechanism for involving citizens in the policy process. CCC participants are afforded the opportunity to review and comment on pending legislation before the city council. In addition, the organization played a key role in selecting the city's chief financial officer for the latter half of the 2001–2004 administration. The CCC is also essential to promoting citizen participation in and facilitating the work of other public participation initiatives, such as the council that oversees the water utility, a committee on transparency, and a public security council. Moreover, the president of the organization at the time of the study proved himself to be a committed individual working hard to ensure the effectiveness of the council.

Unfortunately, however, there are a number of valid criticisms against the CCC. First, participation in the council is restricted to officially established organizations and only organizations that are at least five years old. Therefore, despite its name, the Citizens' Coordinating Council is not actually open to ordinary citizens. Those wishing to join the council would have to form an organization and then wait five years. As a result of this rule, the organization's membership reflects Nuevo Laredo's non-profit sector, which is dominated by business and professional organizations. Of the CCC's more than seventy members, the vast majority represent a business or professional group such as the Colegio de Arquitectos (Association of Architects) or the Colegio de Ingenieros Civiles (Association of Civil Engineers). For some critics, therefore, the CCC is an effort to ensure that Nuevo Laredo's well-organized business community is given a voice in public policy to the exclusion of ordinary community members.

Second, because the CCC is the only legal conduit between government and civil society organizations, other critics contend that the council is really an effort to control and co-opt. For example, one observer stated that the CCC only exists "to validate the decisions of the municipal government." In fact, the council was created despite the presence of an autonomous parallel organization, the Consejo de Instituciones de Nuevo Laredo Nuevo Laredo (CINL; Council of Institutions), which includes an almost identical membership of associations. For many active participants in the CINL, the municipal government's unwillingness to offer a more general arena for participation or to work through the CINL directly suggests that the administration would rather have an intermediary that it can control.

Third, at the head of this extremely hierarchical organization, the president serves as the driving force behind the CCC's efforts. Indeed, some interviewed observers see the position of president merely as a means to groom capable citizens for public office, citing the fact that the CCC's first president made a successful bid for the legislature on the PRI ticket after he completed his term. Because the CCC addresses any number of policy issues, its president is a relatively high profile individual who receives regular media attention. Although it is the right of any citizen to run for public office, political ambitions create a conflict of interest for leaders of such an important citizen oversight commission. A potential candidate might either seek to achieve favor within the party by legitimating government decisions or attempt to gain popular support by using the position to denounce political opponents. Perhaps more important, the present use of such positions for political ends undermines the future credibility of those individuals who claim to be public rather than political entrepreneurs. As argued in chapter 1, citizen trust is the hallmark of civil society organizations.

Unfortunately, using citizen oversight positions as a springboard into partisan politics is not limited to the CCC. The citizen representative on the water utility's governing board during the 2001–2004 municipal administration of José Manuel Suárez López was appointed to head the public works agency in the following administration. Even executive positions within the independent Council of Institutions of Nuevo Laredo are not free from partisan political ambitions, for such posts represent an opportunity to gain political favor within the business and political community. In fact, the municipal president at the time of this study had previously been secretary of the organization.

As stressed in chapter 1, one of the unique aspects of civil society organizations is their independence from political society. This excludes not only partisan and clientelistic organizations but also organizations that use civil society as a platform to gain control of the state. Unfortunately however, Nuevo Laredo's associational life is deeply intertwined with partisan politics and political ambition. What appears to be opportunities

for civil society and associational life to oversee public officials and participate in the policy process, in practice can serve as a means to limit
participation, co-opt, and cultivate political leaders.

However, the CCC is not the only opportunity for civil society participation in the policy process that suffers from perverse incentives. To
finance the rehabilitation of its sewer infrastructure, the city sought the
support of the North American Development Bank (NADB) and the Border Environment Cooperation Commission (BECC). The bank and its
sister agency were created under the side agreements to the NAFTA to
certify and fund the creation of infrastructure for water, sewer, wastewater treatment, and solid waste disposal in the region. Negotiators of the
accord recognized that industrial growth along the border would increase
the demand for water and sewer services. To encourage infrastructure
development, the NADB was established to provide financing for projects,
and the BECC was created to certify the quality of proposed projects. As
one of several certification criteria required by the BECC, project sponsors
must carry out an extensive public participation process: utility agencies
must convene a citizen steering committee with a diverse representation of
society; hold informational meetings with organized sectors of the community; publish and disseminate information about the project; hold two
public meetings with thirty days' advance notice; and generate a report
documenting the public participation process and demonstrating general
public support for the project (BECC n.d.).

Unfortunately, the Nuevo Laredo water utility failed to comply with
either the letter or the spirit of the BECC public participation process.
Despite clear BECC guidelines to the contrary, the citizen steering committee failed to include a diverse representation of society. Half of the
original participants, including the committee's president, were construction contractors of the utility itself. This led to the criticism that the steering committee was merely a tool to divide up contracts for future construction work. Although the committee was expanded in response, other
irregularities persisted. The utility failed to offer written project proposals
to the public, and though it hosted two public meetings, it failed both to
publicize them and to give the required thirty days' notice. Indeed, it
announced the second public meeting only two days beforehand and with
minimal publicity. Despite this lack of notification, the water utility re

ported that 450 people attended (BECC 2004). Unfortunately, this (exaggerated) attendance was the result, not of a yearning for civic engagement among Nuevo Laredo's citizens, but of orchestration by the city and the water utility: they had sent their employees home early to clean up, change out of uniform, and attend the meeting, ostensibly as members of the general public.

As a result, public discussion lasted less than twenty minutes and all speakers offered their support for the project, despite a proposed 30 percent increase in water bills. Such a large increase would normally produce considerable controversy. In fact, in the days and weeks prior to the meeting, articles and op-ed pieces had been published in the local newspaper questioning the project and the rate increases (Flores 2004; Martínez 2004). However, these legitimate questions were not raised at the public meeting. Those concerned about the project either did not attend the meeting or resolved their concerns behind closed doors. Thus it is clear that the public participation process was little more than window dressing to fulfill a requirement of the binational agency. Nonetheless, the board of directors of the BECC certified the project in 2004; having fulfilled its mandate, the citizen steering committee was disbanded.

Informal rules of clientelism and co-option in Nuevo Laredo offer potential public entrepreneurs only limited political opportunity to participate in public affairs without also participating in political and partisan affairs. That some leaders within Nuevo Laredo's associational life use the nonprofit sector to mobilize votes or as a stepping-stone to political leadership serves to discredit any citizen engagement in the public arena. Past and continued manipulation leads the average citizen to question the motives of individuals who appear to be working hard for the benefit of the community. The result is an informal rule that is perhaps more damaging than clientelism and co-option: cynicism and distrust.

Preexisting Networks and Social Infrastructure

Despite the obstacles presented to potential public entrepreneurs by the political arena and by the informal rules governing the relationship between state and society, it is still theoretically feasible for a public entrepreneur to found an organization and act independently of political society. Of the eleven organizations participating in the water policy arena, there is at least one that could be described as a civil society organization, which works independently of government to directly address public problems: the Centro Internacional de Estudios del Río Bravo (CIERB; Río Bravo International Studies Center). In the early 1990s, David Negrete was an up-and-coming engineer working for the Comisión Internacional de Límites y Aguas International (CILA), the Mexican section of the International Boundary and Water Commission (IBWC). He had been transferred to Nuevo Laredo to oversee the construction of a binationally funded wastewater treatment plant and serve as the CILA's representative in the region. After the plant was successfully developed, Negrete began to look for other means to address water problems in his new city. He found an outlet for his energy in the nonprofit sector.

In 1992, the Ford Foundation invited Negrete to participate in a forum on citizen initiatives to protect the Rio Grande. A short time later in Nuevo Laredo, Negrete helped found the CIERB, with the encouragement of the foundation, which also helped tie the center in with a growing network of border environmental organizations. CIERB would later join the Rio Grande/Río Bravo Basin Coalition (based in El Paso, Texas) and partner with Proyecto del Río, based in Las Cruces, New Mexico. CIERB's experience is unique in Nuevo Laredo because, even though Negrete works for the federal government, he has managed to keep his civil society work separate from the political arena.

Under Negrete's leadership, CIERB dedicated itself to a number of different educational programs oriented toward improving environmental quality in the Nuevo Laredo community. The organization became the local coordinator of an annual festival called "Día del Río" (Day of the River), at which communities undertake educational and volunteer activities to improve the environmental quality of the Rio Grande/Río Bravo. As part of Día del Río, CIERB coordinates a massive annual river cleanup. The effort includes everyone from school children, who pick up trash and participate in educational activities, to the Mexican military, which uses cranes to drag discarded washing machines, refrigerators, and cars from the river. Day of the River, which Negrete jokes should really be called "Week of the River," includes essay and drawing competitions and a host of educational activities to raise awareness about water resources.

Even after the Rio Grande/Río Bravo Basin Coalition, which was the driving force behind Day of the River all along the border, ceased operations, CIERB continued to lead the event in Nuevo Laredo.

Unfortunately, however, CIERB's programmatic activities have been limited by a lack of institutionalization. Its directors, like those of many organizations in this study, participate at a low level of intensity and do not provide financial support for the organization. In fact, CIERB has attracted only limited external funds, and the organization has not made major attempts to obtain grant money or alter its legal status to accept tax-deductible donations. As a result, its activities are limited to those few which its volunteer president can organize and maintain.

Despite continuation of one-party rule and the informal rules that support it, it was still possible for CIERB to emerge and blaze a new path toward direct citizen action. There are not more organizations like CIERB because Nuevo Laredo does not have the social infrastructure (defined as preexisting forms of organization that offer a potential source of information and human and financial resources) capable of incubating and sustaining autonomous public entrepreneurial efforts. The city lacks the history of church activism and the democratic social movement that chapter 4 shows to have been important in Ciudad Juárez. It also lacks the vibrant San Diego nonprofit community on the opposite side of the border that has been important to the emergence of civil society organizations in Tijuana. In addition, universities in Nuevo Laredo, such as a branch of the Universidad Autónoma de Tamaulipas, the Instituto Tecnológico de Nuevo Laredo, Universidad Valle del Bravo, and Universidad Tecnológica de Nuevo Laredo are small, oriented toward technical degrees for work in the maquiladora sector, and focused on teaching rather than research and public service. There are no foundations or intermediary organizations to help facilitate the work of public entrepreneurs. Nor is there a strong preexisting set of civil society organizations that could help spin off and produce new organizations.

By contrast, Nuevo Laredo does contain a large supply of clientelistic organizations and business and professional associations, which have served to incubate similar organizations rather than autonomous, public problem–oriented nonprofits like CIERB. Thus, having developed the know-how, skills, and government contacts to intermediate between low-income constituents and the government through their experience and participation in ACOPO, the founders of Lideres Unidos branched off and formed their own organization based on the same model. Thus, too, Nuevo Laredo's business and professional organizations have facilitated the emergence of new business and professional organizations. The Association of Engineers and the Association of Architects, for example, emerged from the Sociedad de Ingenieros, Arquitectos, y Técnicos (Society of Engineers, Architects, and Technical Workers), which was founded back in 1958. In fact, within the Council of Institutions of Nuevo Laredo alone, there are at least twenty-eight business and professional associations.

As distinct from these organizations, CIERB enjoys network ties that are unique in Nuevo Laredo, particularly those to the Ford Foundation, which served as the necessary catalyst for the center's founding and provided it with essential networking support. In addition, CIERB's partnership with organizations such as Proyecto del Río from Las Cruces and its participation in the Rio Grande/Río Bravo Basin Coalition offered new ways of approaching public problems. For example, the idea of Day of the River, the backbone of CIERB's efforts, was in fact conceived 700 miles upstream in the Paso del Norte region.

Negrete's and CIERB's network ties make the organization something of an oddity in Nuevo Laredo. With neither financial, human, and organization resources nor the know-how to create a civil society organization, concerned citizens are likely to dismiss public entrepreneurship as even an option and to follow the paths that have already laid down in front of them, whether it is participation in a clientelistic organization or in a business association. As a result, Nuevo Laredo's nonprofit sector is both quantitatively and qualitatively weaker, more dependent on government, and less solution oriented than the nonprofit sector in Tijuana and Ciudad Juárez.

Conclusion

Even though Nuevo Laredo has a large associational life, very few of its nonprofits meet the definition of a civil society organization. In contrast with Tijuana, Ciudad Juárez, and even Nogales, where organizations undertake programmatic activities to address public problems and do not have ties to political parties, almost all Nuevo Laredo's nonprofits are clientelistic organizations closely tied to partisan politics and business associations with a more parochial orientation. Indeed, several serve as jumping off points for private citizens to enter partisan politics. My explanation for this finding is threefold. First, because one party continues to have a monopoly on the public realm, political brokers are perceived to be a more effective means than independent organizations to address public problems. Second, as a result of decades of one-party rule, informal rules have developed that support clientelism, co-option, and cynicism rather than citizenship. Third, Nuevo Laredo's preexisting forms of social infrastructure have encouraged the continued development of clientelistic organizations and business associations rather than the civil society organizations present in Tijuana and Ciudad Juárez.

4 Ciudad Juárez

Rewriting Informal Rules and Incubating

Organizational Efforts

Introduction

Differing radically from Nuevo Laredo's, the nonprofit sector of Ciudad Juárez has taken on many of the city's complex public problems and worked to hold government accountable. To explain this difference, we need to look at political opportunities in Ciudad Juárez, the process through which norm entrepreneurs have attempted to rewrite the informal rules governing state-society relations, and the available supply of social infrastructure. Although this chapter focuses primarily on Ciudad Juárez, it also adduces corroborating evidence from Tijuana and Nogales, Sonora.

The Need for Civil Society Organizations

As in Nuevo Laredo, there is considerable need in Ciudad Juárez for a strong associational life to help address government and market failures, transcend the border, and ensure the accountability of public officials. When Ciudad Juárez's water utility, the Junta Municipal de Agua y Saneamiento (JMAS; Municipal Water and Sanitation Board), wrote its master plan in 2001, 9 percent of the city's residents lacked water connections and 20 percent lacked sewer. Water infrastructure coverage expanded considerably in 2001 when the water utility extended services to a large area on the city's northwest side called Anapra (Córdova Bojórquez 2003b) Anapra and the surrounding communities have around 14,000 residents, but very few have legal title to the land. As a result, although settlement in the area began as early as 1974, residents had to wait until the 2000s to receive potable water infrastructure; at the time of research, Anapra was still without sewer connections (Córdova Bojórquez 2003b).

The presence of communities with insecure property rights, such as

Anapra, is often attributed to poor urban planning. To combat this problem, in 1995, with the state's support, the municipality created one of Mexico's first municipal planning agencies, the Instituto Municipal de Investigación y Planeación (IMIP; Municipal Institute for Research and Planning). IMIP's founders attempted to shelter the agency from short-term, local politics and the lack of continuity between administrations by granting it autonomy, writing its budget allotment into law, and ensuring that the term of its director spanned successive municipal administrations (for more information on IMIP, see Lozano Fernández 2001 and García Mata 2005). Although the IMIP model has been copied throughout the country, municipal administrations marginalized the institute after their short-term needs ran up against IMIP's long-term planning. Finally, in 2005, after several attempts to reduce the institute's power, legal reforms were passed under PRI leadership to severely cut the agency's budget.

The challenge of developing a long-term approach to urban development is replicated in ensuring future water supply. As mentioned in chapter 2, Ciudad Juárez is dependent on the overexploited Hueco Bolson aquifer, which it shares with neighboring El Paso, Texas. The city has plans to diversify its sources of supply, including purifying water from the Rio Grande and developing wells in other aquifers, but all diversification options entail higher costs, to which state authorities have been adverse. Urban use of Rio Grande water is also controversial: agricultural producers downstream from the city rely on the limited supply of river water to irrigate their crops. Despite the river's name, years of below-average snowpack in the southern Rocky Mountains and drought conditions in the region reduced the water supply upstream in the Elephant Butte and Carrillo Reservoirs to as low as 12.6 percent of capacity in the early 2000s (according to the Bureau of Reclamation), and the river often runs dry during the winter months.

Insufficient flow poses a risk not only to the urban inhabitants of Ciudad Juárez and the agricultural producers of the Valle de Juárez but also to the environment, exposing habitat areas to higher concentrations of urban contamination, including untreated wastewater. Although a 1998 toxicity study by the International Boundary and Water Commission (IBWC 2004) found that the river was not toxic to fish, studies through the Texas Clean Rivers Program (IBWC 2004) have found high levels of fecal coliform bacteria, high chloride and sulfate concentrations, and high total dissolved solids including heavy metals.

In summary, there are serious water-related policy problems in Ciudad Juárez that have been addressed inadequately by government and the market. Even innovative policy initiatives such as IMIP, which at its founding was seen as a harbinger of more effective planning and policy, can be rolled back. In the midst of these problems, civil society organizations have an important role to play in directly confronting public concerns, advocating for better policy, educating citizens, transcending borders, and demanding accountability from government officials.

Evidence That the Nonprofit Sector Is Stronger in Ciudad Juárez

Unlike in Nuevo Laredo, autonomous nonprofit organizations have emerged in Ciudad Juárez to seek solutions to all of these public problems. Several civil society initiatives have already been mentioned in the preceding chapters, including the Paso del Norte Water Task Force's efforts to address the region's water supply, the actions of the Organización Popular Independiente (OPI) to obtain water and sewer services in low-income areas, Plan Estratégico's citywide planning effort, the Centro de Mujeres Tonantzin's promotion of eco-baños in communities without sewer connections, and the response of the Centro de Investigación y Solidaridad Obrera (CISO) to contamination in neighborhoods near the old Condados Presto site.

In addition, the city is also home to the Fundación del Empresariado Chihuahuense A.C. (FECHAC; Chihuahuan Business Foundation), which offers grants and capacity-building workshops to area nonprofit organizations and even funded the construction and operation of a small-scale wastewater treatment plant at the school Centro Educativo Multicultural Yermo y Parras (Yermo and Parras Multicultural Education Center). The Grupo Promotor Parque Río Bravo (Rio Grande Park Promoter Group) rejuvenated a park along the Rio Grande. Two older organizations, the Alianza Internacional Ecologista del Río Bravo (International Environmental Alliance of the Rio Grande) and the Coalición Binacional contra Tiraderos Tóxicos y Bio-Radioactivos (Binational Coalition against Toxic and Bio-Radioactive Trash Dumps) fought against a number of contamination concerns during the 1990s and gained international recognition for their successful opposition to a nuclear waste dump in Sierra Blanca, Texas (Bejarano 2002). A number of groups including Salud y Desarrollo Comunitario de Ciudad Juárez (SADEC; Health and Community Development of Ciudad Juárez) of the Federación Mexicana de Asociaciones Privadas (FEMAP; Mexican Federation of Private Associations), Aqua 21, OPI, Desarrollo Juvenil del Norte de Ciudad Juárez (Northern Youth Development of Ciudad Juárez), and others have trained volunteer community members to promote environmental education and public health. FEMAP–SADEC alone has over 30 years experience training community health and education promoters and claims a massive network of 1,250 active volunteers.

This far from complete list of associational efforts to address public problems related to water in Ciudad Juárez illustrates the depth and breadth of civil society activities in the city. Of the 27 organizations operating in the policy arena, 7 have obtained authorized donee status, 19 have paid employees, 19 have programmatic activities, and 24 meet the definition of civil society organizations (see table 3.1 for reference). To find out why these citizen initiatives are so strong, compared with those of Nuevo Laredo, requires further exploration.

Political Opportunity

Unlike Nuevo Laredo, Ciudad Juárez is no longer dependent on one political party; indeed, residents of Ciudad Juárez and the state of Chihuahua played a key role in Mexico's democratic transition. As in most parts of Mexico, from 1946 to 1983 the PAN had never defeated the PRI in a single mayoral election in the state of Chihuahua (Chand 2001). In 1983, however, the PAN won mayoral races in all of the state's major cities and a number of seats in the state legislature. Ciudad Juárez residents elected Francisco Barrio Terrazas, a wealthy businessman and newcomer to the PAN, as municipal president. Barrio proved to be a popular mayor, and in 1986 he won his party's candidacy for the governorship.

PRI militants blamed federal and state administrations for their electoral defeat in the early 1980s. Governor Oscar Ornelas was pressured to step down, making way for a more aggressive interim governor. Observers and scholars generally agree that the PRI was determined to hold onto power in future elections through all legal and even many extralegal means (Muro González 1994; Aziz 1987; Chand 2001). As a result, before and during the 1986 elections, the state electoral code was modified, the media strictly controlled, the voting rolls altered, voters intimidated, the PRI's clientelistic networks mobilized, ballot boxes stuffed, and election observers expelled (Muro González 1994; Aziz 1987; Chand 2001). According to Vikram Chand (2001), the number of names on the voting rolls exceeded the estimated voting population in 53 of Chihuahua's 67 municipalities. As a consequence of these actions, the official results of the 1986 elections gave the PRI the governorship and all but two of the state's municipalities.

The election provoked 920 complaints of irregularities, a 41-day hunger strike by some of the state's PAN and civic leaders, and a blockade of the international bridges (Chand 2001). Perhaps most important, the archbishop of Chihuahua announced his intention to suspend Mass in protest. Even though the Vatican forced the archbishop to back down, the threat itself was significant: no Church leader had dared suspend Mass since the Cristero War in the 1920s. Despite the popular protests, the government stood by its official election results, although even the victorious PRI candidate Fernando Baeza later admitted in an interview that his administration lacked legitimacy (Chand 2001). More important, the allegations of electoral fraud served to polarize the electorate and turn many people away from the party that had governed the country for several decades.

As PRI legitimacy waned, priista President Carlos Salinas de Gortari, himself accused of winning the presidency through voter fraud, began to recognize opposition victories at the polls. In the 1992 elections, the PAN won back Ciudad Juárez's mayoralty and finally took Chihuahua's governorship. In the subsequent years, the city became a stronghold for this traditional opposition party. Nonetheless, when PAN administrations failed to address the city's many public problems, residents became disillusioned with the party. In the 1998 and the 2001 elections, the PAN won by a margin of less than 1 percent. By the time of this study, neither party could claim the loyalty of Ciudad Juárez's electorate. The emergence of a competitive electoral arena offers potential public entrepreneurs in Ciudad Juárez an environment far different from the one they faced twenty-five years before and the one they still face in Nuevo Laredo. No longer dependent on one, monopolist political party, public entrepreneurs have unprecedented opportunity to organize autonomously and seek alternative solutions to public problems.

Norm Entrepreneurs and Changing Informal Rules

Although the end of one-party rule at the local and national level creates an opportunity, research has shown that informal rules of clientelism, co-option, and cynicism can continue to govern even in competitive electoral environments (Gay 1994; Weyland 1996). Fortunately, however, from the 1970s to the present, norm entrepreneurs in Ciudad Juárez and the state of Chihuahua challenged these informal rules and helped introduce new norms supportive of an autonomous associational life. The following three subsections examine efforts to promulgate norms of independence, professionalism, and philanthropy.

Social Movements: The Norm of Independence

As in the rest of Mexico, neighborhood politics in Juárez's low-income communities was traditionally clientelistic. During the 1970s and the early 1980s, the Comité de Defensa Popular (CDP; Popular Defense Committee) dominated colonia politics in much of Chihuahua (Lau and Quintana Silveyra 1991; Muro González 1994). The CDP was a radical, leftist, social movement that emerged as an alliance between university faculty and students, union workers, and colonia residents. Guided by a combination of leftist philosophies, the movement invaded private property, established communities, and made demands on the political system. In the 1970s and 1980s, the CDP was able to challenge the state as an independent movement and earn considerable material gains. Eventually, however, it joined the PRI–dependent Partido del Trabajo (PT; Workers Party) and formally took its place as part of the PRI corporatist system (Lau and Quintana Silveyra 1991; Padilla 2000). During the rise of the PAN in Chihuahua in the 1980s, the CDP would serve as a primary medium for the PRI to maintain support in low-income neighborhoods (Chand 2001; Muro González 1994).

During the same time period, inspired by liberation theology, the Christian-based communities (CBCs) movement challenged the norms of clientelism, shifting low-income areas "towards new local cultures" that distrusted clientelistic participation in political parties and promoted direct democracy and preservation of autonomy (Núñez González 1990). The Catholic Church's role in introducing new norms was perhaps somewhat surprising, given the history of Church-state relations in Mexico. Throughout the decades of one-party rule, Mexico's clergy had been careful not to enter into public affairs. The 1917 constitution, written after the Mexican Revolution, was opposed to religion generally and to the Catholic Church specifically. The constitution made all education secular: religious associations could not even run their own private schools. Religious orders were banned, and public worship outside of a church was declared illegal. The Church could not own property; the religious clergy was to be limited to Mexican citizens by birth; and priests did not have the right either to vote or to comment on public affairs. State governments had the authority even to set the number of clergy members who could be ordained in their respective states (Núñez González 1990).

The enforcement of these and additional laws passed in 1926 provoked the Cristero War, which lasted for three years, with no clear victor. By the administration of President Manuel Avila Camacho (1940–1946), an informal agreement had been reached: the state would not enforce the constitutional articles directed against the Church, and the Church would stay out of politics.

The Second Vatican Council (1962–1965) and subsequent conferences of Latin American bishops in Medellín (1968) and in Puebla (1979) would challenge the Church's passive role. The Second Vatican Council was convened to adapt Church doctrine and practices to the needs of the modern era. One of the outcomes of the council and the conferences was the Church's acceptance of a responsibility for the temporal as well as the spiritual needs of its members. The Church's progressive turn was promoted by Latin American bishops sympathetic to what would become known as "liberation theology." Written in 1972, Gustavo Gutiérrez Merino's essay "A Theology of Liberation: History, Politics, Salvation" called not only for a liberation from selfishness and sin but a political and social liberation as well. Although liberation theology was later rejected by Pope John Paul II, it had tremendous influence throughout Latin America. Coupled with the principles of collegiality, which offered greater discretion to individual bishops and support for a more active laity, liberation theology and doctrinal change threatened to disrupt the uneasy truce between the Mexican Church and state.

Nonetheless, despite the radical change outlined by the Vatican II Council and the conferences of Latin American bishops, the vast majority of the Mexican Church hierarchy remained far away from public affairs (García 1984; Loaeza 1985). Chihuahua's Archbishop Adalberto Almeida y Merino and Ciudad Juárez's Bishop Manuel Talamas Camandari, on the other hand, were among the few Mexican bishops active in the reform process. Both participated in the Second Vatican Council and as leaders in the conferences of Latin American bishops. As a result, Ciudad Juárez became a center for liberation theology and hosted the first international conference on it in 1971 (Muro González 1994). The Church in Ciudad Juárez not only advocated policies favoring the poor but also pushed for more systemic changes in the relationship between citizens and the state. Following the emergence of a violent guerrilla group and the death of its members while in police custody, Bishop Talamas Camandari wrote, "The dramatic events to which we refer are therefore an urgent call from God for us to conduct a profound and honest review of our political, social, economic, cultural, and religious institutions. We must discern in them all that is obsolete, vitiated, and putrid; and, once discovered, have the courage to change it even if this goes against our own egotistical interests" (Chand 2001, 173).

Although liberation theology's social justice message was considered Marxist by many of Ciudad Juárez's upper and middle class, it resonated with the populace. Christian-based communities sprang up in Ciudad Juárez's western neighborhoods, accompanied by a host of other Christian organizations (Muro González 1994). The new movement promoted self-help, community participation, and independence from the state, and it rejected partisan militancy and clientelism. In so doing, liberation theology challenged the state's informal dominance of societal forms of organization even as electoral competition ended the PRI's formal monopoly on the government. In a sense, Bishops Talamas, Almeida, and others served as norm entrepreneurs. Their ability to introduce new norms into dense and expansive networks of church congregations allowed for the rapid diffusion of these norms throughout society. As this occurred, interviews suggest that independence from political society became an important credential for representing citizens in the public arena. Having challenged the norms of clientelistic dependence on PRI patrons in low-income communities, the CBCs also paved the way for other organizations, such as OPI, which were not affiliated either with political parties or with the Church.

The Chihuahuan Church's recognition of the problems of corruption, clientelism, and authoritarian government under one-party rule also pushed it to the forefront of the state's democratic movement. Prior to the 1986 election debacle, Chihuahua's bishops hoped to use their moral authority to head off electoral fraud through publications advocating democracy, such as one entitled "Christian Coherence in Politics." When that fraud actually occurred, both Archbishop Almeida and Bishop Talamas vigorously decried it. Bishop Talamas declared in a sermon (Chand 2001, 185): "We denounce the fraud, falsehood, manipulation [and] mockery . . . as an extremely grave social sin that Heaven cries out [against]." After Archbishop Almeida's planned suspension of Mass was headed off by the Vatican, he convened a series of weekly "Workshops on Catholics and Democracy" to discuss the Gospels and the Church's relationship with democracy. Of course the Church was only one player in a broad-based movement for greater democracy. Business leaders, newly founded civic associations, and individual citizens all demanded democratic change. Of particular importance was a national coalition of organizations called Alianza Civica, which trained and deployed election monitors. What Chand (2001) called a "political awakening" served not only to bring about competitive elections but also to help rewrite the informal rules of local politics.

Donors: The Norm of Professionalization

Having norm entrepreneurs who are themselves not dependent on the political arena is an important step to ending the informal rules of clientelism, co-option, and cynicism. A second set of such entrepreneurs is working to consolidate new informal rules supportive of an independent nonprofit sector by promoting norms of professionalization. The push to professionalize nonprofit activities in Ciudad Juárez comes from a number of sources, most importantly, from donors who want to see their investment in the nonprofit sector produce tangible results. Although, historically, Mexico has not had a large supply of donor institutions, as the nonprofit sector has grown, there has been a corresponding increase in philanthropy, government grant programs, and local foundations. Such funding opportunities create incentives to professionalize, conduct strategic planning, develop project proposals, manage and account for funds, implement program activities, and evaluate if project goals are being met in order to be a more competitive grant applicant.

From the beginning of the NAFTA debate until the early 2000s, there was a substantial and steady flow of funds from U.S. donors to address environmental concerns along the border. The U.S. environmental community recognized early on that actions taken on one side of the border had environmental impacts on the other side. Worried that greater industrial production stimulated by the free trade agreement would turn the border region into even more of a pollution haven than it already was (Thorup 1993), the U.S. environmental community and donors began looking for partners in Mexico to help fight against the NAFTA and to carry out projects to prevent greater environmental degradation. The William and Flora Hewlett Foundation emerged as a major donor for environmental and particularly water-related policy projects in the region; in 2000 alone, the foundation offered just below $2 million in grants to U.S. and Mexican border nonprofits for environmental concerns (William and Flora Hewlett Foundation 2001).

However, without traditional opportunities for funding from local foundations or private donors, many Mexican nonprofits had grown accustomed to operating without grant money. A large number of organizations within this study were (although many no longer are) based around a few key individuals who carried out organizational activities in their free time and often with their own resources. These organizations were (and in some cases still are) unaccustomed to writing proposals, administering funds, carrying out focused projects, and writing final reports. Investing in these nonprofits represented a risky venture for U.S. foundations, many of which eventually came to believe that granting should be accompanied by "capacity building," which translated to promoting norms of professionalism.

The Paso del Norte Health Foundation serves as a specific example of donor efforts to promote such norms in Ciudad Juárez. In 1996, El Paso's nonprofit Providence Hospital was bought out by the Tennet Corporation, a for-profit hospital administration company. The board of directors of Providence used the proceeds from the sale to establish the Paso del Norte Health Foundation. Recognizing the regional nature of health care the hospital provided, the board chose the historical name of the El Paso–Ciudad Juárez–Las Cruces region for their foundation; indeed, a large percentage of Providence's patients had been residents of Ciudad Juárez. Today, the foundation conducts granting activities in Ciudad Juárez, El Paso, and parts of New Mexico.

Since its establishment, the Paso del Norte Health Foundation has partnered with many organizations in Ciudad Juárez and supported a number of others south of the border through programs entitled "Drinking Water," "When Water Works for Health," and "Healthy Communities." An external review conducted in 2000, however, found that the foundation had become too involved in managing projects and supporting the organizations to which it was donating. As a result, the Center for Civic Engagement and the Center for Environmental Resource Management at the University of Texas, El Paso, were hired to provide technical advice for foundation-funded programs and to help develop the capacity of local nonprofit organizations.

The Center for Civic Engagement works with several of Ciudad Juárez's nonprofit organizations in the Healthy Communities program, including Programa Compañeros (Companions Program), Organización Popular Independiente (OPI), and Centro de Asesoría y Promoción Juvenil (CASA; Center for Counseling and Youth Promotion). Healthy Communities calls for neighborhood residents to attend regular meetings, analyze the problems in their community, prioritize these problems, and develop solutions. This requires that grant recipients carry out workshops with community members, helping them set their priorities, and that they support the implementation of solutions, conduct survey research, and administer project finances. The Center for Civic Engagement has worked with grantee organizations to help them develop the considerable organizational skill and administrative capacity these actions require.

The Paso del Norte Health Foundation also funds the Center for Environmental Resource Management's work with civil society organizations on environmental education and public health promotion projects in Ciudad Juárez. In addition, for several years, the El Paso–based Rio Grande/Río Bravo Basin Coalition has both supported and coordinated environmental organizations along both sides of the border. Among capacity-building organizations operating along the more western part of the border, San Diego–based Pro Peninsula works with environmental organization in Baja California; the Synergos Institute assists philanthropic organizations along the entire U.S.–Mexico border; and the Bureau of Applied Anthropology at the University of Arizona supports the emerging nonprofit sector of Nogales, Sonora.

Not only do norms of professionalism strengthen civil society organizations, making them better able to tackle public problems; the norms also strengthen informal rules of autonomy. The capacity to undertake strategic planning, obtain funding, develop strategic partnerships, and reach out to diverse network partners reduces overdependence on political patrons and creates new opportunities. Professionalization offers public entrepreneurs tactical options besides clientelism and co-option to pursue their objectives. In addition, it sends a signal about the nature of the organization. The aptitude to directly address public problems, follow policies and procedures, hire capable staff, and convene a diverse and respected board of directors demonstrates to others that the organization plays, not by the old informal rules, but by the new autonomous ones. This positive signal can help attract both donations and volunteers.

Although the impetus for professionalization may come from a variety of sources, most often it comes from donors who want to see their money produce results. Because of the dominant role of the U.S. nonprofit sector in supporting organizations along the border, much of the impetus for professionalization has come from the north. Nonetheless, when U.S. donors pulled out of the region in the early 2000s, Mexican philanthropic organizations such as the Chihuahuan Business Foundation helped fill the gap, as the next subsection discusses.

The Norm of Philanthropy and Resources

The new norms of independence and professionalization emerging among Ciudad Juárez's nonprofit community risk being restricted to the networks of existing civil society organizations. To spread through other parts of society, such norms must move beyond existing networks. To reach a tipping point, norm entrepreneurs must attract enough individuals willing to adopt and follow the new informal rules, and, at the same time, public entrepreneurs must attract enough financial resources, information, technical know-how, and organizational experience from the broader community. If, however, other citizens continue to follow the old rules of the game, and if they do not support the efforts of public entrepreneurs, then, just as a business entrepreneur fails to produce a profit, so, too, will norm and public entrepreneurs fail to introduce new informal rules and new forms of organization.

Although one could argue persuasively that norms of independence and professionalism have always operated in pockets of Mexico's nonprofit sector (see, for example, Forment 2003), the establishment of a vibrant civil society requires that these norms be widely diffused. To introduce new informal rules across a community, potential entrepreneurs must first challenge the norms of cynicism and distrust with informal rules of volunteerism and philanthropy. Of particular concern to this process is the business community, which represents a potential source of the human, financial, and social capital necessary for organizational development. That the business community has played an important role in the emergence of professional associations and business groups is obvious, but what has been its contribution beyond parochial associational life?

Only 37 percent of the non-business-oriented nonprofits in this study report any financial or in-kind support from the business community or individual contributors. Moreover, most of the reported contributions entail relatively small donations, one-time contributions, or in-kind support. And despite the important role that boards of directors have played in obtaining resources for the U.S. nonprofit community, the study found this not to be the case in the four research sites. Of forty-eight organizations with boards of directors, only eleven reported that their board members donate or help find funds for the organization. Furthermore, interview respondents repeatedly referred to the absence of a culture of philanthropy as a major obstacle to the growth of the sector, a common observation in the literature on Mexico generally (Castro Salinas 2001; CEMEFI 1996; Layton 2004; Verduzco 2003) and on the border specifically (Bejarano 2002; Kelly 2002; Zabin 1997). Even though the norms of philanthropy and participation in the nonprofit sector have not diffused across Mexican society as a whole, in Ciudad Juárez and the state of Chihuahua, some organizations, most notably, the Chihuahuan Business Foundation (FECHAC), have attempted to rewrite the old, unfavorable informal rules.

In 1990, severe flooding in Chihuahua City brought about a humanitarian disaster. Under the leadership of Chihuahua businessman Samuel Kalisch, businesses agreed to pay an additional tax to help fund the state's reaction to the disaster. Although the arrangement ended with the reconstruction effort, a seed had been planted for more permanent corporate social responsibility. As Kellee James (2002) notes, "The flood-aid, though successful, was reactive in nature. To attend to Chihuahua's social and economic inequalities a more proactive strategy was needed." In 1994, following the election of PAN candidate Francisco Barrio to the governorship, businesses formally agreed to pay the state an additional 0.2 percent tax on earnings to fund a public trust. This trust would in turn provide the resources for the newly created Chihuahuan Business Foundation, to be overseen by a board of primarily business leaders. Although the impetus for the FECHAC began in Chihuahua City, nine local boards currently exist throughout the state, including one in Ciudad Juárez.

The foundation has served as an important means to promote a norm of social responsibility among the business community and to generate support among the for-profit sector for civil society organizations. Over a decade after its founding, the FECHAC has supported over 1,450 projects and programs and invested more than $35 million throughout the state with funds it received from the business community (for more information on the FECHAC, see its Web site, http://www.fechac.org/esp/qs—historia .php). In 2005 in Ciudad Juárez alone, the foundation invested some $2.2 million (FECHAC 2006). In recent years, the foundation's efforts to develop a more "socially responsible" business community have included establishing an 80-hour certificate program on socially responsible businesses for members of the private sector.

The FECHAC has also worked to develop norms of professionalization within the nonprofit sector. Beyond funding organizations, the foundation has traditionally conducted workshops on building civil society capacity. To consolidate such efforts, in 2003, in partnership with the Tecnológico de Monterrey, the foundation helped establish the Centro para el Fortalecimiento de la Sociedad Civil (Center for the Strengthening of Civil Society) to offer workshops, library resources, computer access, and legal and financial advice to the state's nonprofit organizations. The FECHAC, which also hosts an annual conference on civil society, has been lauded as a model of philanthropy in Mexico (Winder 2004).

Although unique in other respects, the FECHAC is not alone in promoting the norm of social responsibility among the business community of Ciudad Juárez. Borrowing on a model from Bilbao, Spain, Plan Estratégico de Juárez (Strategic Plan of Juárez) was established in 1999 by a civic leader and several young members of Ciudad Juárez's business elite to develop a vision for Ciudad Juárez and a plan for how to realize that vision. To do so, the organization implemented an inclusive citywide effort involving studies, surveys, and numerous public meetings and working groups. Whereas the Bilbao model has been replicated in Monterrey and Tijuana, Plan Estratégico's approach has been unique because of its inclusiveness. Interview respondents note that one of Plan's successes has been its ability to bring a diverse group of actors to the table and thus to develop extensive networks throughout the Juárez community, drawing it and many other sectors of society into the public arena.

Theda Skocpol and Morris Fiorina (1999, 2) have defined civil society as "the network of ties and groups through which people connect to one another and get drawn into community and political affairs." Under this definition, initiatives such as the FECHAC and Plan Estratégico are key network actors in Ciudad Juárez's civil society. Their network position within the business community has allowed them to draw others into this "community" and to promulgate norms of volunteerism and participation. These two examples illustrate clearly the possibilities for Mexico's growing third sector as norms of social responsibility and philanthropy diffuse throughout Mexican society.

Social Infrastructure and Resources

Unfortunately, efforts such as the FECHAC and Plan Estratégico are relatively recent and exceptions rather than the norm. In the absence of more widespread support from business and individual community members, civil society organizations in the study draw resources from preexisting social infrastructure. A look at the histories of the seventy-two organizations across the four research sites reveals that most emerged out of already existing social infrastructure, defined as preexisting forms of organization that offer a potential source of information and human and financial resources.

To illustrate, sixteen organizations grew out of civil society networks, such as those of social movements or coalitions of organizations (see table 4.1). For example, in the Tijuana–San Diego area, organizations and individuals working in environmental education came together to found the Bio-Regional Environmental Education Project (PROBEA) to train Baja California's teachers in environmental education. In Nogales, organizations, maquiladoras, and academic institutions formed an association to reforest the Ambos Nogales area. In Ciudad Juárez, community development organizations established a coalition group to promote a citywide social development agenda. And in Nuevo Laredo, the city's social clubs and professional organizations founded the Council of Institutions of Nuevo Laredo, which participates in a broad array of local issues.

As shown in table 4.1, an additional nineteen organizations grew out of the activities or incubating support of a U.S. nonprofit organization, the Church, or universities. The U.S. nonprofit community played a particularly strong role in Tijuana. Although all the cities in this study are close to potential resources in the United States, there is a much greater supply of organizations across the border from Tijuana. Guidestar.com, a Web site that maintains a database of all registered charitable organizations in the United States, lists around 4,800 nonprofit organizations in San Diego, just north of Tijuana, a number that far exceeds the nonprofit communities of the other three U.S. border cities: Nogales, Arizona; El Paso, Texas; and Laredo, Texas (see table 4.2).

U.S. organizations were directly responsible for establishing six organizations in Tijuana, and they play an important role in all four of the civil

Table 4.1   Number of organizations at each city studied and their manner of emergence

Manner of emergence	Tijuana	Nogales	Ciudad Juárez	Nuevo Laredo	Total
Created with support of foreign nonprofit	6	1	2	1	10
Created with support of religious institution	—	—	3	—	3
Created with support of university	2	—	1	—	3
Created with support of other social infrastructure	—	—	3	—	3
Created as coalition of organizations	4	1	5	1	11
Built on previous civil society or social movement network	1	—	4	—	5
Created with support of government	—	—	1	2	3
Created with support of political party	—	—	—	3	3
Academic institution with programmatic activity	2	—	1	—	3
Business or professional organization	2	3	2	4	11
Created by an independent public entrepreneur	5	4	1	—	10
Created with support of business sector	1	2	3	—	6
Unknown	—	—	1	—	1
Total	23	11	27	11	72

society coalitions listed in table 4.1. Several organizations in the study, including Fundación Internacional de la Comunidad (FIC; International Community Foundation), Los Niños (The Children), Fundación Esperanza (Esperanza Foundation), and Centro de Promoción de Salud Esperanza (Esperanza Health Promotion Center), followed a similar emergence trajectory. The case of FIC is illustrative. In the late 1980s, the San Diego Foundation recognized the need for grant making in Tijuana, but its legal mandate was limited to the community of San Diego. As a result, in 1990, the foundation helped establish the International Community Foundation (ICF), which has served as an important donor to address problems related to water in the Tijuana area. ICF seeks to "assist U.S. donors to make tax-deductible gifts to qualified nonprofit organiza-

Table 4.2 Civil society organization presence and city-level explanatory variables

Variable category	Variable	Tijuana	Nogales	Ciudad Juárez	Nuevo Laredo
Civil society presence	Civil society organization presence in policy arena	Medium	Low–medium	Medium–high	Low
	Number of organizations active in policy arena	23	11	27	11
Attributes of community	Population (2005)	1,410,687	193,517	1,313,338	355,827
	Percentage of population over age 5 who lived outside of state in 2000	8.7	6.3	4.2	6.2
	Annual percentage growth rate from 2000 to 2005	3.1	3.9	1.5	2.7
	Percentage of population over age 18 with some college education	16.0	14.8	15.8	17.1
Social infrastructure	History of Christian-based communities movement	No	No	Yes	No
	Supply of nonprofit organizations in U.S. sister city	4,403[a]	71	1,411	275
	Presence of large universities or research institutions[b]	UABC Ibero-americana COLEF	— — —	UACJ Technológico de Monterrey COLEF (branch)	UAT (branch) — COLEF (office)
	Presence of local foundation	Yes	Yes	Yes	No

Source: Attributes of community data are from INEGI 2005; data on number of U.S. nonprofit organizations, from http://www.Guidestar.com.
[a]Includes only city of San Diego rather than greater metropolitan area.
[b]Full names of universities or research institutions are Universidad Autónoma de Ciudad Juárez (UACJ), Universidad Autónoma de Baja California (UABC), Universidad Autónoma de Tamaulipas (UAT), Tecnológico de Monterrey, Universidad Iberoamericana, and Colegio de la Frontera Norte (COLEF).

tions" primarily in Baja California but in other states and countries as well (ICF 2006). In the late 1990s, ICF and several large foundations saw the need for a greater supply of foundations indigenous to Mexico. As a result, the ICF helped establish the first foundation native to Baja California, Fundación Internacional de la Comunidad (FIC).

In like fashion, in the mid-1970s, a San Diego–based parish began building houses in Tijuana. Over time, the effort formalized itself into the nonprofit organization Esperanza International. According to the organization's director, an office was later opened in Tijuana, and eventually the Tijuana office became its own separate agency, Fundación Esperanza. The new organization was able to benefit from its parent organization's resources, office space, and organizational experience until it could develop its own financial base, board of directors, and professional staff. These examples highlight the incubatory process that collective action at times requires. Indeed, only ten organizations (less than 14 percent) in the study emerged solely from the initiative of a public entrepreneur.

Though it played less of a role in the founding of civil society organizations in Ciudad Juárez, the foreign nonprofit community was essential to the establishment of two of the city's twenty-seven organizations. Carlos Vázquez and others had been working tirelessly on educational and community development issues in several of Ciudad Juárez's marginalized eastern neighborhoods in the 1980s when they heard about Kölping International, a Catholic social organization, founded by Adolph Kölping in Germany in the mid-1800s, that was promoting activities along the lines of Vázquez's work in Ciudad Juárez. Kölping had projects in Veracruz and Chiapas and wanted to expand into other parts of Mexico. According to Vázquez, he and others were invited to attend a meeting about the association, and soon after they were incorporated into the family of Kölping organizations as "Promoción Social Kölping." In 1997, Kölping International helped fund the construction of a large community center, which now houses the once fledgling organizational effort.

Religiously inspired organizations such as Kölping International and the incubating support of the Church and monastic orders have been essential to the establishment of several of Ciudad Juárez's civil society organizations. As discussed above, OPI emerged out of the Christian-based communities movement, inspired by liberation theology. Although the organization is expressly nonreligious, the network of organizers who formed the group was brought together by the CBCs movement. Several religious orders have also started groups in Ciudad Juárez that are active in water-related policy arenas. These include the Centro de Mujeres Tonantzin (Center for Women, Tonantzin), a project of Sisters of the Charity of the Incarnate Word and Desarrollo Juvenil del Norte (Northern Youth Development), an initiative of the Salesians of Don Bosco.

Mexican academic institutions have also been important to associational efforts. Of particular note is Ecoparque (Ecopark), which emerged as a binational confluence of academic research, innovative public policy, and environmentalism in 1993, but which has been sustained by the Colegio de la Frontera Norte (COLEF; College of the Northern Border) in Tijuana. Advocates of Ecoparque note that Tijuana and its low-income neighborhoods face a number of environmental and economic problems. First, the city does not have the capacity to treat the amount of wastewater that is being generated by its rapidly growing population. Second, poorly planned urban growth and limited water resources have led to a lack of green spaces throughout the city. Third, Tijuana's steep hills and urban development combine to produce bare hillsides subject to erosion during the region's occasional heavy rains. Ecoparque addresses all of these problems in one low-cost project. Essentially a wastewater treatment facility, the park draws wastewater from a nearby neighborhood, treats it through an aeration process as it descends one of Tijuana's many hills, then pumps it back up to irrigate soil-stabilizing vegetation along the hillside. Not only does the park address all three of these public problems but it also serves as an environmental education center. Although Ecoparque originated on the U.S. side of the border, when the facility's lease was not renewed, it was moved to its current Tijuana location under the COLEF's stewardship (Medina 2000).

Academic institutions play an even more important role in coalition-based organizations. For example, universities are the driving force behind an effort to develop a binational plan for the Tijuana River watershed (the Tijuana River Watershed Binational Vision Project); a task force to address water scarcity in the El Paso–Las Cruces–Ciudad Juárez region (the Paso del Norte Water Task Force); and an effort to reforest the Ambos Nogales area (Asociación de Reforestación en Ambos Nogales Ambos, or ARAN). For these efforts, academia has been indispensable.

The importance of social infrastructure and preexisting civil society networks to Ciudad Juárez's and Tijuana's nonprofit communities appears to go a long way toward explaining the dearth of civil society organizations and associational efforts directly addressing public problems in Nogales, Sonora, and Nuevo Laredo. Table 4.2 shows a much greater supply of social infrastructure in the two larger cities. Despite increasing electoral competition in Nogales, Sonora, a limited culture of philanthropy within the business community, a less historically activist Church, a small nonprofit community on the U.S. side of the border, a limited university presence, and little preexisting civil society organizations and networks have resulted in a small nonprofit sector with few programmatic activities. Although Nogales is a much smaller city, these findings suggest that it is the absence of social infrastructure, rather than the size of the city per se, that helps define the limits of the sector.

Of the seventy-two nonprofits examined in this study, thirty-five — almost half (49 percent) — emerged with the essential support of social infrastructure. These preexisting forms of social organization offer public entrepreneurs diverse options in creating and developing an association. The social infrastructure argument is thus an argument about networks.

Chapter 1 compared the experiences of ACOPO and Lideres Unidos in Nuevo Laredo with those of OPI in Ciudad Juárez. Lideres Unidos followed the informal rules of clientelism because its members had learned these tactics as former participants in ACOPO and because they were networked to PRI government and party officials. In contrast, the leaders of OPI followed norms of independence from government because of their connection to the Christian-based communities movement. Within these contrasting networks, different norms produced distinct prescriptions for how to best address water and sanitation deficiencies in the community.

A look at the social networks of ACOPO and OPI is instructive. Figure 4.1 illustrates that in policy arenas related to water, ACOPO connects only with agencies in the municipal government. Because. however, OPI connects to a large variety of groups, it is able to obtain new ideas from the Rio Grande Park Promoter Group, technical know-how from Aqua 21, financial resources from the Center for Environmental Resource Management, and in-kind services from the Municipal Planning and Research Institute (see fig. 4.2). These ties have not only allowed the organization to survive; they have also brought information and resources to address a host of public concerns.

An even more impressive network example is Tijuana's Proyecto Fronterizo de Educación Ambiental (PFEA: Border Environmental Education Project). As figure 4.3 illustrates, PFEA's network ties cross the border, connect to government, link to academia, and provide access to foundations. Because PFEA has such a diversity of ties, overdependence on government or political patrons is not even a remote possibility. More important, organizations such as PFEA find themselves in a central network position capable of bringing together the complementary resources of government, foundations, U.S. nonprofits, and Mexican civil society organizations. PFEA has actually led the charge in confronting important public problems in the Tijuana–San Diego region, where it has been instrumental in coordinating efforts to advance environmental education, promote environmental and right-to-know legislation, and develop a vision for the binational Tijuana River watershed.

As these examples illustrate, network ties are important both to develop and transmit norms, on the one hand, and to bring together the diverse resources needed to confront complex policy problems in the border region, on the other.

Conclusion

This chapter has further examined the role of political opportunities, informal rules, and social infrastructure in the emergence and development of civil society organizations. The end of one-party rule in Ciudad Juárez and Tijuana and the increase in electoral competition in Nogales, Sonora, have ended monopoly dependence on traditional power holders. Nonetheless, political change by itself is an insufficient condition to produce a vibrant set of civil society organizations. Additional efforts are required to combat the informal rules of clientelism, co-option, and cynicism that developed during decades of one-party rule.

In Ciudad Juárez, norm entrepreneurs have introduced new ideas about

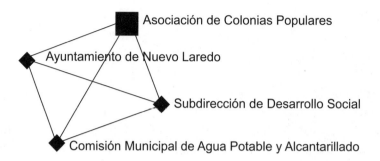

Figure 4.1.   Social network of the Asociación de Colonias Populares (ACOPO)

Figure 4.2.   Social network of the Organización Popular Independiente (OPI)

how citizens should relate to the public realm. The Christian-based communities and democratic movements have shown the effectiveness of autonomous association. In addition, funding opportunities and capacity-building efforts from donor institutions have promoted new norms of professionalism. Nonetheless, there is a very legitimate fear that such norms will be limited to the networks of preexisting civil society organizations and fail to diffuse through society more generally. This concern highlights the importance of organizations such as the Chihuahuan Busi-

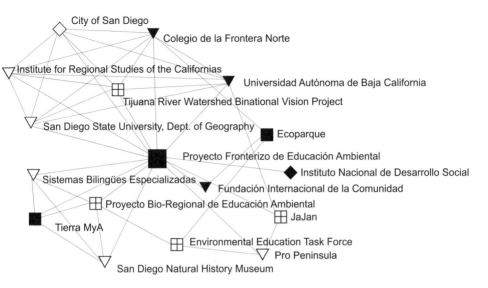

Figure 4.3. Social network of the Proyecto Fronterizo de Educación Ambiental (PFEA)

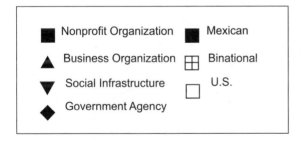

ness Foundation and Strategic Plan of Juárez, which demonstrate the enormous potential if norms of social responsibility and philanthropy replace the informal rule of cynicism among a broader public.

Absent widespread norms friendly to the emergence of autonomous associational life, public entrepreneurs have found the human, in-kind, and financial resources necessary to incubate nascent civil society initiatives through preexisting social infrastructure. The importance of social infrastructure to the development of civil society organizations has both positive and negative implications. On the positive side, it suggests that, even given the history of informal rules of clientelism, co-option, and cynicism, there are nonetheless networks governed by different norms with the resources necessary to sustain organizational efforts. On the negative side, however, even though the importance of social infrastructure might bode well for cities with an activist Church, a history of autonomous social movements, research institutions, foundations, or geographical proximity to a large nonprofit sector in the United States, many cities in Mexico, indeed throughout the developing world, lack such advantages. Unless greater efforts are made to promote philanthropic and voluntary norms throughout society, such cities will likely be left with only a small nonprofit community dominated by parochial associations.

Central to the argument of this chapter has been the role of networks. Although closed networks can foster new norms, dense, interconnecting networks are able to disseminate such norms and can more readily obtain resources to sustain organizations and address public problems than organizations with only one resource base.

Given the importance of networks to understanding how informal rules persist, how they are reformed, how resources are obtained, and how organizational efforts are incubated, chapters 5 through 7 explore the development of network ties between nonprofits and other sectors. Given that the U.S. nonprofit community is an important source of new norms and resources and that binational problems along the border require binational solutions, chapter 5 seeks to explain the emergence of cross-border ties. Given the dearth of ties to the business community and the need for greater philanthropic support of the third sector in Mexico, chapter 6 explores how civil society organizations cross this "other border." Finally, given that ties between associational life and the state have traditionally been governed by informal rules of co-option but that addressing many policy problems requires cross-sector cooperation, chapter 7 examines the current relationship between nonprofit organizations and government.

II Crossing Borders

5 Binational Collaboration

Introduction

The U.S.–Mexico border region is defined by the geopolitical boundary that divides the two countries. More than a line on a map, this border divides cultures and languages, priorities and interests, and rules and political systems. As shown in chapter 4, ties that cross this border are important for three key reasons: they help (1) bring human and financial resources to strengthen Mexico's growing body of civil society organizations; (2) introduce new ideas and diffuse new norms; and (3) solve binational public problems.

The U.S.–Mexico border is not the only border that makes up the boundary of Mexican civil society organizations. There are two others: a border between these organizations and the for-profit sector and a third one between them and government. Ties across these divisions are indispensable if the norms of autonomous, solution-oriented, collective action are to spread across society more broadly. They are also necessary to draw in human and financial resources to the sector, which can be used to address "cross-border" problems more effectively, develop better public policy, and hold government accountable.

Regardless of the public benefits to be realized by cross-border or cross-sector cooperation, individual actors must benefit from collaboration for it to be feasible. Indeed, there are very good reasons why an organization would seek ties beyond the borders of the third sector. Network ties offer organizations a means to obtain resources in an environment of scarcity (Granovetter 1973; Cook 1977; Burt 1992); because organizations are dependent on the actions of others to successfully pursue their goals, these ties also offer an opportunity to address problems of interdependence and uncertainty (Gould 1993; Gulati and Gargiulo 1999). For example, the ability of an environmental organization in San Diego to enjoy the Tijuana River estuary is dependent on the actions of government, private sector, and civil society groups in Mexico. Cooperation with Mexican groups, therefore, serves as a way for U.S. organizations to address their dependence on them.

Of course, as exchange theorists point out, for there to be cooperation between two potential collaborators, it must benefit both (Blau 1964; Levine and White 1961; Cook 1977). And, in fact, there is considerable opportunity for profitable exchange across the three borders surrounding civil society organizations. For example, U.S. organizations can obtain local knowledge and address their dependence through collaboration with Mexican groups. In turn, Mexican organizations can obtain resources and technical knowledge from U.S. nonprofits. For-profit businesses can improve their image in the community through socially responsible practices and can benefit greatly from the human and financial resources available in the business community. Government agencies can help ensure effective policy implementation with civil society support, and associational life can benefit from public policies that complement organizational activities.

Nonetheless, even though there are benefits to cooperative activities, to negotiate and carry them out involves considerable transaction costs of time, money, and effort. These transaction costs are increased dramatically by borders, as can be most easily seen across the U.S.–Mexico border, where language barriers are considerable, telephone calls expensive, cultural norms and expectations different, and travel complicated by long waits and often prevented entirely for many Mexicans (see Staudt and Coronado 2002). Similar difficulties exist across other borders. For example, in their study of cooperation between a chamber of commerce and a public school system, James Austin and colleagues (2004b, 63) found that communication was complicated by the businessmen's and -women's use of the term "clients" to refer to students: "When faced with disparate organizational cultures, partners had to invest time and energy in building the communication bridge."

A transaction cost perspective on the obstacles to cross-border and inter-sector cooperation suggests that different interests are not necessarily irreconcilable, even though they require greater effort to overcome.

Different interests may, however, provoke collective action problems and strategic interaction, which pose a more pervasive threat to cooperation (Kollock 1994). Scholars have pointed to many situations where two parties could benefit considerably from collaborating, yet in fact do not (Olson 1965). Given that there are different interests on opposite sides of the third sector's borders, what appear to be overtures of cooperation might be attempts at co-option.

As was discussed throughout chapters 1 through 4, cooperation has its dark side. Asymmetric relations between associational life and government in Mexico have historically produced clientelism and co-option rather than effective public policy, the resolution of public problems, and accountable government. Although co-option is most frequently discussed in terms of civil society and government relations, it can occur across any of the sector's borders. A U.S. organization might force a Mexican association to prioritize U.S. environmental concerns over local ones. Alternatively, a for-profit company might widely publicize support for civil society initiatives while only making a very limited contribution to them. In all these cases, there are very legitimate reasons to be suspicious of cooperation.

Given these risks, actors can be expected to work only with partners they can trust. "Organizational decision-makers were willing to forfeit the opportunity of getting the 'best deal' on the resources they needed," Joseph Galaskiewicz (1985, 288) observed, "in exchange for the greater security derived from working with organizational leaders who were like themselves and thus more trustworthy." Indeed, a long sociological tradition argues that network development is based on similarities among actors (Burt 1990; Fischer 1982; Marsden 1987; Popielarz and McPherson 1995).

In summary, actors on different sides of a border have different resources that, if combined, could lead to profitable exchange for both partners. Cooperation might also produce a number of positive externalities, including the strengthening of Mexican civil society, the resolution of policy problems, and the diffusion of norms of autonomy, professionalism, and philanthropy. On the other hand, different organizations have different cultural norms and interests that increase the transaction costs of finding and working toward common goals and that threaten to produce distrust and strategic interaction rather than coordination of activities. To identify the factors that make cooperation on public problems more or less likely to occur, this chapter uses the institutional analysis and development (IAD) framework developed by Elinor Ostrom (1999), who explored how three sets of key contextual variables — (1) the physical nature of a problem, (2) the attributes of the community, and (3) the rules-in-use — explain the success or failure of cooperation.

Noting numerous cases where groups have successfully solved collective action problems, several scholars have attempted to understand how these variables increase or decrease the likelihood of cooperation (Ostrom 1990; Ostrom, Garner, and Walker 1994). Elinor Ostrom, Roy Gardner, and James Walker (1994, 44) have argued that, to understand actions and outcomes, we need first to examine a first set of contextual variables, the physical environment in which they take place: "The physical possibility of actions, the producibility of outcomes, the linkages of actions to outcomes, and the knowledge of actors all depend on the physical world and its transformations." In a sense, the physical geography and the physical attributes of a policy problem lay the backdrop to understand interdependence in the research sites. For example, a civil society organization might be dependent on the United States because water flows from north to south; dependent on an industrial plant because of its location near an aquifer recharge point, or dependent on government because the water supply is too large an issue to be solved by an organization acting alone.

A second set of variables are the attributes of the community "that are important in affecting the structure of an action arena." These "include generally accepted norms of behavior, the level of common understanding about action arenas, the extent to which the preferences are homogeneous, and distribution of resources among members" (Ostrom, Gardner, and Walker 1994, 45). Because different policy problems involve different individuals, groups, networks, and communities, we need to explore how different actors and the relationships between different networks create incentives for cooperation or conflict. For example, do different understandings about water problems, different norms of behavior, and different preferences between civil society organizations and for-profit sector actors negatively impact the potential for collaboration? And if so, can these differences be overcome?

A third set of variables that impacts actions and outcomes are the rules that govern the policy arena or the "rules-in-use," as Ostrom, Gardner, and Walker (1994) have called them; these include both formal rules, such as laws and regulations, and informal rules, such as expectations of appropriate behavior. Many rules, though not compulsory, may create incentives for particular behavior (Crawford and Ostrom 1995). Among the rules that might impact cross-border and cross-sector cooperation are decentralization reforms (Do these facilitate cooperation between civil society organizations and local government?) and tax incentives given to actors in the for-profit sector (Do these encourage contributions to nonprofits?).

Each focusing on these three sets of contextual variables, the next three chapters explore when and how cooperation is developed across the borders of civil society organizations.

The Importance of Binational Ties

Economic growth in the region has come at a social and environmental cost that the market has failed to internalize: problems of water supply, environmental degradation, and public health have persisted despite job growth. Although market failures are often posited to produce a governmental response, the division of the border region into two separate political systems hinders the ability of either the U.S. or Mexican government to address transborder policy problems unilaterally. Henry Hansmann (1987) and Burton Weisbrod (1988) argue that where both markets and governments fail to confront policy problems, solutions might be produced by the nonprofit sector.

Along the border, life for many residents, called "transfronterizos" or "borderlanders" by Oscar Martínez (1994), is binational in nature. Binational citizen efforts have produced broad-based coalitions to address a variety of public problems. Perhaps the most celebrated example of civil society leadership is the Paso del Norte Air Quality Task Force, a coalition of members of civil society, business leaders, nonprofit organizations, academics, and government officials in the Paso del Norte region of Ciudad Juárez, El Paso, and Las Cruces. The task force was formed in 1993 to respond to air-quality concerns resulting from the region's economic development and exacerbated by topographical and meteorological factors. The group took on a number of projects to improve air quality in the region, including working with brick manufacturers to burn cleaner fuels, holding workshops for paint shop owners, pushing for the creation of a dedicated commuter lane on the international bridges, and training auto mechanics in auto emissions diagnostic technologies (Ketter 1998; Safa Barraza 1997). Most important, the task force led the way to establishing the permanent Joint Advisory Committee for the Improvement of Air Quality (JAC), a twenty-person group made up of government officials and members of civil society from both sides of the border. Its mandate is to develop and present recommendations to the Binational Air Work Group (established under the 1983 La Paz Agreement) to prevent or control air pollution in the Paso del Norte air basin (Ketter 1998; Safa Barraza 1996; see also JAC's Web site, http://www.jac-ccc.org/index.html). These advances, which directly addressed the region's severe air-quality problems and created new institutions, were only achieved because of binational civil society collaboration and leadership.

Network scholars and social capital theorists argue that, through repeated interaction, individuals or groups of individuals develop norms of trust, reciprocity, and tolerance (Granovetter 1973; Coleman 1988; Putnam 1993; Mutz 2002). As a corollary, the absence of such ties can result in distrust, a lack of reciprocity, and intolerance. All of these could conspire to increase the probability of binational conflict rather than cooperation.

Indeed, in the early 2000s, a serious binational conflict exploded between the United States and Mexico over scarce water resources (TCPS 2002; Woodhouse 2005). A 1944 treaty on the division of shared surface water in the Rio Grande and Colorado River gives the United States the right to receive one-third of the water from Mexico's Río Conchos, which feeds into the Rio Grande. Throughout the 1990s and early 2000s, however, Mexico experienced a prolonged drought, making it difficult to comply with its water deliveries to the United States for the course of a decade. Even though the treaty contemplates reduced deliveries in drought years, U.S. actors charged that the decade-long water debt violated its terms and that Mexico was actually expanding agricultural production (Woodhouse 2005). The conflict produced protests by farmers and farmer associations on both sides of the border, inflammatory statements by Texas Governor Rick Perry and Chihuahua Governor Patricio Martínez, a provocative resolution by the Mexican Congress, and cancelled binational meetings between Presidents George W. Bush and Vicente Fox (TCPS 2002). Although the conflict was eventually resolved and Mexico repaid the water debt, the incident hurt farmers on both sides of the border and complicated the overall binational relationship.

In summary, cross-border, civil society cooperation can build bridges of trust and reciprocity capable of overcoming the political division between nations. It can result in cooperative solutions rather than conflictive reactions to binational problems. Recognizing the importance of cross-border cooperation brings us to the central theme of this chapter: how cooperative ties develop.

Explaining Cooperation

Using the institutional analysis and development framework, this chapter examines the impact of the physical attributes of the policy problem, the attributes of the community, and the rules-in-use on binational collaboration. It argues that, even though the physical nature of water-related public problems creates an interdependence between binational actors that makes cooperation desirable, differences in priorities, norms of interaction, and interests on either side of the border can result in strategic interaction and distrust. Moreover, the rules-in-use create incentives to look for policy solutions through domestic political institutions rather than binational ties. Despite these challenges, however, key network actors have emerged to bridge the binational division, foster trust on both sides of the border, and work toward policy solutions.

Physical Attributes and Interdependence

As discussed in chapter 2, water-related problems in the border region are typically binational in nature: what happens on one side of the border impacts the other side. In the Tijuana–San Diego region, the United States and Mexico are connected by the Tijuana River watershed. Sewage leaks and non-point-source pollution draining into the river have historically brought wastewater, sediments, and contaminants across the border and into the Tijuana River estuary and the Pacific Ocean. This has endangered habitat in the estuary and contaminated beaches in the California city of

Imperial Beach. In other words, the health of the estuary and Imperial Beach's ocean water quality are dependent on actions taken in Mexico.

In the Ambos Nogales region, the Nogales Wash flows from south to north through the two cities until it drains into the Santa Cruz River. The wash is fed by leaks from potable water lines and sanitary sewer overflows in Nogales, Sonora. In the 1990s, the International Boundary and Water Commission was forced to establish a chlorination station at the border to treat errant sewage (for a detailed discussion, see Ingram, Laney, and Gillilan 1995). Although conclusive scientific evidence has not supported the claim, lupus and cancer clusters in Nogales, Arizona, have often been blamed on pollution detected in the aquifers under the Nogales Wash (Varady and Mack 1995). Furthermore, both Nogaleses draw drinking water from the Santa Cruz River basin several miles east of the cities, and several miles north of Nogales, Arizona, an out-of-compliance international wastewater treatment plant treats both cities' wastewater.

Within the Rio Grande River basin, which includes the research sites of Ciudad Juárez and Nuevo Laredo, water flows primarily to the southeast and forms the international border between Mexico and the United States. Ciudad Juárez and El Paso both draw groundwater from the overexploited Hueco Bolson. As a result, groundwater use by one impacts the future supply available to the other. In Los Dos Laredos, both cities rely on the Rio Grande/Río Bravo for drinking water, and both face risks from contamination in the river. Despite the presence of a wastewater treatment plant in Nuevo Laredo, as of 2002, an estimated 4.2 million gallons of untreated sewage flowed into the river daily (Parsons Engineering 2002).[1]

These brief descriptions of each of the four research sites illustrate the considerable interdependence that exists in the region. U.S. and Mexican cities depend on one another for water quality and water availability. Numerous scholars have recognized the need for cross-border cooperation to address these transnational concerns (Brown et al. 2003; GNEB 2005; Ingram 2000; Ingram, Laney, and Gillilan 1995). David Brooks and Jonathan Fox (2002) suggest that binational cooperation occurs not because of ideological conviction or farsighted strategy but out of simple necessity. Even though dependence and interdependence make cooperation desirable, however, they do not make it inevitable. Alternatively, interdependence could produce a zero-sum competition between the United States and Mexico. Rather than work together to address contamination, each country could attempt to export it to the other. Rather than work together to ensure a long-term supply of water, each country could attempt to obtain a larger share of the resources before it was fully consumed.

Some scholars find that interdependence does in fact produce transnational cooperation. For example, in the social movements literature, Margaret Keck and Kathryn Sikkink (1998) argue that transborder social movements are precisely the result of interdependence created by globalization. From this perspective, disparate organizations recognize their mutual dependence and come together in cooperation to solve problems that jointly affect them. In fact, when environmental problems are binational in nature, Mexican and U.S. groups have much to gain from cross-border cooperation. Both sides stand to benefit from sustainable water use, protected environmental resources, and reductions in untreated wastewater. There is a particularly favorable opportunity for mutually beneficial exchange when the United States is dependent on Mexico. U.S. nonprofits can exchange greater financial resources and technical know-how for Mexican local knowledge and legitimacy.

In fact, cases of cooperation to address interdependence have been documented all along the border. For example, the Sonoran Institute, based in Tucson, Arizona, has been concerned with environmental degradation in the upper Santa Cruz River basin, which crosses the U.S.–Mexico border twice in the rural region to the east of Ambos Nogales. An important stopping point for a variety of migratory birds in the Sonoran Desert, this waterway has unfortunately become threatened by environmental deterioration. As a result, the Sonoran Institute and other U.S. environmental organizations have been supporting local Mexican initiatives to ensure that its riparian habitat is preserved. Other examples of note include cross-border efforts to address environmental degradation in the Colorado River delta (Angulo 2004); promote a wastewater treatment facility in Naco, Sonora (Kelly 2002; Safa Barraza 1997); and conserve the San Pedro River watershed (Browning-Aiken et al. 2004). Numerous articles and books have been written on cross-border organizing in the region (see, for example, Brooks and Fox 2002; Lara 2000; Staudt and Coronado 2002; Verduzco Chávez 2001; Zabin 1997).

There are, of course, limits to cross-border ties. Jonathan Fox (2002,

343), for example, expresses frustration with the tendency to overstate the degree of binational collaboration: "Sympathetic journalistic coverage often features headlines like 'budding cross-border resistance,' . . . yet we have been reading similar headlines about relations between social movements in Mexico and the United States for more than a decade. For reasons not yet fully understood, these 'buds' have had difficulty flowering. Consolidating cross-border partnerships turns out to be easier said than done."

Also writing in the social movements literature, Sidney Tarrow (2000, 8) has argued that cooperation is "most likely to take root among pre-existing social networks in which relations of trust, reciprocity, and cultural learning are stored" and that there are formidable obstacles to collaboration when political borders divide social networks. Although he is writing about social movement development, a similar argument could be applied to cross-border nonprofit collaboration.

As the above-mentioned water crisis of the early 2000s illustrates, limited water supply could produce zero-sum competition between interdependent Mexican and U.S. water users rather than cooperation. In fact, competition over limited water resources is often posited to produce a "tragedy of the commons" (Hardin 1968). Rather than work out cooperative agreements to manage shared water resources, water users may knowingly extract water at unsustainable rates. Indeed, reducing one's use of the common resource when others are not reducing theirs would only entail forgoing a short-term gain with no long-term benefit. The problem is summed up in the often quoted words, "Whiskey is for drinking, water is for fighting over."

Attributes of the Community

The most striking attributes of the border community are its ethnic, linguistic, and cultural differences. At the very least, such heterogeneity raises the transaction costs of cooperation. Collaborating parties may need to hire translators and spend more time at the negotiating table to overcome cultural differences and find common ground. More fundamentally, however, as in the case of the tragedy of the commons, differences in interests and priorities between people living on either side of the border raise the possibility that cooperation is not even desirable.

Northern co-option of southern nonprofit organizations is a well-documented phenomenon, whereby transnational cooperative efforts respond to the preferences of foreign donors and foreign offices rather than local needs (Alvarez, Dagnino, and Escobar 1998; Bailey 1999; Bandy 2004; Biekart 2004; Khalid 2004). Indeed, Mexican organizations may be wary of U.S. nonprofits, which often have a greater supply of financial and staff resources than their Mexican counterparts. Some activists along the border fear that such co-option has already occurred. One member of civil society in Carol Zabin's 1997 study attributes the rapid growth of Mexican organizations devoted to environmental issues rather than broader issues of poverty and democratization to U.S. border nonprofits and U.S. foundations. A long history of state co-option of societal forms of organization has provided more than sufficient justification for Mexican organizations to be skeptical about asymmetric partnerships.

Of course, there is a risk of overstating the schism between associational life on either side of the border. Lawrence Herzog (1990) describes the border, not as a division between two countries, but rather as a place of coming together. As Helen Ingram, Nancy Laney, and David Gillilan (1995) write, "But if boundaries can separate, they can also connect." Several scholars have noted the presence of *transfronterizos* (borderlanders), or people who travel back and forth across the border, have family on either side, and effectively function in either country (Ingram, Laney, and Gillilan 1995; Martínez 1994; Staudt and Coronado 2002). With the important exception of San Diego County, the other three U.S. counties examined in this study (Santa Cruz County, Arizona; El Paso and Webb Counties, Texas) have very large Hispanic populations, representing over 75 percent of the total population, and a similarly high proportion of Spanish speakers (see table 5.1). These preexisting network ties and ethnic homogeneity across the border offer a potential basis to build cross-border trust between U.S. and Mexican civil society.

Nonetheless, even within the Hispanic population, there are what Oscar Martínez (1997) calls "national borderlanders," or people who live along the border but identify with the country they live in rather than with

Table 5.1   Attributes of the community: U.S. border communities

	Tijuana– San Diego	Ambos Nogales	Paso del Norte	Los Dos Laredos
Percentage of persons of His- panic/Latin origin in U.S. sister county (2005)	29.5	80.5	81.2	94.9
Percentage of Caucasian persons not of Hispanic/Latin origin in U.S. sister county (2005)	52.3	18.4	14.6	4.3
Percentage of persons speaking language other than English at home in U.S. sister county (2000)	33.0	80.5	73.3	91.9

Source: U.S. Census Bureau, http://www.quickfacts.census.gov/qfd/index.html

the binational region. Claire Fox (1999) finds that, despite their common cultural heritage, considerable suspicion exists between Mexican-Americans living in the United States and Mexican nationals. Many scholars, including Claire Fox (1999), accept the normative idea of a borderless culture; however, they are forced to recognize that severe cultural divisions exist. Therefore, collaboration will require not only physical interdependence but also the construction of trust across the border.

The Rules-in-Use

In addition to the physical environment and the degree of trust among heterogeneous actors, the rules-in-use profoundly shape incentives for cooperation. At the most basic level, security at the border raises the transaction costs of binational cooperation. Security measures to protect the U.S. side of the border are particularly problematic, resulting in long waits for those wishing to cross from south to north and preventing many Mexicans from crossing at all. As transaction costs increase, the net benefits to be derived from binational cooperation decrease.

More fundamentally, however, the geopolitical border delimits two different legal systems with two distinct centers of power in Washington, D.C., and Mexico City. Tarrow (2000, 2) has argued that, despite global problems, social movement organizations operate within the context of domestic political institutions: "In contrast to the 'strong' thesis — which proclaimed a transnational civil society developing willy-nilly across national borders — empirical work in this tradition is beginning to focus on beyond-border activism on the part of actors whose interests continue to be framed by domestic political opportunities and constraints."

Because U.S. groups do not have legal rights in Mexico, and Mexican organizations lack legal rights in the United States, nonprofits have incentives to turn toward state and national political institutions to redress public problems in the region. This is particularly the case when civil society organizations are highly dependent on governments for policy solutions. For example, there are limits to the ability of these organizations to treat wastewater or determine policies under which water resources are distributed.

Given dependence on government and the presence of domestic political institutions, it might be more effective for a local San Diego group to contact their representative 2,700 miles away in Washington, D.C. than to cooperate with a Mexican citizens' organization just across the border. In fact, concerned U.S. citizens have at their disposal (1) city council members and state and federal congressmen and women, (2) local, state and federal bureaucracies, and (3) state and federal court systems. Consequently, even though they may depend on the same natural resources, domestic political opportunities create strong incentives for U.S. and Mexican members of civil society to look to their respective political institutions for assistance rather than to one another.

Nonetheless, some attempts have been made to establish binational government institutions to address problems shared by the two countries. For example, the side agreements to the NAFTA–created Commission for Environmental Cooperation (CEC; Comisión de Cooperación Ambiental). As discussed earlier, through the CEC, citizens and civil society organizations can lodge formal complaints against a participating NAFTA country for failing to enforce its own environmental laws. In an examination of the NAFTA–created Commission for Labor Cooperation (CLC; Comisión de Cooperción Laboral), a similar agency created to address labor complaints, Tamara Kay (2005) finds that the commission has encouraged and indeed brought about binational collaboration between non-state actors.

In addition to the CEC, the side agreements created the binational Border Environment Cooperation Commission (BECC; Comisión de Cooperación Ecológica Fronteriza) and the North American Development Bank (NADB) to encourage public infrastructure development in the region. Finally, to increase local level government and civil society participation in the resolution of border environmental problems, the U.S. and Mexican federal governments created the binational Border 2012 program. Through the program, binational task forces have been convened with open public participation, bringing both U.S. and Mexican groups to the same table and providing grant money to civil society organizations. Through the CEC, BECC, NADB, and the Border 2012, NAFTA governments have initiated programs and established agencies with something akin to transnational or binational jurisdiction. Although these initiatives pale in comparison to the set of domestic opportunities in the United States and Mexico, Francisco Lara (1999) has argued that they do create binational opportunities for cross-border civil society cooperation.[2]

In summary, even though the potential benefits to cooperation among interdependent actors may result in cross-border ties, different interests or the perception of different interests may lead either to no cooperation or to actual conflict. Given the region's heterogeneity in culture, language, priorities, and interests, interdependence will be mediated by the degree of trust between actors and affected by the rules governing the policy arena. This gives rise to two contradictory expectations: (1) that U.S. and Mexican organizations will use well-established domestic political opportunities and institutions to redress binational problems; or (2) that they will collaborate across the border to take advantage of the transnational political opportunities that exist under Border 2012, the CEC, BECC, and NADB.

Analysis of Binational Collaboration

Nonprofit business and professional organizations such as the Camera Nacional del Comercio (CANACO; National Chamber of Commerce) and the Association of Engineers, though active in water-related policy arenas, have as their primary objective private sector work. Their binational collaboration reflects this objective, concentrating on economic rather than on water-related policy arenas. To provide a more conserva-

Table 5.2   Incidence of cross-border cooperation

	Tijuana–San Diego	Ambos Nogales	Paso del Norte	Los Dos Laredos	Totals and average[a]
Total number of U.S. nonprofits in U.S. sister city	4,403	71	1,411	275	6,553
Total number of Mexican nonprofits studied	21	8	20	8	57
Number of Mexican nonprofits with with cross-border ties	16	4	10	1	31
Percentage of Mexican nonprofits with cross-border ties	76.2	50.0	50.0	12.5	54.4

Source: Data on U.S. nonprofits are from http://www.Guidestar.com.
[a]Data for Tijuana–San Diego include only city of San Diego rather than the greater metropolitan area; for Ambos Nogales, Santa Cruz County; for Paso del Norte, El Paso County; and for Los Dos Laredos, Webb County.

tive analysis of cross-border collaboration, these business associations are excluded and the focus placed on the remaining sixty Mexican nonprofits and their ties or lack of ties to U.S. groups. Included as well are forty-three U.S. organizations that address binational water issues in the four border areas (for a full listing, see the appendix).

The dependent variable for this chapter is "collaboration," which occurs if (1) there is a flow of resources between two organizations, (2) two groups cooperate on a mutual project, or (3) two organizations are a core part of a binational coalition. Mere membership in a binational coalition or communication with an organization on the opposite side of the border does not constitute a binational tie in this study.

As shown in table 5.2, of the 57 Mexican organizations in this binational network study, 31 (54 percent) collaborate with U.S. organizations, universities, or foundations; the study also finds an impressive 12 cross-border coalitions. Tijuana has the highest percentage of cross-border links (see also Lara 2000). Of the 21 organizations examined there, 16 (76 percent) have collaborative ties to U.S. nonprofits. Tijuana is followed by Ciudad Juárez (50 percent), Nogales (50 percent), and Nuevo Laredo (12.5 percent).

An important control factor that helps explain differences in cross-border collaboration between the different cities is the supply of civil society organizations on either side of the border, also shown in table 5.2. The high number of such organizations in the Tijuana–San Diego area helps explain greater cooperation there. In like fashion, the dearth of organizations on either side of the border in Los Dos Laredos accounts for the lack of binational cooperation in that region. Nogales, Sonora, also faces a limited associational life on the Nogales, Arizona, side of the border, although groups from Tucson, Arizona, and other towns north of Nogales are active in binational water issues. Despite the closeness of San Antonio, Texas, to Los Dos Laredos, no San Antonio organizations were found to have Mexican civil society partners in Nuevo Laredo.[3]

The Tijuana–San Diego Region: Missed Opportunities and Cooperation

During the early 1990s, Tijuana had only one wastewater treatment plant for the city's growing population. The San Antonio de los Buenos plant, southwest of the city, went into operation in 1987. Although it had the capacity to treat 17 million gallons of sewage a day, the city was actually producing much more. In addition, as late as 2003, 21 percent of Tijuana's households were not even connected to the sewer system (Camp Dresser & McKee Inc. 2003). Even in communities with sewer services, damaged infrastructure prevented some sewage from reaching the plant. As a result, errant and untreated sewage crossed the border in the Tijuana River or through one of three canyons that feeds into the Tijuana River estuary before being introduced into the ocean just south of the California city of Imperial Beach.

Not surprisingly, this untreated sewage was of considerable concern on the U.S. side of the border. U.S. residents in the Tijuana River Valley were forced to contend with bad odors, health risks, and mosquito proliferation. Under the leadership of David Gomez, several area residents formed Citizens Revolting against Pollution (CRAP). The organization, which began operations out of Gomez's garage, sought to represent the area's residents in seeking a solution to the problem and at its peak claimed to have six hundred supporters.

Not only CRAP but also environmental groups such as the Sierra Club and the Audubon Society, the San Diego Baykeepers, and the Southwest Wetlands Interpretative Association were and continue to be worried about the effects of the sewage on plant and animal life in the Tijuana River estuary and in the Pacific Ocean. Given Tijuana's heavy industry, environmental groups rightly suspected that the sewage posed a risk to the environment (Wakida and Riveles 1997). The errant sewage was also a major concern to the San Diego region's many beachgoers, surfers, and tourism industry.

For close to two decades, these different groups have participated in a contentious political debate. Though all of them wanted to resolve the sewage problem, they disagreed, sometimes vehemently, about how to do so. Unfortunately, according to U.S. government officials interviewed, their involvement often seems to have hindered rather than helped.

In 1990, following political action by CRAP and the city of Imperial Beach, a state of emergency was declared by city, county, and state officials. Not long afterward, the U.S. and Mexican sections of the International Boundary and Water Commission signed Minute 283, committing their countries to the construction of an international wastewater treatment plant (Michel 2000; Salazar 1999; and Parsons Engineering 2004).[4]

In 1995, after a long and continuous debate about appropriate treatment methods, ground was broken on an advanced primary treatment facility. The plant, which included an ocean outfall to transport the treated wastewater 3.5 miles from the coast, cost $400 million after overruns, according to IBWC estimates, and was not completed until 1999.

The plant has had an important impact on contamination of the region; to the credit of policy makers on both sides of the border, its construction was complemented by development of a master plan by the Tijuana water utility, infrastructure rehabilitation, and an industrial pretreatment program. Nonetheless, a number of wastewater treatment problems remain. Despite the multimillion-dollar price tag, the plant was only meant to be a partial solution, both in terms of quantity and quality of treatment (Parsons Engineering 2004). Even with the plant, Tijuana's wastewater production in 2004, fueled by population growth and industrial development, exceeded treatment capacity by 6 million gallons a day (Parsons Engineering 2004), which flowed directly into the environment with only chlorine injections. Moreover, the plant can only operate during dry weather. Rains swell the volume of wastewater to overwhelming levels, at which point the sewage, albeit diluted by rainwater, is flushed out into the estuary. As a third problem, the quality of treatment at the plant does not comply either with the U.S. Clean Water Act or with an international agreement between the two countries (IBWC Minute 283). A U.S. federal district court order demands that the plant's insufficiencies be resolved by September 2008.[5] Unfortunately, how best to address the deficiencies of the plant and to comply with the court order continues to be a matter of contention. As provided in legislation sponsored by local Congressman Bob Filner (Public Law 104-37), the IBWC chose a private-public partnership called "Bajagua LLC" to pump the partially treated sewage back into Mexico for secondary treatment. However, some of the environmental organizations and activists in the area are vehemently opposed to the Bajagua solution: they question the validity of a private sector response to a public problem and fear abdication of U.S. government responsibility for the issue.

Throughout this almost twenty-year public debate, U.S. organizations involved in the water-related policy arena have used diverse strategies to promote a policy solution. Admittedly, associational life has somewhat limited options given its dependence on a governmental solution. Nonetheless, among the strategies adopted, none has involved the development of partnerships on the opposite side of the border. Rather, citizens and organizations pursued a domestic solution through legislative, executive, and judicial branches of government at the city, county, state, and federal levels. For example, when asked to identify what partners the organization had worked with to find a solution to the wastewater problem, CRAP's president identified the Tía Juana Valley Authority Water District, the Metropolitan Sewage Commission, the Public Utilities Commission, the San Diego County Environmental Health Board, the International Boundary and Water Commission, the Environmental Protection Agency, the San Diego mayor's office, and the governor's office. In addition, he stated that he has worked closely with Congressmen Duncan Hunter and Bob Filner. Hunter had even appointed David Gomez to participate in a congressional border task force and Filner invited him to testify before Congress. By contrast, the organization had no links to groups across the border, even though many of the organization's members are fluent Spanish speakers with family ties to Mexico.

Environmental organizations such as the Sierra Club and the Audubon

Society also identified interaction with an impressive list of U.S. government actors and agencies — but no Mexican organizations. In 1994, the Sierra Club and others filed a lawsuit against the U.S. government in federal court alleging that it had failed to conduct sufficient environmental studies.

The lack of binational civil society ties has produced obstacles to resolving the sewage problem. One long-term environmental activist involved in the dispute admitted in an interview that local nonprofit organizations and government agencies originally pursued a strategy of exaggerating the gravity of the sewage problem to gain national attention, a strategy that, however successful in the short term, eventually backfired. First, it gave the area just north of the border a horrible reputation as a sewage dump, frightening away both residents and tourists. More important, however, it made it appear that Tijuana and Mexico had no interest in addressing the sewage problem. Indeed, one of the strange ironies of the controversy surrounding the wastewater treatment plant in the Tijuana–San Diego region is that political action has occurred almost entirely on the U.S. side of the border, despite widespread acceptance of the binational nature of the problem.

This unilateral action incurred a significant cost: U.S. organizations exhausted their financial, human, and political capital in lobbying, litigating, and convincing officials on the U.S. side of the border to address a problem over which they did not have full decision-making authority. The failure of the unilateral approach would give rise to new binational efforts in the 2000s.

Growing out of an environmental workshop at Tijuana's Universidad Iberoamericana in the early 2000s, JaJan, which means "good water" in the Pai Pai indigenous language, is a coalition of organizations and members of civil society from both sides of the border, including San Diego Baykeeper, ProEsteros, Centro Educativa Tipai, Grupo Ecologista Gaviotas, and a host of other groups. The organization monitors the quality of ocean waters along the coast at locations such as the mouth of the Tijuana River estuary and where effluent from the San Antonio de los Buenos plant enters the Pacific Ocean and produces a weekly bulletin of its findings. According to its members, JaJan does not engage in activism, but rather seeks to produce a source of information on water quality and to help educate citizens about the importance of clean water through active involvement in water monitoring. The need for public information is a necessity for good policy making that has at times been lacking in Tijuana. For example, in the summer of 2003, the city suspended full treatment of wastewater at the San Antonio de los Buenos facility to conduct ten-year maintenance. Although the maintenance was necessary and even to be applauded, Tijuana's citizens were not notified of the suspension despite the health risks it presented to summer beachgoers. Groups like JaJan are able to fill such information gaps.

Another binational collaborative effort has been promoted by the Tijuana River National Estuarine Research Reserve (TRNERR), composed of a number of U.S. government institutions and an Imperial Beach non-profit organization, but highly dependent on actions taken in Mexico. Not only are there a variety of pollutants that flow into the reserve; urban development, poor planning, de-vegetation, and illegal settlements cause massive erosion that threatens to fill in the estuary and endanger this important habitat. In the early 2000s, the reserve used government funds to construct catchment basins to trap sediment coming from the Mexican canyons. Designed to last for several years, the multimillion-dollar basins filled up after one major rain event, providing yet more evidence of the limits of unilateral action. To strengthen its binational efforts, the reserve brought on a high-profile Mexican national who had served as an advisor to binational institutions and the Mexican federal government to help implement cross-border work in Tijuana; through him, the reserve has been able to cultivate collaborative ties to a variety of Mexican government agencies and civil society organizations.

In cooperation with the International Community Foundation and U.S. government agencies, funds have been channeled to Tijuana and Mexican federal planning agencies to conduct studies and develop plans to improve urban infrastructure in the three Tijuana canyons. The Border 2012 program has also provided grants to local Tijuana nonprofit organizations to reduce erosion and conduct environmental education in the Tijuana canyons. Thus Eco-Sol is working with residents to develop gardens, revegetate the hillsides, and compost organic trash. Thus, too, a neighborhood organization from nearby Playas de Tijuana, in cooperation with the Universidad Iberoamericana, is working with communities to develop a type of retaining wall that allows water to pass through while keeping the topsoil intact. JaJan is also being funded to conduct environmental education by involving the canyon's residents in water monitoring.

Another example of binational cooperation worth mentioning is the Tijuana River Watershed Binational Vision Project. Inaugurated in 2002, the project is promoted by the binational academic community of San Diego State University, the Colegio de la Frontera Norte (COLEF), and the Southwest Consortium for Environmental Research and Policy (SCERP). The project, which became an official water task force for the Border 2012 program, comprises a number of civil society groups and government agencies; its "vision" is to promote the restoration of important conservation areas, to protect groundwater supplies, to develop a binational water-quality-monitoring system, and to create mechanisms for transborder watershed management (IRSC and Department of Geography, SDSU 2005).

These examples from the San Diego–Tijuana region illustrate the consequences of both the presence and the absence of effective binational cooperation. In light of this discussion, the following three subsections examine the effect of interdependence, attributes of the community, rules-in-use, and efforts to build trust on the presence and absence of U.S.–Mexican nonprofit collaboration.

Physical Attributes and the Rules-in-Use

Interdependence proves to be a powerful and yet illusive concept across the four study sites. Organizations engaged in cross-border relationships agree that most issues along the border produce high degrees of interdependence and require binational cooperation. Organizational names such as the Bio-Regional Environmental Education Project stress how the political border has unnaturally divided the region. Collaborative efforts refer to their geographical areas of operation in ways that emphasize the regional rather than national. They use names such as "the Californias," "Ambos Nogales," the "Paso del Norte" region, and "Los Dos Laredos." Despite these normative claims, the empirical relationship between dependence and cooperation is actually quite mixed. On the one hand, recent efforts undertaken by JaJan, the Tijuana River National Estuarine Research Reserve, and the Tijuana River Watershed Binational Vision Project represent important binational efforts to address interdependence. On the other hand, however, the long-standing problem of wastewater in the Tijuana–San Diego region illustrates how strong interdependence can still fail to elicit binational civil society cooperation.

In the Tijuana–San Diego region, U.S. organizations perceived and continue to perceive the court system, U.S. bureaucracies, and legislative representatives to be more productive avenues to pursue policy solutions than binational approaches. The lack of binational cooperation and a reliance on domestic institutions is not specific to this region, however. The communities of Nogales, Arizona, and Laredo, Texas, are also directly impacted by the degree to which their Mexican sister cities treat their wastewater, and yet no cooperation has emerged to address this interdependence. As noted in chapter 2, wastewater from Nogales, Sonora, is treated along with that from Nogales, Arizona, at an international plant 9 miles north of the two communities. Unfortunately, however, the plant does not have sufficient capacity to handle flow increases during rainy periods, and recent changes in U.S. regulations have brought the facility out of compliance with the Clean Water Act. U.S. organizations responded with litigation in Arizona courts. As in San Diego, the courts have demanded a solution to the problem; however, the controversy remains.

These wastewater cases illustrate that, as a result of perceived and real dependence on a governmental solution and the presence of frequently used mechanisms within U.S. governmental institutions, civil society organizations north of the border have chosen to pressure their own government rather than seek binational ties.

Domestic political opportunities are not the only rules that serve as disincentives to collaboration. There is no shortage of examples of how rules governing security at the border have frustrated cooperation. An anecdote from JaJan's early history told by one of its founding members is illustrative. The organization originally tested its water samples at a laboratory in the United States. The samples had to be processed within a set number of hours after sampling, but the wait to cross the border often exceeded that number, invalidating the test results. To expedite the process, the samples were carried through the faster pedestrian line, and a U.S. partner would drive to the border to pick them up. Unfortunately however, the security X-ray detection equipment spoiled the samples, and the tests were again invalidated. Finally, through the support of the national Sierra Club, the coalition was able to purchase equipment to do the testing on the Mexican side of the border.

The Tijuana Watershed Binational Vision Project has also found a means to address the problem of border security. Long waits to cross the border and prohibitions on Mexicans without a visa from crossing north severely limited attendance at its meetings on both sides of the border. To ensure that all can attend, the group always meets on the Tijuana side within walking distance of the border crossing. This allows Mexican attendees to avoid having to cross the border altogether and U.S. attendees to avoid the long line of cars on the return trip by parking on the U.S. side and walking across. These two examples show that the obstacle of border security, though significant, can nonetheless be overcome. As a result, security rules are best viewed as an increase in transaction costs, raising the cost-benefit ratio of collaboration but not precluding it. Although domestic political opportunities and border security create disincentives to binational cooperation, not all rules operating in the policy arena do.

Rules-in-Use: Binational Political Opportunities

Theoretically, binational political opportunities should foster cross-border collaboration, yet only the Border 2012 program was found to do so. Citizens or civil society organizations can submit a complaint to the Commission for Environmental Cooperation (CEC) charging that a NAFTA member government has failed to implement or enforce its own environmental laws. Of 56 submissions to the CEC, 12 involve transnational cooperation; of those 12, 9 collaborations are between U.S. and Canadian organizations, 1 is a case of tri-national cooperation, and only 2 are between U.S. and Mexican organizations (see table 5.3). Because of the small number of cases, one cannot say with confidence whether the transnational opportunity represented by the CEC submission process has encouraged U.S.–Mexico civil society collaboration.[6]

On the other hand, the CEC did promote binational collaboration through a grant-funding program in the late 1990s. One of the expressed objectives of the North American Fund for Environmental Cooperation

Table 5.3 Formal complaints submitted to the commission on environmental cooperation, 1996–2006

Case	Alleged violating country	Bi- or tri- national status	Result
Aquanova (1998, 2003)[a]	Mexico	No	Factual record[b]
BC hydro (1997, 2000)	Canada	U.S. and Canada	Factual record
BC logging (2000, 2003)	Canada	U.S. and Canada	Factual record
BC mining (1998, 2003)	Canada	No	Factual record
Cozumel (1996, 1997)	Mexico	No	Factual record
Metales y Derivados (1998, 2002)	Mexico	U.S. and Mexico	Factual record
Migratory birds (1999, 2003)	U.S.	U.S., Mexico, and Canada	Factual record
Molymex II (2000, 2004)	Mexico	No	Factual record
Oldman River II (1997, 2003)	Canada	No	Factual record
Ontario logging (2002, 2007)	Canada	U.S. and Canada	Factual record
Ontario logging II	Canada	U.S. and Canada	Factual record
Pulp and paper (2002, 2007)	Canada	—	Factual record
Río Magdalena (1997, 2003)	Mexico	No	Factual record
Tarahumara (2000, 2006)	Mexico	No	Factual record
Alca-Iztapalapa II (2003)	Mexico	No	Open
Coal-fired power plants (2004)	U.S.	U.S. and Canada	Open
Environmental pollution in Hermosillo (2005)	Mexico	No	Open
Ex-Hacienda El Hospital II and III (2006)	Mexico	No	Open
Lake Chapala II (2003)	Mexico	No	Open
Montréal Technoparc	Canada	U.S. and Canada	Open
Quebec Automobiles (2004)	Canada	No	Open
Los Remedios National Park (2006)	Mexico	No	Open
Species at risk (2006)	Canada	U.S. and Canada	Open
AAA Packing (2001)	Canada	—	Not pursued
Aage Tottrup (1996)	Canada	No	Not pursued
Alza Iztapalapa (2002)	Mexico	No	Not pursued
Biodiversity (1997)	Canada	No	Not pursued
El Boludo Project (2002)	Mexico	No	Not pursued
CEDF (1997)	Canada	No	Not pursued
Coronado Island (2005)	Mexico	U.S. and Mexico	Not pursued
Crushed gravel (2005)	Mexico	No	Not pursued
Cytrar I (1998)	Mexico	No	Not pursued
Cytrar II (2001)	Mexico	No	Not pursued
Cytrar III (2003)	Mexico	No	Not pursued

Table 5.3   (*continued*)

Case	Alleged violating country	Bi- or tri-national status	Result
Dermet (2001)	Mexico	No	Not pursued
Devil's Lake (2006)	Canada	U.S. and Canada	Not pursued
Ex-Hacienda El Hospital I (2006)	Mexico	No	Not pursued
Fort Huachuca (1996)	U.S.	No	Not pursued
Gasoline spill in Tehuantepec (2004)	Mexico	No	Not pursued
Great Lakes (1998)	U.S.	No	Not pursued
Guadalajara (1998)	Mexico	No	Not pursued
Hazardous waste in Arteaga (2004)	Mexico	No	Not pursued
Home Port Xcaret (2003)	Mexico	No	Not pursued
Jamaica Bay (2000)	U.S.	No	Not pursued
Lake Chapala I (1997)	Mexico	No	Not pursued
Logging rider (1995)	U.S.	—	Not pursued
Methanex (1999)	U.S.	No	Not pursued
Mexico City Airport (2002)	Mexico	No	Not pursued
Molymex I and II (2000)	Mexico	No	Not pursued
Neste Canada (2000)	U.S.	No	Not pursued
Oldman River I (1996)	Canada	No	Not pursued
Oldman River III (2004)	Canada	No	Not pursued
Ontario power generation (2003)	Canada	U.S. and Canada	Not pursued
Ortíz Martínez (1997)	Mexico	No	Not pursued
Quebec hog farms (1997)	Canada	No	Not pursued
Spotted owl (1995)	U.S.	No	Not pursued

Source: Commission for Environmental Cooperation (CEC), http://www.cec.org/citizen/index
.cfm?varlan=english.
aFor formal complaints resulting in CEC factual record, two dates are provided: date complaint
was filed and date factual record was issued; for all others, only date complaint was filed.
bIf CEC decides to pursue formal complaint submitted by citizen or civil society organization, it
will issue "factual record," which offers objective history for that case, legal obligations of
United States, Canada, or Mexico, and evidence supporting or contradicting alleged failure to
enforce environmental law.

(NAFEC) was to encourage binational ties. In the early years of CEC
granting, binational collaboration was clearly an important priority in
terms of both the total amount of the grants and the percentage of grants
involving Mexican organizations; binational cooperation seems to have
tapered off, however, in the last four years of the NAFEC granting pro-

Table 5.4 North American Fund for Environmental Cooperation, 1997–2003

	1997	1998	1999	2000	2001	2002	2003
Number of grants	34	28	26	16	17	18	17
Grants involving a Mexican non-profit	21	12	11	9	6	8	8
Transnational coalitions involving a Mexican nonprofit	9	6	6	3	4	2	2
Coalition per Mexican grant ratio	.26	.21	.23	.19	.24	.11	.12
Coalitions involving both Mexican and Canadian nonprofits	4	1	3	2	1	0	0

Source: Commission for Environmental Cooperation (CEC), http://www.cec.org/grants/proj ects/index.cfm?varlan=english.

gram (see table 5.4). Whether this was due to a change in funding priorities or in grant submissions is unclear. In either event, the question is now moot: the program was terminated in 2003.

There is also little evidence that the Border Environment Cooperation Commission (BECC) or the North American Development Bank (NADB) elicit binational civil society cooperation. BECC and NADB projects are focused on specific infrastructure projects, and although public participation criteria contemplate a public meeting in the sister city of a BECC applicant, these criteria have been largely ignored. In addition, even though the BECC had a civil society representative on its board of directors and several representatives on its advisory board, the directors have not played an important role in cross-border cooperation and the advisory board was dissolved by the George W. Bush administration.[7] In the early days of the BECC, there was a binational monitoring effort to ensure that the side agreements to the NAFTA were properly implemented, but this has now fallen off. One interesting by-product of BECC–NADB monitoring is an ongoing e-mail network called "BECCnet," run by the University of Arizona. With hundreds of subscribers on both sides of the border, BECCnet continues to be an important border-wide, often bilingual, communicative tool linking government, civil society organizations, and academia.[8]

There is, however, evidence that the Border 2012 program has encouraged binational cooperation. The mission of the Border 2012 program is "To protect the environment and public health in the U.S.–Mexico border region, consistent with the principles of sustainable development" (EPA and SEMARNAT 2003, 2). To achieve this objective, the program has established a variety of task forces and funding opportunities to maintain a federal commitment to the region while increasing the participation and input of local governments and civil society actors from both sides of the border. Under Border 2012, there are border-wide work groups, policy forums, and four sets of regional work groups, each comprising task forces set up to address specific environmental issues. For example, in the Ambos Nogales region there is a Water Task Force, Air Task Force, Children's Environmental Health Task Force, Emergency Preparedness and Response Task Force, and a Waste and Enforcement Task Force. These task forces serve as an important venue to bring together citizens and government actors from both sides of the border. Furthermore, task forces are provided with funds to offer simultaneous translation at meetings, which reduces the language barrier. Of particular importance, the Border 2012 program has embraced existing binational projects and organizations. For example, the Tijuana River Watershed Binational Vision Project became the Border 2012 task force for the Tijuana River watershed. Task force status provides existing organizations with funding to alleviate the cost of meeting, broadens the network of potential participants, facilitates cooperation between civil society initiatives and government, and increases the credibility and legitimacy of citizen initiatives.

Finally, the Border 2012 program offers a granting program for small projects along the border. Organizations eligible to submit grant proposals include civil society organizations, colleges and universities, border states, multistate or tribal organizations, and local governments. Proposed projects must address a binational or transborder issue and meet the goals and objectives of Border 2012. Although final granting decisions are made by the regional offices of the Environmental Protection Agency (EPA), the offices consult with their Mexican counterparts, and selected projects must meet the priorities established by the binational task forces. Despite the binational focus of the grants, however, as a U.S. federal agency, the EPA could legally give grants only to U.S. entities at the time of this study. These funding rules created incentives for Mexican organizations to seek out U.S. partners to obtain EPA funds and for U.S. organizations to seek Mexican partners to improve their chances of receiving a grant.[9] Border 2012 has helped fund a number of binational initiatives in this study, including efforts to reduce erosion in Tijuana's canyons and to reforest the Ambos Nogales area.

In summary, of the transnational mechanisms established since the NAFTA, only the Border 2012 program has directly produced binational civil society collaboration. The CEC submission process has resulted in very limited U.S.–Mexico collaboration, and the NAFEC funding program has been discontinued. Although BECCnet remains an important communicative tool across the border, the BECC and NADB's focus on local infrastructure issues and the elimination of the binational BECC advisory board have limited their impact on collaboration. Thus, compared to domestic political opportunities, the incentives to binational civil society cooperation offered by these different institutions are minimal.

Attributes of the Community: Heterogeneity and Building Trust

Another potential barrier to binational collaboration are the many differences in culture, language, priorities, and interests between civil society organizations on either side of the border. There is a great deal of anecdotal evidence from the border region that illustrates how heterogeneity hinders collaboration. For example, Nuevo Laredo and Laredo each have one small environmental organization, both the product of the same initiative and centered on a few, key, dedicated individuals. Although both also share the same name, the "Rio Grande International Study Center/ Centro Internacional de Estudios del Río Bravo," they have had very limited interaction over the fourteen years since their founding in 1992, largely because the key actors on both sides of the border do not speak the others' language. Heterogeneity is also an obstacle in the Tijuana–San Diego wastewater treatment case, where some of the most active members of the U.S. environmental community are not Spanish speakers.

In addition, interviews reveal a series of concerns about partnering with organizations on the other side of the border. The strong tradition of autonomous associational life in the United States and the greater available wealth there have produced an asymmetry in resources and organizational capacity. As a result, some Mexican organizations view U.S. partners as paternalistic. On the other hand, some U.S. groups fear that Mexican organizations only seek partnerships as a means to access resources. In addition, U.S. organizations, highly dependent on the availability of funds, have been known to receive a grant for binational work, but then pull out of the community at the termination of the funding cycle. This has created a perception of unreliability among some members of Mexican civil society. Mexican organizations in turn are sometimes perceived as lacking the capacity to administer funds, critically evaluate their work, and develop and submit reports.

Despite these obstacles, more than half of the Mexican organizations in the study have ties to U.S. groups. In addition, if the differences between the United States and Mexico were a decisive impediment to cooperation, then one would expect to find less cooperation in the heterogeneous Tijuana–San Diego region than in the other three areas, whereas the study finds the reverse to be true. Clearly, heterogeneity is an obstacle that, however significant, can be overcome.

Binational coalitions are the most common mechanism to bring a number of organizations from both sides of the border to the same table. Table 5.5 lists twelve binational coalitions present across the four research sites. These coalitions tend to take the form of a core set of organizations or actors who shoulder most of the organizing costs, surrounded by numerous other groups that filter in and out of the coalition, for which participation in coalitions offers a way to communicate with groups across the border at minimal cost and risk. The Tijuana River Watershed Binational Vision Project is a perfect example of one such coalition. Organizations and members of civil society can attend project meetings, obtain information, and network with other citizen initiatives without surrendering any autonomy or committing any resources. With limited risk and investment, coalitions circumvent the need for trust even as they serve to foster it.

One of the most interesting solutions to cross-border differences is found in eight U.S. organizations that have hired Mexican staff members to lead their cross-border efforts (see table 5.5), best exemplified by Oscar Romo of the Tijuana River National Estuarine Research Reserve. With a long history working on environmental issues along Mexico's northern border, Romo served as an advisor to both Presidents Zedillo and Fox on border environmental concerns and was formerly a member of the BECC

Table 5.5   Cross-border collaborations

	Region[a]
Coalitions	
Coordinadora Regional Fronteriza de Organizaciones No Gubernamentales	Ciudad Juárez
Paso del Norte Environmental Health Task Force	Ciudad Juárez
Paso del Norte Water Task Force	Ciudad Juárez
Rio Grande / Río Bravo Basin Coalition	Ciudad Juárez
Ambos Nogales Revegetation Partnership (ARAN)	Nogales
Bio-Regional Environmental Education Project (PROBEA)	Tijuana
Environmental Education Council of the Californias (EECC)	Tijuana
JaJan	Tijuana
Tijuana River Watershed Binational Vision Project	Tijuana
Southwest Network for Economic and Environmental Justice	Tijuana and Nogales
U.S.–Mexico Border Philanthropy Partnership	Tijuana, Nogales, and Ciudad Juárez
Southwest Center for Environmental Research and Policy	Tijuana, Nogales, and Ciudad Juárez
U.S. organizations with essential Mexican nationals as staff members	
Center for Environmental Resource Management (CERM)	Ciudad Juárez
Environmental Defense	Ciudad Juárez
Rio Grande / Río Bravo Basin Coalition	Ciudad Juárez
Environmental Education Exchange	Nogales
Sonoran Institute	Nogales
Environmental Health Coalition	Tijuana
San Diego Baykeeper	Tijuana
Tijuana River National Estuarine Research Reserve (TRNERR)	Tijuana
Organizations founded by a U.S. organization	
Proyecto del Río	Ciudad Juárez
Borderlinks	Nogales
Centro de Promoción de Salud Esperanza	Tijuana
Colectivo Chilpancingo	Tijuana
Fundación Esperanza	Tijuana
Fundación Internacional de la Comunidad (FIC)	Tijuana
Los Niños	Tijuana
Medicinas Comunitarias Sociales	Tijuana

Table 5.5   (*continued*)

	Region[a]
Professional intermediaries	
Center for Civic Engagement at University of Texas, El Paso	Ciudad Juárez
Center for Environmental Resource Management	Ciudad Juárez
Rio Grande / Río Bravo Basin Coalition	Ciudad Juárez
Bureau of Applied Anthropology at the University of Arizona, Tucson	Nogales
ProPeninsula	Tijuana
Synergos Institute	Tijuana
Longtime cross-border actors	
Proyecto Fronterizo de Educación Ambiental	Tijuana
San Diego Natural History Museum	Tijuana
Environmental Health Coalition (EHC)	Tijuana
International Community Foundation (ICF)	Tijuana
Tijuana River National Estuarine Research Reserve	Tijuana
Center for Environmental Resource Management	Ciudad Juárez
Federación Mexicana de Asociaciones Privadas de Salud y Desarrollo Comunitario	Ciudad Juárez
Environmental Defense	Ciudad Juárez
Aqua 21	Ciudad Juárez
Institute for Regional Studies of the Californias (IRSC)	Tijuana

[a]No cross-border collaborations were found in Nuevo Laredo region.

advisory council. Because of his experience in the region, Romo was brought onto the reserve staff to coordinate binational efforts in Tijuana's canyons. An employee on the U.S. side of the border with long-standing ties to government and civil society actors on the Mexican side of the border, he is able serve as a bridge between the two. A meeting between Romo and representatives from Mexican civil society seemed more like a discussion among Mexicans about how to address erosion in their community than an instance of binational collaboration. It just so happened that one of the attendees was employed on the opposite side of the border, that the funding for the projects came from the United States, and that the estuary on the U.S. side of the border would benefit immensely from their actions.

Thus Mexican nationals, born and raised in Mexico but working for U.S. organizations, represent the most effective means to bridge the border. Perhaps surprisingly, in only two cases did Mexican-Americans (born in the United States but of Mexican descent) serve as the vital link to Mexican civil society (see table 5.5).

As discussed in detail in chapter 4, on eight occasions, U.S. nonprofits actually helped establish Mexican organizations (see table 5.5). For example, San Diego's Environmental Health Coalition (EHC) helped empower women in the pollution-affected Colonia Chilpancingo. The neighborhood lies literally in the shadow of the closed-down site of the contaminated Metales y Derivados Plant. With the EHC's support, the women founded Colectivo Chilpancingo (Chilpancingo Collective) to help push for a cleanup of the Metales y Derivados industrial site and to address other environmental health concerns in the community. In cases like Fundación Esperanza (Esperanza Foundation), a U.S. organization either needed a Mexican partner where none existed or decided to help start a new organization rather than work with existing organizations. Today, all of the Mexican spin-off nonprofits are independent, but they maintain strong cross-border ties to their parent organizations.

The border is also bridged by six U.S. organizations that can be considered professional border crossers (see table 5.5), dedicating much of their work to assisting civil society organizations on the Mexican side of the border. In many cases, they are contracted by foundations to develop cross-border ties and facilitate binational efforts. In the Tijuana–San Diego region, Pro Peninsula was formed by two young graduates of the graduate program in International Relations and Pacific Studies at the University of California, San Diego. The organization works to build the capacity of Baja California environmental nonprofits in the areas of strategic planning, fund-raising, board development, membership planning, and Web presence. Another excellent example is the Center for Environmental Resource Management (CERM) of the University of Texas, El Paso, mentioned in chapter 4. With grant support from the El Paso–based Paso del Norte Health Foundation, CERM works with its Mexican partners to build capacity and assist in the administration of grant projects in water-related policy arenas in Ciudad Juárez, employing Mexican staff members and consultants to facilitate its work.

Several U.S. nonprofits and Mexican organizations interact directly without a Mexican employee, a U.S. parent organization, or professional intermediaries. In almost all of these cases, key Mexican or U.S. actors have developed a reputation as an organization or individual trusted on both sides of the border through a long history of cross-border activity (see table 5.5). For example, the central actor in Proyecto Fronterizo de Educación Ambiental (PFEA), Laura Silvan, worked for a U.S. environmental group before launching her own organization in Tijuana in 1991. With over a decade and a half of experience in binational collaboration, Silvan and PFEA are well trusted by U.S. foundations and U.S. organizations. PFEA is a key network node in a number of binational coalitions including the Tijuana River Watershed Binational Vision Project, the Environmental Education Council of the Californias, and the Bio-Regional Environmental Education Project. The organization was also responsible for managing a multimillion-dollar series of border-wide meetings of environmental organizations called the "Encuentro Fronterizo." Other organizations in the Tijuana–San Diego region have followed a similar trust-building route. For example, the San Diego Natural History Museum and the Institute for Regional Studies of the Californias have also invested heavily in developing cross-border trust.

In summary, even though heterogeneity raises the transaction costs of cross-border collaboration, precluding it for many individuals who are not bilingual, key network actors serve to bridge differences in cross-border relationships, even as they operate within the physical context of policy problems and within the rules-in-use. Examining the challenges of supplying cities with sufficient water lets us explore all three factors simultaneously, and in so doing, tie together the theoretical argument of this chapter.

Illustrative Case: Obtaining Water Resources for Growing Cities

In the Ambos Nogales and Paso del Norte regions, sister cities share scarce groundwater. Whereas surface water along the border is governed, albeit imperfectly, by a 1944 treaty, there are no binational agreements on the use of groundwater. In the absence of an agreement or hierarchy, overexploitation of groundwater has the potential to bring about a tragedy of the commons. Although the threat of such a tragedy has provoked numerous calls for groundwater-sharing agreements (GNEB 2005; Mumme 2000b), even the exact size of many of the region's shared aquifers remains un-known. Under such conditions, the United States and Mexico could reach a mutually advantageous cooperative agreement that sustainably governs the commons, or they could strategically attempt to obtain a larger por-tion of the commons through unconstrained pumping and eventually de-plete the resource. In fact, in the Paso del Norte region, extraction rates from the aquifer far exceed recharge estimates (Turner, Hamlyn, and Ibáñez Hernández 2003). El Paso has acted to diversify its water supply sources; Ciudad Juárez has been slower in its response.

Civil society organizations, including water user associations, commu-nity groups, and environmental groups are of extreme importance in re-solving this dilemma. They are able to make decisions about their own water use, take action independent of government, and place pressure on government actors. Generally speaking, these organizations have two op-tions in this binational dilemma: (1) they can utilize domestic political institutions to ensure that their nation's government fights for more water rights, a scenario more likely to produce a zero-sum game between the United States and Mexico; or (2) in the absence of a domestic governmental solution, they can lead public officials, who are constrained by domestic rules and political pressures, toward a cooperative binational agreement.

The presence of domestic political opportunity structures would favor civil societies proceeding down already familiar paths. As a result, one would not necessarily expect binational cooperation to emerge. This is what actually occurred in Ambos Nogales. In the early and mid-1990s, Nogales, Sonora, needed to increase its water exploitation to serve its growing population. Mexican water officials considered drilling addi-tional wells in the binational Santa Cruz River basin, to the east of Ambos Nogales (SIUE 1995). However, U.S. water users in the arid Sonoran Desert region, such as the Groundwater Users' Advisory Council (GUAC), knew that they would be negatively impacted by any new wells. More-over, environmental groups, such as the Friends of the Santa Cruz River, feared that continued groundwater pumping would further decrease sur-face water flows in the Santa Cruz River. U.S. civil society actors found political institutions to be the most effective avenue to pressure Mexico, and no cross-border ties were developed (GUAC 1996). According to several participants in this study, conflict was avoided when Nogales,

Sonora, delayed plans to drill more wells in the Santa Cruz River basin and instead brought additional water from the Los Alisos River basin, 20 miles south of the city.

In the Paso del Norte region, however, the binational academic community, with a long history of promoting cross-border collaboration, is leading the Paso del Norte Water Task Force, rooted in an earlier binational effort, the Paso del Norte Air Quality Task Force, founded in 1993 by members of the environmental and academic community. This first task force was open to the public and drew the participation of government officials, concerned citizens, and members of civil society organizations from both sides of the border. The Paso del Norte Water Task force involves many of the same key players, most notably the U.S. environmental organization Environmental Defense. To facilitate its work with the task force, Environmental Defense hired Carlos Rincon, a Mexican national with strong ties in the Paso del Norte community. When asked why Mexican farmers on the outskirts of Ciudad Juárez would be willing to participate in a water task force promoted by a U.S. environmental organization, Rincon replied that farmers in Mexico simply did not think of him as part of a U.S. environmental group. Prior to joining Environmental Defense, Rincon, a hydrologist by training, had been director of the Instituto Nacional de Investigaciones Forestales y Agropecuarias (INIFAP; National Institute of Forestry, Agriculture, and Animal Research) and had had a long history in the academic, governmental, and private sectors. Like Oscar Romo, Rincon has been able to serve as a bridge across the border.[10]

Under the leadership of Environmental Defense and the academic community, the Paso del Norte Water Task Force, with the participation of the water utility, enlisted one water expert and one major water user from each of the three states in the Paso del Norte region: Chihuahua, Texas, and New Mexico. The task force has analyzed water markets and conservation techniques and promoted technology transfers in the region. To date, its greatest accomplishment has been to normalize and standardize information flows between the three jurisdictions, an important first step toward addressing the larger problem of sustainable water supply for the region.

The Paso del Norte case differs from the Ambos Nogales case in several respects. The Paso del Norte Water Task Force is built on the success of the

Paso del Norte Air Quality Task Force. Binational network actors had already won each other's trust and the trust of government officials on both sides of the border. Furthermore, the U.S. organization Environmental Defense, staffed by a Mexican national, has been a vital bridge for both the air-quality and water coalitions. Binational cooperation in the Paso del Norte, therefore, has been made possible by preexisting networks, past success, trust, and an internalized bridge to Mexican civil society. In the Ambos Nogales case, on the other hand, no such long-term binational ties have been created. Not surprisingly, no significant binational collaboration has emerged.

In summary, this comparative case study of water supply problems illustrates the importance of the physical nature of the problem (mutual dependence), the rules-in-use (the lack of a treaty governing groundwater), and the attributes of the community (the presence or absence of preexisting networks). By examining how these factors interact, we can explain how cooperation emerged in the Paso del Norte region, but not in the Ambos Nogales region.

Conclusion

In a speech on binational collaboration, longtime observer and participant in border environmental issues Mary Kelly (2002, 134) stated, "If one had tried to organize a border wide conference of non-governmental actors interested in environmental issues in the U.S.–Mexico border in 1990, getting fifty people to attend would have been considered lucky — and most of them would have been academics." Today the situation is different, and binational collaboration abounds, serving to strengthen Mexican civil society, diffuse norms supportive of associational life, and solve binational policy problems.

The good news for binational civil society cooperation is that the obstacle of heterogeneity can be overcome. Differences in culture, language, and interests in the border region, much like security rules there, serve to raise the transaction costs of collaboration rather than to preclude it. But even though heterogeneity does not preclude binational collaboration, collaboration is dependent on key individuals or organizations to serve as bridges and negotiate differences between the two countries.

The bad news is that interdependence, or the need to work together to address binational problems, is insufficient to produce binational civil society collaboration (particularly when civil society actors are dependent on government). Given that governments are constrained from addressing binational policy problems by the limits of their legal jurisdictions, it was hoped that more flexible civil society organizations would have greater potential to organize binationally and lead governments to seek binational solutions. And, in fact, such cases have been well documented (Ketter 1998; Safa Barraza 1997). However, this study has found that when solutions to policy problems require governmental involvement, civil society organizations are sensitive to domestic political opportunities and more likely to pursue policy concerns through domestic governmental channels rather than through collaboration with actors on the other side of the border. Political and legal divisions between the United States and Mexico thus not only directly limit responses by governments to binational policy problems but also indirectly limit responses by the nonprofit sector.

6 The Other Border

Civil Society Organizations and the For-Profit Sector

Introduction

Reliance on foreign contributions raises serious questions about the sustainability of the nonprofit sector in Mexico's border region. Overdependence on single-source funding is risky: U.S. foundations may change their geographical or substantive focus unexpectedly. In fact, the border environmental community has been deeply impacted by changes in funding priorities. The NAFTA provoked a major response from U.S. foundations, such as the Ford, William and Flora Hewlett, and Charles Stewart Mott Foundations, but a decade after the agreement was signed, these foundations had significantly decreased their contributions to the region. Thus, having long supported water-related projects in the border region with millions of dollars annually, after a change in leadership, the Hewlett Foundation moved away from both water issues and the U.S.–Mexico border; by 2005, the foundation had withdrawn support entirely (see table 6.1). The decline in funding provoked concern in the border environmental community, which had become dependent on funds from major U.S. foundations.

The problem of overdependence is clearly illustrated in the case of the binational Rio Grande/Río Bravo Basin Coalition, which received substantial funding from large foundations such as Hewlett. The coalition was a much-celebrated binational effort to protect the Rio Grande. It claimed sixty-seven members at its peak and was favorably profiled in news sources and academic works (Staudt and Coronado 2002). Despite the success of the coalition, it was forced to close its doors in 2004. The director of the organization blamed the closure on funding problems and complained about the reductions in U.S. foundation and government support to the region. Although, on paper, the coalition still exists, it no longer operates with a paid staff, offices, or funding.

Table 6.1 Hewlett Foundation environmental grants to U.S.–Mexico border communities, 2000–2005

	2000	2001	2002	2003	2004	2005
Grants to Mexican nonprofits	6	6	3	0	0	0
Grants to U.S. nonprofits	5	5	9	2	1	0
Grants to bi-national non-profits	0	0	1	1	1	0
Total grants to border non-profits	11	11	13	3	2	0
Total grant amounts	$1,925,000	$4,850,000[a]	$2,850,000	$525,000	$350,000	0

Source: William and Flora Hewlett Foundation
[a]Includes $2 million given to Mascareñas Foundation and Fundación Internacional de la Comunidad for regranting in border region for environmental projects. This money was to be used in future years.

Overdependence on foreign or single-source funding highlights the importance of local philanthropy for the long-term sustainability of the nonprofit sector. Yet commentators on associational life in Mexico are quick to point out the country's historic and current lack of philanthropy (Castro Salinas 2001; CEMEFI 1996; Layton 2004; Verduzco 2003). In a cross-national study, Gustavo Verduzco, Regina List, and Lester Salamon (1999) find that more than 85 percent of the revenue of Mexico's relatively small nonprofit community comes from fees, and less than 6 percent from philanthropy. At the same time, however, Mexico is among the largest economies in the world, with a 2005 GDP of $768 billion. Indeed, as representatives of the Sonoran Business Foundation noted ironically in a recent conference on the nonprofit sector, Mexico has the greatest number of billionaires in Latin America. This creates a puzzle: given the presence of such economic resources amid such tremendous social need, why is there so little philanthropy? Although there is a real danger that strong ties to and overdependence on the for-profit sector will lead to co-option and a loss of critical voice, the lack of such ties has limited the growth of the sector and failed to bring sufficient human, financial, and organizational capital to bear on salient public problems. The lack of ties between non-profits and the business community suggests that there exists a very real boundary between these two sectors, one I refer to as the "other border."

With an eye toward strengthening civil society organizations, spreading norms of volunteerism and philanthropy, and resolving public problems, this chapter first examines the extent and limitation of cross-sector coop-eration between the business community (a term I use interchangeably with the "for-profit sector" and define to include both for-profit corpora-tions and the men and women who run them) and civil society organiza-tions at all four research sites.[1] It then seeks to explain how collaborative ties are constructed across the other border.

Socially Responsible Behavior and the Potential for Exchange

Cooperation between civil society organizations and the business commu-nity can manifest itself in a number of ways. First and foremost, members of the for-profit sector can make financial donations to civil society orga-nizations. These might be straightforward cash donations, or they might involve more innovative fund-raising. For example, in 2002, the Johnson & Johnson Corporation donated $90,000 to the Center for Environmen-tal Resource Management at the University of Texas, El Paso for sanita-tion and hygiene programs in the Paso del Norte (Kiy et al. 2005).

Cause-related marketing represents an additional means to support nonprofit organizations. In 1998, Nestlé México launched a campaign called "Join us in reforesting Mexico." The company donated one penny from every bottle sold of Agua Santa María to Espacios Naturales y De-sarrollo Sustentable (Natural Spaces and Sustainable Development) for reforestation (M. Lara 2000).

Support might also entail in-kind services rather than just financial contributions. For example, in Nogales, Sonora, maquiladoras painted leftover barrels green with a "reduce, reuse, and recycle" triangle. They drilled holes in them to ensure they would not be used to store water and donated them as trash containers to city residents. In fact, Richard Kiy and colleagues (2005) find that in-kind services are the preferred form of corporate contributions in the border region.

Nonprofit and for-profit actors might also collaborate on a joint project. The Mexican corporation Cementos Mexicanos (CEMEX) has worked with nonprofit organizations to preserve 55,000 acres in the Boquillas del Carmen area across the Rio Grande from Big Bend National Park on the U.S. side. In total, the company has contributed over $1.4 million to this environmental protection initiative in the border region (Kiy et al. 2005).

Alternatively, for-profit sector actors can participate directly in the activities of nonprofit organizations. For example, in the United States, members of the business community have commonly sat on the boards of directors of local nonprofits (Useem 1987), bringing both human and financial resources to the organizations.

In these examples, the advantages of cross-sector cooperation for nonprofit organizations are obvious; those for the business community are perhaps less evident. In the research on corporate philanthropy, there has been a lively debate about the role of the for-profit sector in supporting nonprofit organizations. At one extreme, the U.S. economist Milton Friedman has famously argued that corporations have an obligation to return a profit to their shareholders and that siphoning funds off for philanthropic purposes is therefore outside their mission. At the other, some argue that corporations have a social responsibility to their communities and that they should therefore give regardless of the impact on the bottom line (Shaw and Post 1993). Speaking of his company's response to the flooding of the Mexican border town Piedras Negras, one manager stated: "We did not track the daily hours or cost, we did what we felt was our duty and our responsibility" (Kiy et al. 2005, 47).

Altruism need not be the sole motivation for giving, however, and many commentators contend that socially responsible behavior actually leads to greater profits (Kotler and Lee 2004; M. Lara 2000). Although the debate on the financial benefits of corporate giving continues (for a discussion, see Sinclair and Galaskiewicz 1997; Useem 1987), there is evidence that many socially responsible firms are motivated by what Tocqueville termed "enlightened self-interest" (Sinclair and Galaskiewicz 1997). From this point of view, socially responsible behavior leads to an improved public perception, which in turn positively impacts the bottom line. For example, the cause-related marketing strategy mentioned above offers a means to gain market share. Given the choice between Agua Santa María and a competitor, it is more likely consumers will choose Santa María because they will know that part of the proceeds will go to protect the environment.

Others argue that a business sector devoted to socially responsible activities will create a stronger community and a better investment climate (Stendardi 1992). James Austin and colleagues (2004a, 7) state: "There is a growing recognition that market forces alone will not alleviate the gamut of social problems. Business leaders increasingly are seeing the improvement of those conditions as vital to the development of more vibrant and sustainable business environments." Echoing this sentiment, María Luisa Lara (2000, xix) writes: "It is important to understand that social development is a condition for the development of business, which cannot ignore illiteracy, criminality, poverty, environmental problems, and droughts; these are phenomena that affect a business's performance and demonstrate the need to integrate social development into business objectives." Such statements, which have particular resonance in the border region, recognize the interdependence that exists between businesses and the communities in which they operate. Businesses along the border do in fact stand to benefit from helping to solve water-related public problems in the region. Unsustainable water use very likely would result in high water prices and even water shortages, which would harm business interests considerably.

Though perhaps a less profound benefit, participation in nonprofit efforts also serves a social function. Volunteer work or participation on nonprofit boards allows business elites to meet, exchange information, and interact with one another in a nonbusiness setting (Salzman and Domhoff 1983).

In summary, there are considerable advantages to cross-sector collaboration for both nonprofit and for-profit actors. Cross-sector collaboration offers nonprofit actors a means to obtain human and financial resources, diversify funding sources, and address dependencies on the local environment; it offers for-profit actors the opportunity to improve their reputation in their respective communities, it strengthens the business climate of those communities, and it provides a medium through which to interact with other business elites. Such collaboration also produces positive externalities that impact society as a whole. Contributions of human, financial, and organizational resources not only help an individual organization; they also strengthen Mexico's nascent civil society. Regular cross-sector interaction also helps spread norms of social responsibility and philanthropy from nonprofit sector networks to the broader society. Furthermore, cross-sector ties bring a diversity of resources to bear on complex policy problems. Any one civil society, governmental, or for-profit entity may be unable, on its own, to solve a policy problem, whereas the combination of resources unique to each sector more likely could.

Factors Impacting Cooperation

In addition to documenting the extent of cross-sector ties, this chapter seeks to explain when cooperation occurs across the "other border" that divides the nonprofit and business communities. Although there are considerable potential benefits to be gained from cooperation across this border, there are also costs. The following three subsections, like chapter 5, use the institutional analysis and development framework to identify the physical attributes of the policy arena, rules-in-use, and attributes of the community that could be expected to impact the likelihood of cross-sector collaboration.

Physical Attributes

Jeffrey Pfeffer and Gerald Salancik (1978) argue that much of organizational activity is in fact an effort to manage dependencies. They contend that interdependence exists when an actor does not control all of the conditions necessary for the achievement of a goal, and that organizations attempt to internalize dependencies by bringing other actors, on whom they are dependent, into a cooperative relationship. For example, Jeffrey Pfeffer (1973) finds that nonprofit hospitals, which are dependent on the local environment for funds and political support, have boards composed of key community leaders, whereas government and religiously affiliated for-profit hospitals, which are relatively immune from the local environment, have boards that specialize in hospital administration.

Just as water-related public problems produce interdependence across the U.S.–Mexico border, they also produce interdependence across the division between the nonprofit and for-profit sector. If, for example, a civil society organization is concerned with improving the quality of a water resource, then it is dependent on all the individuals and businesses that contribute to contamination of that resource. Or if an association is concerned with overexploitation of water resources, then it is particularly dependent on large water users. Given such dependence, it would be desirable for these organizations to seek collaborative ties with contaminating industries and major consumers of water resources. Theoretically, an organization could work with industry to reduce contamination and adopt water-saving technology. Nonetheless, the previous chapter found that the presence of interdependence alone was insufficient to produce cooperation and, in fact, at times resulted in conflict. It concluded that, although physical interdependence makes cross-sector cooperation desirable, it does not make it inevitable or even likely. This chapter reexamines the interdependence hypothesis across associational life's other border.

Attributes of the Community

One of the obstacles to cooperatively addressing interdependence is the heterogeneity that exists across borders. Just as there are differences in culture, priorities, and interests across the U.S.–Mexico border, so there are comparable differences across the other border between the for-profit and nonprofit sectors. At the very least, these differences raise the transaction costs of cooperation; more fundamentally, they raise the possibility of strategic interaction. Unfortunately, there are plenty of reasons for distrust across the other border. The nonprofit community in Mexico has been controversial and has not engendered the same respect and trust it receives in the United States.[2] Clientelism and heavy involvement in the partisan arena during one-party rule damaged the legitimacy of associational life and called into question the motivation of third sector leaders.

Unfortunately, as chapter 3 shows, many nonprofits still maintain clientelistic ties to political patrons. Present-day scandals have not helped the nonprofit sector gain credibility. For example, Fundación Vamos México (Let's Go Mexico Foundation), directed by Marta Sahagún de Fox, the wife of former President Vicente Fox (2001–2006), was the center of political controversy over the possible illegal use of public funds (Layton 2004). In the 2005 National Survey on Philanthropy and Civil Society (ENAFI), 45 percent of respondents reported some or much distrust when asked for donations. Michael Layton (2004) cites a 2004 survey by the Mexican newspaper *La Reforma* in which, of 855 Mexico City respondents, 72 percent said that they distrusted fund-raising campaigns on behalf of the needy. Along the border, there is additional reason for distrust. As one observer told me: "NGO [nongovernmental organization] attacks . . . on the maquiladora industry in the debates over approval of NAFTA and since have engendered greater mistrust on [the] part of [the] private sector."

Reasons for distrust cut both ways, however. As noted above, Mexico does not have a history of philanthropy (Castro Salinas 2001; CEMEFI 1996; Verduzco 2003; Layton 2004). Mexico's business community is perceived by some critics to be isolated from the social and environmental problems of the country. Instead of helping to address such needs, wealthier segments of the population are able to use their superior resources to seek individual solutions to public problems. For example, if water is contaminated, then bottled water can be purchased. If there are no parks or nature reserves or if the environment is contaminated on the Mexican side of the border, then those with visas can travel or even live across the border and enjoy the parks that are available there. These actions represent private solutions to public problems. In the worst-case scenario, the business community might not only be apathetic to Mexico's troubles; it might actually contribute to the country's social and environmental hardships through labor exploitation and environmental contamination.

Given their divergent interests, support from the business community might only be a disguised effort to co-opt civil society. Such co-option would not be without precedent. In the environmental arena, activists John Stauber and Sheldon Rampton (1995) argue that industries that produce potentially harmful waste have an incentive to engage in "greenwashing," defined by the environmental group CorpWatch (2001) as "the phenomenon of socially and environmentally destructive corporations attempting to preserve and expand their markets by posing as friends of the environment and leaders in the struggle to eradicate poverty." For example, in northern Mexico, the Mitsubishi Corporation provided a lucrative contract to a Mexican university to produce a positive environmental impact statement about the effects of a proposed salt-producing operation in Baja California (Barkin 1999). Although key network bridges overcame the problem of heterogeneity across the U.S.–Mexico border, differences are expected to be an even greater obstacle across the border shared by the for-profit and nonprofit sectors.

Although the two sectors are clearly divided from one another, it would be a mistake to view them as homogeneous blocks. In fact, there are considerable divisions within each sector. For example, a large body of literature has noted that for-profit sector actors are more or less likely to engage in socially responsible activity depending on the nature of the industry where they are employed (Sinclair and Galaskiewicz 1997; Useem 1987). In a U.S. study, Louis Fry, Gerald Keim, and Roger Meiners (1982) found that businesses having more contact with the public spend more on contributions to nonprofit organizations. One of the most salient attributes of the business community in the border region is the predominance of the maquiladora industry, which, at its peak in 2000, employed a staggering 255,740 workers in Ciudad Juárez (Turner, Hamlyn, and Ibáñez Hernández 2003). Using 2005 statistics from the Secretary of the Economy, Kiy et al. (2005) found that there were 925 maquiladoras in Tijuana, 144 in Nogales, 350 in Ciudad Juárez, and 55 in Nuevo Laredo. Norris Clement (2002, 11) has observed that, by the twenty-first century, "the assembly-manufacturing sector had become one of the main drivers, if not the main driver, of the Mexican border economy."

What does the predominance of the maquiladora industry mean for nonprofit and for-profit relations? In their study of corporate giving in the U.S.–Mexico border region, Kiy et al. (2005) document maquiladora support for the local nonprofit community. Of the 110 maquiladora participants in their study, two-thirds gave financial contributions to a local nonprofit (see table 6.2). In another study, Austin et al. (2004b) found that the socially responsible businesses were primarily multinational corporations (MNCs). They argue that MNCs export a culture of social responsibility from advanced industrial democracies to developing countries. Furthermore, economic development advocates Nancy Birdsall and David Wheeler (1993) have argued that foreign direct investment is actually more sympathetic to environmentalism than domestic industry because it

Table 6.2   Maquiladora philanthropic activities in the border region, 2004

Type of giving	Response (percent)		
	Yes	No	DK/NA[a]
Donated cash to local groups	64.4	23.6	10.0
Donated products to local groups	46.4	46.4	7.3
Matched contributions of employees	25.5	59.1	15.5
Provided scholarships	44.5	45.5	10.0
Gave support[b] to local schools	51.8	40.0	8.2
Paid employees for volunteer time	17.3	70.9	11.8
Sponsored a youth team	51.8	39.1	9.1
Sponsored a community event	63.6	29.1	7.3
Implemented written charitable guidelines	30.0	52.7	17.3

Source: Kiy et al. 2005. Authors give results of mail-in survey responses from 110 maquiladoras: 51 (46%) from Baja California; 14 (13%) from Sonora; 12 (11%) from Chihuahua; 12 (11%) from Coahuila; 2 (2%) from Nuevo León; and 19 (17%) Tamaulipas. Because 800 companies were sent survey questionnaire, however, this number(110) represents a response rate of only 13.75 percent. It is reasonable to assume that nonrespondents demonstrated lower levels of giving.
[a]"Don't know"/"No answer."
[b]Nature of support (whether cash, in-kind, or both)is not specified by authors.

allows for the importation of more advanced technological processes that incorporate better pollution standards. These arguments suggest that the maquiladoras may be more supportive than domestic businesses of the nonprofit sector and even the environmental community.

On the other hand, foreign companies may lack the local commitment of their domestic counterparts. Julian Wolpert and Thomas Reiner (1980) found that corporations give disproportionately in their headquarter city over other locations of operation, a finding that appears to hold true in the border region. Kiy et al. (2005) found that maquiladora managers had limited discretionary authority for charitable giving, that nearly two-thirds of maquiladora managers in their study sample only had the authority to provide contributions of up to $1,000. The authors singled out a major U.S. multinational corporation with 15 percent of its workforce in Ciudad Juárez. If 15 percent of the MNC's annual giving were spent in the border region, the contribution would exceed $4 million. Instead, the company donated a mere $100,000—less than 3 percent of its annual giving—in the region.

In addition, activists and critics of the NAFTA argue that foreign corporations move to the border specifically to reduce costs and avoid environmental regulations (García and Simpson 2004). Barry Castleman (1987) has found that, across the globe, weak environmental regulations are a motivation for the migration of industry from north to south. Given this motivation, it would be surprising to find maquiladoras increasing costs through contributions to nonprofit efforts or working with environmental groups to curb natural resource degradation.

Perhaps most important, because they operate within a different legal and fiscal framework than local industry, maquiladoras cannot deduct their charitable contributions under the Mexican tax code (Kiy et al. 2005). Indeed, because the taxes they must pay are based on their total cost of operations, donations actually increase their tax liability (Kiy et al. 2005). In light of these conflicting findings, this chapter asks whether foreign maquiladoras or Mexican national corporations have stronger ties to associational efforts at the four research sites.

There also exists a salient division within the nonprofit organizations of this study based on attitudes toward economic development, on the one hand, and protection of the environment, on the other. A broad array of groups can be found within policy arenas related to water, including environmental organizations, public health groups, community development organizations, professional associations, foundations and city improvement groups. Although there are many exceptions, generally speaking, environmental organizations are more likely than other groups to find themselves opposed to private sector economic development. In the border region specifically, different environmental organizations have stood against the NAFTA and the growth of the maquiladora sector (Thorup 1991), liquefied natural gas (LNG) plants (Lindquist 2004), tourism development (Pesenti and Dean 2003), a saltworks plant in Baja California (Barkin 1999), a waste dump in Texas (Kelly 2002), and a number of other economic initiatives. At the same time, the environmental community is not always well looked upon by economic interests. In many countries with numerous social needs, protecting the environment is often prioritized below more salient concerns of promoting economic development and reducing poverty (Inglehart 1987). More fundamentally, the environmental community has often been accused of overstating its case to obtain public attention and promote its own agenda (Bandow 1993). Environmental groups could thus be expected to have fewer ties to the for-profit sector than other organizations in the study.

In summary, there are considerable differences both within and between the business and nonprofit communities in Mexico that might impact relations between the two sectors. Generally speaking, differences and distrust between the for-profit and nonprofit sectors could be expected to prevent cross-sector collaboration. Nonetheless, given the diversity within them, we need to disaggregate the two sectors. With that in mind, this chapter explores whether foreign-owned maquiladoras or nationally owned businesses are more sympathetic to nonprofits, on the one hand, and whether environmental organizations have fewer dealings with the for-profit community than do other nonprofit organizations, on the other.

Rules-in-Use

Regardless of their nationality or focus, the nonprofit and the for-profit sectors do not operate in an institutional vacuum. Formal and informal rules can create incentives and disincentives for cross-sector cooperation. In the U.S. literature on nonprofit organizations, a number of authors view the governing board of directors as a primary point of interaction between a civil society organization and the for-profit sector (Grønbjerg 1993; Hall 1975; Middleton 1987; Pfeffer and Salancik 1978). Pfeffer and Salancik (1978) argue that board members are strategically selected to bring resources into the organization and control external dependencies. "For example," writes Melissa Middleton (1987, 143–144), "a social service nonprofit may place on its board an active member of the local chamber of commerce, who it is hoped will link the organization to the business community." In Mexico, a civil association (AC) is required to form an assembly of associates (*asamblea de asociados*) and a board of directors (*consejo directivo*). Because boards have served as an important point of interchange in the United States, and because they are also legally required in Mexico, they could be expected to serve as bridges in the research sites. In fact, Alejandro Natal (2002) found that Mexican foundations (*instituciones donantes*) did use their boards to develop ties to the business community. Nonetheless, both U.S. nonprofit organizations and Mexican foundations could be expected to exhibit greater administrative capacity than a typical Mexican nonprofit organization. This chapter examines whether Natal's findings apply to the organizations in this study.

Another primary incentive for private sector support to nonprofit organizations in the U.S. experience is the tax deduction (Scrivner 2001). Like many countries, Mexico allows private sector actors to deduct donations to nonprofit organizations from their taxable income, but it offers less incentive for giving than in the United States. To begin with, income taxes are considerably lower in Mexico, especially for the wealthy. Instead, the Mexican government obtains most of its revenues from a value-added tax (a form of sales tax) and oil revenues. Moreover, by allowing wealthy individuals to bequeath their entire fortunes to their descendents, Mexican law reduces the incentives for business leaders to create foundations and donate to the nonprofit sector.

Incentives for giving also depend on how an organization is incorporated. Civil society organizations typically incorporate under one of two auspices: private assistance institutions (IAPs) or civil associations (ACs). As discussed in chapter 1, the category of IAP, created in 1899, allows for the existence of private philanthropy but under the scrutiny of an oversight committee called the "Junta de Asistencia Privada" (JAP; Private Assistance Board; Rico Valera 2002; Carillo Gamboa 1997). IAPs can offer tax-deductible receipts for contributions; however, each month they must pay a fee equal to 0.06 percent of their income and provide financial reports to the JAP, which has the power to grant or deny IAP status, authorize an IAP's annual operating budget, certify its annual reports, and dissolve the organization.

As a result of this strict governance regime, most nonprofit organizations incorporate as civil associations (ACs), which do not face the strict regulations of IAPs. To offer tax-deductible receipts, civil associations must become authorized donees (donatarias autorizadas or DAs), which entails additional incorporation costs; reporting requirements are strict and benefits uncertain, discouraging many organizations from surrendering the relative informality of their civil association status. Despite the differences between the U.S. and Mexican systems, DA organizations could be expected to have stronger ties to the for-profit sector than their AC counterparts. This chapter examines the rules-in-use (the need to form a board of directors, the existence of DA status) as well as the physical attributes of the policy arena and the attributes of the community to better understand cross-sector relations.

Analysis of Cooperation across the Other Border

Like chapter 5, this study focuses on fifty-seven nonprofit organizations that address problems related to water in the four research sites, examining the business and professional organizations separately as potential intermediaries. To gauge their relationship with the for-profit sector, interview respondents were questioned about sources of funding, the makeup of and the role played by their organization's board of directors, collaboration with for-profit actors, and attitudes toward the business community.[3]

As suggested in chapter 4, this study finds relatively weak ties between the business community and nonprofits in terms of financial contributions, participation in organization activities, or collaboration. Indeed, most nonprofits harbor some distrust of the for-profit sector's profit-making motive. Nonetheless, the few examples of cross-sector collaboration offer significant insight into how trust can be built across the for-profit–nonprofit divide.

The gap between the two sectors can first be seen in the attitudes of civil society respondents toward the business community. Interview participants were asked an open-ended question about the main obstacles to greater cooperation between the business community and civil society organizations. While some organizations were pleased with the level of interaction between the two sectors, many respondents charged that the for-profit sector lacked commitment toward social issues. As one typical interview respondent stated: "Our objectives are different. They don't worry about society's problems. Instead, the private sector looks for [its own] benefits from its actions." This response, among others, illustrates a common perception that the business community does not offer potential partners to address public problems.

Examining financial contributions, this study finds that only 22 of the 57 reporting organizations (just over 38 percent) have received financial

Table 6.3   Nonprofit organizations and their relationship to the business community

Relationship	Organizations having relationship	
	Number	Percent[a]
Receive financial donations	22	38.6
Receive in-kind donations	9	15.8
Based in business community	6	10.5
Partnered with business community	6	10.5
No tie to business community	24	42.1

[a]Based on total of 57 respondents.

or in-kind support from the for-profit sector (see table 6.3). Moreover, with the exception of groups such as the Chihuahuan Business Foundation, most of these organizations draw only minimal support from the business community. Indeed, most support took the form of relatively small, one-time, or in-kind donations, including food and soft drinks for public events, gloves and trash bags for garbage cleanup programs, a used computer, and cleaning and first aid supplies.

Participation in the activities of civil society organizations is another way the business community can support the third sector. This study focuses on voluntary participation on an organization's board of directors. Of the 57 organizations studied in the chapter, 48 (84 percent) have a board of directors, a legal requisite for civil association status in Mexico. Of these, 17 organizations have drawn businesspeople and an additional 8 have drawn professionals (doctors, lawyers, scientists) to their board of directors.[4] Although this number is significant (25 of 48, or 52 percent), unfortunately, as we will see below, many of these boards are inactive and few produce financial or human capital for the organization.

Partnering between actors of the nonprofit and for-profit sectors is also infrequent. Nonetheless, the few examples of participation are highly successful, several being multi-sector, often binational coalitions. For example, individual maquiladoras and the private sector–based Asociación de Profesionales en Seguridad Ambiental (APSA; Environmental Security Professionals Association) have worked with other civil society efforts to reforest and revegetate Nogales. In addition, in six cases, nonprofit organizations were actually created by a group of business leaders, eliciting both financial support and cooperation from the for-profit sector. Two are business foundations created in the states of Chihuahua and Sonora. The Chihuahuan Business Foundation and the Sonoran Business Foundation are of primary importance to civil society organizations in Ciudad Juárez and Nogales, Sonora, respectively, as a source of funds, technical support, information, and organizational capacity.[5]

In summary, although there are some impressive examples of cross-sector collaboration, such as the Chihuahuan Business Foundation, on the whole, for-profit ties to the nonprofit sector are typically weak, involve inactive boards, and often result in occasional and minimal support. Ironically, despite marked differences in language and culture, the U.S.–Mexico border provides less of an obstacle to overcome than the for-profit–nonprofit divide. Binational collaboration typically entails a far greater transfer of resources and more intensive relations than cross-sector collaboration.

That said, the following paragraphs focus on successful cases of cross-sector collaboration, which, though less common than might be desired, have led to the strengthening of the nonprofit sector and produced efforts aimed at resolving public problems. Perhaps more important, they demonstrate the potential for greater cooperation across the other border.

Efforts by the Business Community to Support Civil Society Organizations

Chapter 4 profiled and highlighted the importance of the Fundación del Empresariado Chihuahuense A.C. (FECHAC; Chihuahuan Business Foundation), which traces its roots to disaster relief following a 1990 flood. In 1994, the foundation was given the responsibility of administering a trust funded by a voluntary tax on state businesses; today, it is divided into nine local councils and has a strong presence in Ciudad Juárez. Over its first decade of existence, the FECHAC provided some $10 million in funding for Ciudad Juárez's association life and social development projects. In partnership with the Tecnológico de Monterrey, the foundation established the Centro para el Fortalecimiento de la Sociedad Civil (Center for the Strengthening of Civil Society) to provide workshops, library resources, computer access, and legal and financial advice for civil society organizations. The center offers a 48-

hour course on nonprofit professionalization, which includes classes on legal issues, financial management, planning, organization, and fund-raising. Thus the FECHAC not only serves as a source of financial resources for Ciudad Juárez's civil society organizations but also offers services to help strengthen and consolidate organizational efforts.

The FECHAC model has been celebrated as a unique Mexican innovation, whose success in mobilizing for-profit sector support for nonprofits inspired the creation of the Fundación del Empresariado Sonorense A.C. (FESAC; Sonoran Business Foundation) in neighboring Sonora in 1997 (James 2002; Kiy et al. 2005). Unlike the FECHAC, the FESAC has been unable to obtain tax-based trust funding; nonetheless, the Nogales chapter of the foundation has promoted philanthropic giving among the city's business community and also has attracted grant monies from U.S. foundations. The FESAC has used these funds to support charitable projects and to build the institutional capacity of Nogales's nonprofit sector; it has helped budding organizational efforts formally establish themselves as legal entities and has developed a detailed directory of all the nonprofits operating in the city. The foundation has also promoted innovative fund-raising techniques such as the "rounding-up" program, in which cashiers at major grocery store chains round purchases up to the next highest peso (9 cents); the difference is then donated to fund social programs. In addition, the FESAC has hosted the Foro sobre Experiencias en el Servicio a la Comunidad (Forum of Experiences Serving the Community) to allow for interaction and information sharing among the city's small nonprofit community; it has convened government, business leaders, and nonprofits in its Foro de Desarrollo Local (Forum for Local Development).

Tijuana has its own recent initiative to promote philanthropy and fund nonprofit organizations: the Fundación Internacional de la Comunidad (FIC), founded in 2000 with the support of the International Community Foundation in San Diego and the William and Flora Hewlett Foundation. The FIC describes its mission as one of promoting philanthropy, helping to professionalize civil society organizations, and improving the quality of life and well-being of the Baja California community. Though it remains dependent on larger foundations for the bulk of its funding, the FIC has worked to promote a culture of philanthropy in Baja California: the foundation listed forty-nine local donors in its 2004 annual report. The FIC has also been active in addressing water-related public problems, providing some $20,000 Hewlett Foundation mini-grants to nine organizations to address environmental and water-related concerns in the state in 2004. The organization has also worked to build the institutional capacity of Baja California's nonprofit sector by offering seminars on institutional development and convening a conference on accounting issues for nonprofit organizations.

All three of these grant-making organizations are tied together through the U.S.–Mexico Border Philanthropy Partnership, which consists of more than twenty community foundations in both Mexico and the United States partnered to promote local community foundations along the border, supported by national and international donors, and coordinated by the Synergos Institute. Community foundations, which are intended to be both representative of and accountable to the community, are promoted by the partnership as a key tool to fostering local giving. Even as the FECHAC, FESAC, and FIC seek to build the capacity of their respective local nonprofit communities, the partnership in turn seeks to strengthen and support these nascent philanthropic efforts.

Efforts by the Business Community to Help Solve Water-Related Policy Problems

In Ciudad Juárez and Nogales, significant business community cooperation with civil society organizations has led to major advances in addressing water-related public problems. Worried about the future of Ciudad Juárez, Miguel Fernández Iturriza, one of the city's wealthy businessmen involved in everything from bottling soft drinks to real estate, in 1999 brought together a group of young professionals who would one day be the city's economic leaders. Together, they asked two simple questions: What kind of Ciudad Juárez do we have? And what kind of Ciudad Juárez do we want? From this core group, the Plan Estratégico de Juárez (Strategic Plan of Juárez) was born.

Unlike other civil society efforts promoted by members of the business community, the Strategic Plan's focus was not on the economic arena. Director Lucinda Vargas argues that the Strategic Plan's goal is to raise the quality of life in Ciudad Juárez, which she contends is more of a social goal than an economic one. From the beginning, the plan sought to involve virtually all sectors of society in a massive, transparent effort to develop a vision of the "Juárez que queremos" (the Juárez that we want) and make the vision a reality: to that end, it established a broad-based committee of promoters, held well-attended meetings, and conducted opinion surveys. According to Vargas, the promoters of the Strategic Plan wanted it to be owned by the entire community. When people ask her how the Strategic Plan is going to implement a specific idea, she has to correct them: "No, how are *all of us* going to implement it?"

A widely distributed document entitled "La Propuesta" (The Proposal) outlines the organization's plan to achieve the envisioned Ciudad Juárez; it addresses issues from improving education and culture to promoting a binational metropolitan area. Though not focused on water-related issues, "The Proposal" does recognize the need for sustainable development and water use in the region. More important, during a meeting, a diverse group of businessmen and -women, citizens, and representatives of nonprofit organizations sat at one of the Strategic Plan's many working group tables and discussed the lack of green spaces in Ciudad Juárez. Out of this initial conversation, the Grupo Promotor Parque Río Bravo (GPPRB; Rio Grande Park Promoter Group) was born. With diverse aims in mind, the group's founding members came together to promote a park along Ciudad Juárez's 19-mile stretch of the Rio Grande. Cyclists wanted a safe place to bike; environmentalists wanted to protect the endangered river; community organizers wanted a place where people could relax on the weekends. According to the GPPRB's coordinator, many participants saw the river, which runs the length of Ciudad Juárez, as a symbol that could bring a greater sense of identity and community to this city of people born mostly somewhere else.

With start-up funding from the FECHAC, the GPPRB hired a consulting firm to organize its activities and meetings. It set about attracting the support of key actors, whether from government agencies, civil society organizations, concerned citizens, or the business community, to form a multi-sector coalition. Its first project was to renovate a run-down park along the city's northwestern side, an area of low-income, longtime residents. The participation of businesspeople proved to be invaluable: the housing construction company BRASA Desarrollos donated the services of its personnel and heavy machinery for the project.

Collaboration between the business community and nonprofit organizations in search of solutions to public problems is not unique to Ciudad Juárez. The Ambos Nogales Revegetation Partnership (ARAN), a coalition that features considerable participation by the business community, is quite literally transforming the landscape of Ambos Nogales. ARAN "aims to increase the planting and maintenance of native vegetation and the incorporation of water harvesting principles in order to reduce erosion, increase habitat, and reestablish communities of native vegetation within the communities of Nogales, Arizona, and Nogales, Sonora" (see ARAN's Web site, http://www.aran.bara.arizona.edu). In a community with few civil society organizations, ARAN's emergence is somewhat unusual. When the coalition was founded in 2001, several groups in Nogales, Sonora, had been involved in tree-planting initiatives. Comité Tarea Reforestación Educación (Reforestation Education Work Committee), or Comité TRE, a student organization at the Instituto Tecnológico de Nogales (Nogales Technological Institute), and SUMEX, the Mexican division of Xerox Corporation based in Nogales, were independently using a poorly maintained tree nursery established by the federal government to conduct occasional tree-planting projects. At the same time, the University of Arizona's Bureau of Applied Research in Anthropology and the Instituto Tecnológico de Nogales obtained a grant to work with local schools on both sides of the border on revegetation and water-harvesting projects. These groups along with APSA, government officials, and concerned citizens all found a home within ARAN, a truly diverse multi-sector, binational coalition, all the more notable for the particularly strong participation of the maquiladora sector. In addition to APSA, the Asociación de Maquiladoras (Association of Maquiladoras) and a number of individual maquiladoras form key components in the coalition.

The successes of the Strategic Plan, the GPPRB, and ARAN show the tremendous potential of greater cooperation with the business community, which can mobilize greater financial, human, and even political resources than most civil society organizations to address public problems. Unfortunately, however, these exemplary efforts of multi-sector cooperation are exceptions rather than the rule. To explain when and how such cross-border ties emerge, this chapter uses the explanatory framework employed in chapter 5, beginning with the physical nature of policy problems.

Physical Attributes: Environmental Aspects of Water Policy

Chapter 5 argued that, when public problems cross political borders, binational efforts are needed. Public problems can also cross the other border between the for-profit and nonprofit sectors, and in like fashion, the resolution of such problems also requires cross-sector cooperation. The greatest dependence of civil society organizations on the for-profit sector surrounds the issue of industrial waste disposal. As with other variables, however, even though physical dependence might create a need for cooperation, it does not ensure its emergence. Not surprisingly, this study finds that problems of industrial contamination tend to produce conflict and distrust between the for-profit and nonprofit sectors.

Across the four research sites, eight civil society organizations actively address industrial contamination concerns. They have no cooperative ties either to corporations or to individual businesspeople. Nor do they have ties to the different business associations that address industrial waste concerns, such as environmental committees convened by the Cámara Nacional de la Industria de Transformación (CANACINTRA; National Chamber of the Manufacturing Industry). On the contrary, most of the eight are engaged in conflict with specific companies or industries. In Tijuana, together with its partner, the Environmental Health Coalition in San Diego, Colectivo Chilpancingo has been leading the campaign to clean up the abandoned Metales y Derivados plant in Tijuana. In Nogales, two informal associations of concerned citizens, Grupo Ecologista Independiente de Nogales (Group of Independent Ecologists of Nogales) and Proyecto COMADRES de Nogales (Project COMADRES of Nogales), have taken on a number of industrial contamination issues over the last two decades. And in Ciudad Juárez, two organizations successfully challenged contaminating industries and proposed waste dumps during the 1990s: the Alianza Internacional Ecologista del Río Bravo (International Environmental Alliance of the Rio Grande) and the Coalición Binacional contra Tiraderos Tóxicos y Bio-Radioactivos (Binational Coalition against Toxic and Bio-Radioactive Trash Dumps). Members of the Alianza Internacional and the Coalición Binacional are now helping two labor organizations, the Centro de Estudios y Taller Laboral A.C. (CETLAC; Labor Workshop and Studies Center) and the Centro de Investigación y Solidaridad Obrera (CISO; Center for Labor Research and Solidarity) continue the fight against industrial contamination in Ciudad Juárez.

Beyond the area of industrial contamination, the study finds only two cases of cross-sector cooperation to address physical interdependence. The Paso del Norte Water Task Force has convened a group of water experts, water utilities, and large water users, including industry representatives, to address the overexploitation of aquifers in its multi-jurisdictional region. The industrial park development company Grupo Bermudez participates in the task force as a representative of water users in the state of Chihuahua, with a recognized interest in resolving overexploitation of the region's aquifers.

The Tijuana Watershed Binational Vision Project, a planning effort to preserve and protect the Tijuana watershed, has also tried to draw for-profit sector actors into the policy arena. The project's organizers recognize that the business community has an important stake in the preservation of environmental resources in the watershed. Although the project has attracted some private sector participation, including that of the CANACINTRA, it has been unable to obtain wider involvement.

On the other hand, cross-sector cooperation is much more likely to occur in noncontroversial policy arenas, where physical dependence is not an issue. In the environmental arena particularly, for-profit sector cooperation with nonprofit organizations has occurred around noncontroversial topics such as environmental education, tree planting, trash cleanup, and the creation of parks. For example, businesses have supported Nuevo Laredo's Centro Internacional de Estudios del Río Bravo (CIERB; Río Bravo International Studies Center) in its promotion of Day of the River and efforts to clean trash from the Rio Grande. For-profit actors have contributed trash bags and gloves to the Border Environmental Education Project (PFEA) for beach cleanup efforts in Tijuana. In Ciudad Juárez, Aqua 21 received a large grant from a maquiladora to conduct environmental education programs. As discussed above, local construction companies have lent their personnel and equipment to help build a park along the Rio Grande/Río Bravo. Perhaps, the most impressive cooperation between the environmental community and the for-profit sector can be found in Nogales, where the business association APSA and individual maquiladoras have partnered with universities and organizations to re-vegetate Nogales under the auspices of ARAN.

In summary, although there are important cases of cross-sector cooperation between civil society organizations and industry, these are less likely to occur around conflictive contamination problems and more likely to occur around less controversial issues. As argued in chapter 5, dependence makes cooperation desirable but not inevitable.

Attributes of the Community

Potentially divergent interests highlight the important role of trust in understanding cooperation. As noted above, trust and cooperation vary based on the type of actor involved in the policy arena. Here we are specifically concerned with differences between environmental and other nonprofit organizations and between foreign- and nationally owned businesses.

Not surprisingly, respondents from organizations with an environmental focus exhibited greater distrust of the for-profit sector than did other organizations in the study. This division can be seen most clearly among the above-mentioned eight nonprofits concerned with industrial contamination. Although these organizations' conflicts are typically limited to specific companies or industries, most respondents appear distrustful of the for-profit sector as a whole. When representatives were asked their position on the statement that the for-profit sector shared the same interests as their organizations, three respondents very much disagreed, four simply disagreed, and only one agreed. Moreover, the respondent who agreed qualified her response, noting that, though the for-profit corporations shared common interests with nonprofits, they were unaware of those commonalities. Several respondents complained that for-profit personnel were not even willing talk to them. For their part, they expressed no interest in cooperation.

Distrust of the for-profit sector is the general tendency in the broader environmental community, a group of twenty-six organizations. Environmental organizations and those working with environmental issues are in fact more likely than other nonprofits (e.g., community development or public health groups) to believe that the private and nonprofit sectors have different interests.[6] One interview respondent said he avoided reaching agreements of any kind with for-profit sector actors, even though he recognized that sustainable development required cooperation between environmental groups and industry. Neither industry nor civil society, he contended, had developed the culture of trust to make cooperation possible. Several respondents stated that they would not want to compromise their independence by accepting contributions from for-profit sector actors. Two respondents referred to other organizations that had lost their critical voice after accepting grant monies. Another member of the environmental community claimed that a businessman had attempted to bribe him with $3,500 to stop protesting contamination in his neighborhood. The perception of conflicting interests and the fear of co-option are thus alive and very real among organizations dealing with environmental problems.

It is interesting to note that the few instances of for-profit sector support for environmental activity, as opposed to water-related community development and public health campaigns, have come primarily from maquiladora rather than domestic businesses. Thus CIERB's Day of the River/Día del Río celebration, Aqua 21's environmental education programs, and ARAN's reforestation efforts all draw support from maquiladoras. This cooperation in the face of inter-sector distrust raises a question: does it signify a greater commitment to protecting the environment on the part of the maquiladoras (or at least an effort to compensate for their environmental impact) or is it little more than greenwashing? In the few cases of high-intensity involvement with nonprofit organizations, the maquiladoras' initiatives appear genuine. For example, SUMEX has been central to ARAN's reforestation efforts in Ambos Nogales. True, reforestation is a noncontroversial environmental activity that does not address the corporation's physical dependencies. However, SUMEX has received ISO-14001 environmental management and practice certification from the International Standards Organization and won several environmental awards both in Mexico and within the Xerox Corporation. Finally, according to SUMEX documentation, 80 percent of its product, primarily toner cartridges, is recycled.[7]

To comply with environmental legislation, most maquiladoras have a department dedicated to safety, hygiene, and the environment. The individuals that head these departments are typically professionally trained environmental engineers who have the potential to serve as key bridges between environmental efforts and the maquiladora sector. In Nogales, several of these professionals formed the Asociación de Profesionales en Seguridad Ambiental (APSA; Environmental Security Professionals Association). APSA, which holds an annual conference on environmental regulation, works with member organizations to understand environmental legislation and ensure compliance. The association emerged as a major supporter and central participant in ARAN's reforestation efforts. When the coalition was short on money and waiting for news of a potentially large grant from the Border 2012 program, APSA pledged extra money to support the coalition's efforts and became the coalition's fiscal agent for a large grant obtained through the Border 2012 program. An APSA executive board member stated that, because they are part of the community and their actions affect the community, APSA members have an obligation to become involved in community affairs.

Although the maquiladoras are more involved than domestic businesses in environmental efforts, they are less involved in civil society efforts more generally. Only 20 percent of civil society organizations in the study have ties to the maquiladoras, whereas 54 percent have ties to domestic businesses (see table 6.4). A slightly higher number of study respondents also perceived the domestic for-profit sector to be more supportive of civil society organizations.[8] To further illustrate the point, many respondents questioned the maquiladoras' commitment to the needs of the community and its nonprofit organizations. For example, two respondents in Ciudad Juárez echoed the common perception that, because their upper management lives in neighboring El Paso, maquiladoras have less commitment to the community. Furthermore, four of the five civil society organizations that emerged from the business community grew out of domestic businesses. Only APSA grew out of the maquiladoras.[9]

Evidence from this study suggests that because of their environmental impact and negative environmental image, maquiladoras paradoxically have greater incentives than many national businesses to undertake socially responsible initiatives in environmental affairs. Many of these initia-

Table 6.4   Ties between nonprofit and for-profit sectors

Category	Number	Percent[a]
Nonprofits having ties to domestic for-profit sector	31	54.4
Nonprofits having ties to maquiladora sector	11	19.3
Nonprofit having no ties to either domestic for-profit or maquiladora sector	24	42.1

[a]Based on total of 57 respondents.

tives, particularly those led by environmental professionals, are genuine efforts to compensate for the maquiladoras' negative environmental impact. Nonetheless, outside of the environmental arena, national businesses appear to have closer ties to the nonprofit sector and maintain a better image in the civil society community.

Rules-in-Use

This analysis examines two sets of rules that could be expected to impact interaction between the for-profit and nonprofit sectors, including the requirement to have a board of directors and different legal auspices for incorporation as a nonprofit organization. It was predicted above that the obligation to have a governing board of directors would encourage cross-sector ties: nonprofit organizations would fill their board positions with members of the business community to attract both human and financial resources and address dependencies. Unfortunately, as stated earlier, although businessmen and -women do participate on boards of directors, many are inactive or play a minimal role in governing or assisting the organization. Civil associations face little legal oversight by the Mexican government; after an organization is established, there is therefore no legal incentive to maintain its board of directors. One director of a successful organization in Tijuana stated frankly that her organization's board exists only on paper. Several interview respondents offered similar answers.

Even when boards are active, board members are not a significant source of resources for most of the organizations studied. Of the 24 organizations with either a businessperson or a professional on the board of directors, only 11 (46 percent) stated that their board members provide or help find funds for the organization. In other words, fewer than 20 percent of the organizations in this study use a governing board to attract funds. One interview respondent admitted that he was able to convince five people to join only by releasing several from any obligation to provide funding.

In the eleven cases where a board of directors does contribute to the financial well-being of an organization, members play an important role in providing resources. Thus the 8-person board of Salud y Desarrollo Comunitario de Ciudad Juárez (SADEC; Health and Community Development of Ciudad Juárez), which, among other things, trains health promoters in low-income neighborhoods, provides 8.3 percent of the organization's sizable annual budget; nearly half of the board members participate as volunteers in the organization. Thus, too, board members of Tijuana's Centro de Promoción de Salud Esperanza (Health and Promotion Center, Esperanza) are responsible, directly or indirectly, for all of the organization's individual contributions. In summary, the governing boards of civil society organizations across the four research sites play a potentially important, but widely underutilized role both as sources of funding and personnel and as bridges between the for-profit and nonprofit sectors.

It was also predicted that authorized donees (DAs), tax-exempt organizations able to offer tax-deductible receipts for donations, would have greater for-profit sector ties and support than other nonprofits. In fact, there is a statistically significant correlation between organizations with DA status and financial or in-kind support from the business community.[10] Of 14 organizations with such status, 11 (79 percent) receive private sector funds. Moreover, as in cases like the Strategic Plan and SADEC, this support is generally substantial. It should be mentioned that DA status does more than allow for tax benefits; it also demonstrates a certain level of institutional capacity to potential donors. All of the DAs in the study are professional organizations with strong assets and paid staff.

Unfortunately, however, of the 57 nonprofit organizations included in the cross-sector study, only 14 (fewer than 25 percent) are incorporated as authorized donees (DAs), so that, like the board of directors, DA status is an underutilized route to obtain for-profit sector support. On the other hand, there are significant obstacles to incorporation as a DA. According to local foundations, legal expenses run between $800 and $1,200, and the approval process can take up to two years. Nonprofit organizations found the Servicio de Administración Tributaria (SAT), the Mexican equivalent of the U.S. Internal Revenue Service, unprepared both legally and administratively for applicants. Indeed, interview respondents complained that, unable to process applications at all, the SAT regional offices, even in metropolitan areas such as Tijuana and Ciudad Juárez, had (after much delay) to send them on to Mexico City for approval.

Particularly problematic is the requirement that DA applicants obtain a letter of support from the relevant federal, state, or local government agency operating within the same policy arena, all the more so where the applicants have been openly critical of government agencies.[11] At a more basic level, several organizations complained that there was often no mechanism to obtain such a letter.

Building Trust

Despite distrust between the nonprofit and for-profit sectors, and despite the relatively low intensity of cooperation across the divide, there are several mechanisms being used to build cross-sector trust. In the case of crossing the U.S.–Mexico border, chapter 5 found that the distrust is overcome through (1) coalitions, (2) Mexican citizens working in U.S. organizations, (3) professional border crossers, (4) U.S. parent organizations that have helped establish Mexican associations, and (5) key network actors that have earned the trust of groups on the opposite side of the border. This chapter finds that similar factors are also supporting cross-sector collaboration.

Coalitions offer an important means to link the two sectors. Of 20 civil society coalitions in the study, 7 (35 percent) involve some degree of private sector participation (see table 6.4). These include the participation of maquiladoras in the Ambos Nogales Revegetation Partnership (ARAN) and of businesspeople in Ciudad Juárez's Rio Grande Park Promoter Group (GPPRB). Coalitions represent important opportunities for a diverse set of actors to come together to address specific public concerns. In both the ARAN and the GPPRB, donating to a coalition effort in which they directly participated gave for-profit donor-actors a say in how their donated funds were allocated; moreover, it allowed them to monitor those allocations and thus to circumvent the problem of distrust.

Just as Mexicans working in U.S. organizations are able to bridge the binational division, environmental engineers have the potential to bridge the divide between the environmental and business communities. APSA in Nogales, Sonora, is perhaps the best example of a group of business-based environmental professionals supporting civil society initiatives; however, it is not the only one. José Carmelo Zavala runs a profitable hazardous waste disposal service in Tijuana. He is also very active in Tijuana's local chapter of the National Chamber of the Manufacturing Industry (CANA-CINTRA). From these two positions, he has become a major player in Tijuana's environmental community, participating in civil society efforts and serving on public participation committees. One interviewed colleague said that he did not know whether to consider Zavala, a businessman, a concerned citizen, or an environmentalist. It is precisely for this reason that Zavala is able to effectively serve as a bridge between these different communities. With the support of the CANACINTRA, Zavala would later help form Centro Industrial de Gestión Ambiental (CIGA; Industrial Center for Environmental Management), an organization similar to APSA, which has developed air-quality-monitoring and environmental education projects.[12] Genuinely concerned about the environment, industry professionals with environmental training can serve as key bridges in inter-sector collaborations.

In the case of cross-border inter-sector cooperation, professional border crossers such as Pro Peninsula in San Diego and the Center for Environmental Resource Management in El Paso, funded by foundations on the U.S. side of the border, regrant, build capacity, and support Mexican associational life; they dedicate a large portion of their work to supporting Mexican civil society initiatives. In a sense, the Chihuahuan and Sonoran business foundations are professional border crossers between the business community and nonprofits. The FECHAC offers the business sector a trustworthy means to support the nonprofit community. Intermediary institutions such as the FECHAC are able to evaluate a solicitation for funds through a competitive granting process and to monitor the use of funds through reports or more direct oversight. By donating to the FECHAC or FESAC, individual members of the business community do not have to invest time or effort to ensure that their donations are being used effectively. Reliable intermediary organizations thus offer concerned members of the business community an additional method to circumvent the trust problem.

In eight cases, U.S. nonprofits helped establish Mexican organizations. Although these Mexican associations all became independent, they maintain close relations with their U.S. parent organizations. A similar phenomenon occurs in the five cases of civil society organizations created directly by the business community. Although the Strategic Plan of Juárez was formed by a group of businessmen, it has developed into a transparent organization that encourages widespread civil society participation. The organization has maintained its credibility among the business community while also earning the support of nonprofit organizations. Through its highly inclusive methods, transparency, and visible effort to steer clear of partisan politics, the Strategic Plan has created a neutral space where a diversity of people and interests can interact.

It should be mentioned, however, that professional and business associations such as the Chamber of Commerce and the Association of Engineers have not, on the whole, been a key point of contact between civil society organizations and the business community. Indeed, business organizations in all four cities studied interact with their civil society counterparts almost entirely through government-created public participation committees. This finding bodes ill for the future of cross-sector relations, all the more so in light of the proliferation of business organizations in all four cities.

As noted above, one of the obstacles to trust in and thus collaboration with the nonprofit sector is its lack of professional development. Efforts currently under way by the Center for the Strengthening of Civil Society in Ciudad Juárez and foundations in Nogales, Sonora, and Tijuana to overcome this obstacle through workshops that directly address issues such as fund-raising and board development and through legal and financial advice are expected to facilitate future cross-sector collaboration.

Trust can also be built through a third party. Thus, largely because of their strong ties to the Catholic Church, the Centro de Mujeres Tonantzin (Tonantzin Women's Center) and Desarrollo Juvenil del Norte (Youth Development of the North) receive regular support from for-profit sector actors. First, the Church provides a neutral venue where actors from the two sectors are able to develop network ties. Second, having strong ties to the Church, a trusted social institution, serves to validate the dependability of an organization.

Although some bridges have been built across the other border, Kiy et al. (2005) identify many missed opportunities in the region. In their survey, maquiladora managers report that they are seldom approached for nonprofit support: a surprising 70 percent receive fewer than six requests per year for assistance. Many nonprofits are unaware of opportunities for funding from businesses or feel they need personal contacts within the sector to pursue support. Kiy et al. (2005, 36) conclude that there is "still much work to be done in educating the civil society sector on more effective ways to outreach to [domestic] corporations and maquiladoras."

Conclusion

This chapter finds that, unfortunately, for most of the study's nonprofit organizations, ties to the business community are relatively few and have not attracted significant resources or support. Indeed, the U.S.–Mexico border appears to be easier to bridge than the other border between the for-profit and nonprofit sectors. Although a great deal of academic attention has been given to binational collaboration, more needs to be given to cooperation across this other border.

Because physical dependence generates possibilities both for cross-sector cooperation and for conflict, collaborative ties generally address noncontroversial public problems that do not involve dependence. Although such collaboration is still highly desirable, the inability to address more complex issues, such as industrial contamination, reveals the limits of civil society–led initiatives. Interestingly, however, it is the maquiladoras that are more likely to engage civil society organizations on environmental topics, even though domestic businesses are perceived to be slightly more amenable to the third sector in general. Boards of directors and DA status, though important mechanisms to bridge the gap between the two sectors, are currently underutilized. To create incentives for maquiladora giving, legal and administrative reforms are needed to facilitate incorporation of nonprofits as authorized donees.

Fortunately, the chapter also finds several additional mechanisms through which trust can be built or assurances given across the cross-sector divide. By actively participating in coalitions, for-profit actors can maintain control over donated resources. Environmental engineers can serve as important bridges between industry and the environmental community. Professional border crossers, like the business foundations of Chihuahua and Sonora, can guarantee that private sector contributions are well used. And organizations started by for-profit sector actors can serve as an additional mechanism to bridge the two sectors. Through these relatively new mechanisms, several unprecedented cross-sector ties have been developed that have both strengthened the nonprofit sector and led to initiatives addressing water-related public problems. Despite these advances, however, there is cause for only cautious optimism. These ties across the other border between for-profit and nonprofit sectors will need both to take hold and to develop much further if norms of philanthropy and volunteerism are to spread throughout the business community and society as a whole.

7 Continuity and Change

Nonprofit-Government Relations

Introduction

This chapter focuses on relations between nonprofit organizations and the government bureaucracy. Like cooperation across the other borders of the third sector, cooperation with government officials can lead to better solutions to public problems and to a stronger nonprofit sector. Nevertheless, relations between civil society organizations and government are analytically distinct from other "cross-border" ties. Although co-option is always a fear of Mexican nonprofits collaborating with wealthier U.S. organizations and for-profit sector actors, it has been a historical reality of their relations with government officials in Mexico. Links between the nonprofit and government sectors are distinct in other respects as well. Cross-sector links offer a means to ensure that government officials are held accountable and that citizens may participate in governmental decision making. Fortunately, Mexico's political transformation has opened not only the electoral arena but also public administration. It is now common practice for most agencies, at all three levels of government, to convene citizen committees or offer formal opportunities for citizens to participate in the affairs of the agencies. Most information produced by the federal government is now available to the public. Public meetings are increasingly common, and many agencies offer citizens formal complaint mechanisms to report everything from abuses of authority to environmental contamination. Indeed, scholars of water issues along the border have dealt extensively with these increased opportunities for citizen participation (Brown and Mumme 2000; de Mello Lemos and Luna 1999; Mumme 2000a; Spalding and Audley 1997). Democratic reforms in public administration have the potential to facilitate both the work of nonprofit organizations and the participation of these organizations and concerned citizens in government, giving them the opportunity and the means to affect policy and hold government officials accountable.

Unfortunately, however, as discussed in chapter 1, change is often path dependent and far less radical than it appears. Just as the development of civil society organizations requires the introduction of new norms of autonomy, more democratic public administration requires the creation of informal rules that value the contribution citizens can make in the public arena.

To understand the evolving relationship between nonprofit organizations and government officials and the democratization of public administration, this chapter examines (1) the persistence of clientelism in low-income areas, (2) the creation of committees for public participation, (3) the ability to access information, (4) the availability of formal complaint mechanisms, (5) the level of government support and funding for nonprofit organizations, and (6) government willingness to cooperate with civil society initiatives. The chapter seeks to document the current relationship between the nonprofits of this study and the government bureaucracy. Like previous chapters, it uses the institutional analysis and development framework to identify and examine factors that could be expected to affect that relationship.

Why Open Up to Civil Society?

As noted in chapter 1, nonprofit-government relations have been traditionally governed by clientelism and co-option (Bizberg 2003; Chalmers and Piester 1995; Cornelius 1975; Eckstein 2001; Fehrenbach 1995; Hernández and Fox 1995; Mitchell 2001; Olvera Rivera 2004; Verduzco 2003; Wiarda 1973). Although Mexico has undergone significant electoral reform and witnessed the rise of opposition parties, these developments do not necessarily produce a democratic public administration. Indeed, there is evidence of considerable continuity. Thus Tonatiuh Guillén López (2001) has found that, once in power in Baja California, the National Action Party (PAN) rejected power-sharing arrangements they had once championed as an opposition party. Even after reforms to municipal government went into effect in 1994, the party of the victorious mayor was still guaranteed a supermajority on the city council. In addition, despite demands for a transparency law, it would take the PAN–controlled Baja California state legislature sixteen years to pass such legislation, an act it undertook only as its power began to wane in the state. Thus, too, Yemile Mizrahi (2003) has found that, despite its pro-reform rhetoric, the PAN has been hesitant to create spaces for public participation, precisely to avoid encouraging participation that favors the PRI. Furthermore, according to Alberto Olvera Rivera (2004), the PAN has distrusted civil society as being predominantly on the political left despite the party's own deep roots in civil society. These research findings suggest that, even as electoral competition increases, there has been resistance to reform.

However, there are also compelling reasons why government officials should support the democratization of public administration. It allows them to (1) shift transaction and production costs away from the bureaucracy and tap into local resources, (2) manage their dependence on stakeholders, and (3) ensure continuity for their programs.

One of the criticisms of decentralization in the developing world generally and Mexico specifically is that it has shifted responsibility for the provision of public goods and services to local government without, however, also shifting the resources needed to accomplish these tasks effectively (Willis, Garman, and Haggard 1999; Rodríguez 1997). As a result, local government agents must look for innovative ways to fill resource gaps, and nonprofit organizations, with their human and philanthropic resources, present one such way. This is especially the case for smaller local governments that lack the financial resources of the larger cities. Thus, given his limited staff (three) and even more limited budget, the motivated director of the newly created municipal environmental agency of Nogales, Sonora, has looked to civil society to overcome his agency's limitations. Local governments in small cities are not alone in facing the problem of inadequate resources. The delegation of the Federal Attorney General's Office for Environmental Protection (PROFEPA) in Tamaulipas sought to augment the eyes and ears of its limited staff by creating regional citizen councils for monitoring and reporting environmental contamination.

Even given sufficient financial resources, most government efforts are dependent on the actions and responses of other agencies, civil society, and private citizens for successful policy implementation (Pressman and Wildavsky 1984). Scholars of coproduction have long found citizen engagement to be necessary in the production of public services as diverse as policing and security (Percy 1981), education (Davis and Ostrom 1991), infrastructure development and maintenance (Ostrom 1996), and solid waste disposal (Savas 1977). That the state is dependent on other sectors runs contrary to the fundamentally statist ideology of Mexico under one-party rule; thus it has not always been recognized in a meaningful way. For those who nevertheless recognize this dependence, engaging nonprofit organizations can attract key stakeholders to government efforts. To illustrate, efforts to build parks, revitalize aquifer recharge zones, and protect rivers have been a particular challenge at the four study sites. Parks are subject to being vandalized, invaded and settled by marginalized groups, contaminated by nearby residents and businesses, and ignored or abandoned by their intended beneficiaries. Accordingly, government actors have embraced civil society efforts to construct a park along the Rio Grande. They look to citizens and nonprofit organizations not only to absorb some of the costs of planning and implementation, but also to directly participate in building the park and thus to instill a public sense of ownership over it.

Continuity is another important benefit to engaging civil society actors. Municipal administrations are elected for only three years in Mexico, and many worthwhile government projects are cancelled by succeeding administrations (Rodríguez 1997, 36; Guillén López 1996, 23), resulting in disorderly growth and inefficient service provision. Effective planning requires a long-term vision; civil society's commitment to important initiatives offers a way to ensure that future administrations face pressure to continue and complete them. In Ciudad Juárez, the involvement of the nonprofit sector has created a counterbalance to the shortsightedness of elected officials. When the Chihuahuan state administration of Patricio Martínez attempted to shut down Ciudad Juárez's Instituto Municipal de Investigación y Planeación (IMIP; Municipal Institute of Research and Planning) in the early 2000s, civil society organizations strongly protested and the institute's doors remained open. Unable to make the transparency policy of the José Manuel Suárez López administration (2001–2004) legally binding absent a corresponding state law, the Nuevo Laredo city council passed a resolution creating a citizen committee to help ensure that the practice would continue into the next administration.[1]

Despite these benefits, there are perhaps more compelling reasons why government officials would be resistant to democratic reforms. First, the implementation of policies friendly to citizen participation involves considerable transaction costs. Citizen committees, public access to information, and complaint mechanisms all require the time and energy of staff, as well as considerable managerial and organizational skills.

More important, however, opening up public administration means a partial loss of control over agency direction and activities. For the technocrat, public access means reduced discretion to do what he or she believes to be technically and administratively most sound. For the political opportunist, public access means a reduced ability to extract personal benefits. And for the authoritarian, citizen participation means a reduction in political patronage. It is therefore often perceived to be in the best interest of government actors to maintain control over information and the policy process.

On the other hand, the issue of democratic change in public administration is not simply a question of whether or not to reform. Government officials can reap the electoral and legitimacy benefits of implementing democratic reforms without actually surrendering any control. Indeed, many efforts by the Mexican state to co-opt citizen initiatives during one-party rule were accompanied by the rhetoric of democratization and public participation. For example, the National Solidarity Program (PRONASOL) of the Carlos Salinas de Gortari administration (1988–1994), first mentioned in chapter 1, appeared to be a unique policy innovation because public spending priorities were to be set by local citizen committees rather than by bureaucrats. Although the program was billed as a democratic and decentralizing reform, scholars agree that its targeted spending was designed to co-opt grassroots PRI networks in competitive electoral areas (Cornelius, Craig, and Fox 1994; Fox 1994).

Alternatively, citizen committees and other opportunities for public participation may be mere window dressing. For example, officials may create a space for citizens to voice their opinions but not allow that voice to have any impact on policy. Through the creation of such spaces, policy makers can appear to be opening up the policy process while continuing business as usual. Unfortunately, although elections produce incentives for government actors to open public administration, they also create incentives to pay lip service to democratic measures.

With that in mind, this chapter seeks to understand when and how genuine opportunities are created and when mechanisms for public participation are merely window dressing or means to co-opt associational life. To do so, it uses the institutional analysis and development framework to identify the physical nature of policy problems, the attributes of the community, and the rules-in-use that could be expected to impact opportunities for public participation.

Physical Attributes: Water and Clientelism

As it did for binational and cross-sector collaboration in chapters 5 and 6, the physical nature of policy problems sets the stage for nonprofit-government relations in chapter 7. Water-related policy problems involve a diversity of policy issues, from obtaining water resources for a city as a whole, water and sewer services for individual neighborhoods, and wastewater treatment to urban planning, protecting natural resources, industrial contamination, water-related public health, and environmental education. The nature of different policy arenas will produce distinctive nonprofit-government relations. This chapter concerns itself with one particular policy arena: the extension of water and sewer services into low-income communities. Whereas protection of the environment may not be a priority for low-income residents in the arid border region, access to water resources is a matter of survival. However, given their precarious economic situation, many low-income residents are unable to pay the costs of service extension. The need for water has traditionally been exploited by political opportunists seeking votes, setting the stage for clientelistic relationships that do not exist in other policy arenas.

Attributes of the Community

Government-nonprofit relations could be expected to vary, based on the communities involved. Authors such as Sidney Tarrow (1994), writing in the social movements literature, have observed the mutually reinforcing interaction between political opportunities and social movement mobilization. Even as political opportunities can facilitate the work of the third sector, so civil society can create its own political opportunities. Vikram Chand (2001) contends that the political reforms in Mexico have not been a result of actions taken by the state, but an awakening of Mexican society. In fact, the well-documented role of civil society in facilitating democratic transitions in Mexico and other countries is testament to its ability to create opportunity (Bernhard 1993; Glenn 2001; Linz and Stepan 1996; Olvera Rivera 2001). In the border region, interviewed civil society actors and government officials contend that the nonprofit community played a major role in the creation and opening of binational institutions such as the Commission for Environmental Cooperation (CEC; Comisión de Cooperación Ambiental), the Border Environment Cooperation Commission (BECC; Comisión de Cooperación Ecológica Fronteriza), NADB, and Border 2012. One would therefore expect stronger civil society initiatives to force the democratization of public administration.

The nature of nonprofit organizations is important for an additional reason. Deborah Yashar (1999) argues that governments seek to actively include supporters and passively exclude opponents. It is less risky to open up the policy process to a small group of elite actors, such as businesspeople and academics, than to common citizens. Different government administrations can be expected to respond differently to the nonprofit sector and to citizens in general.

Rules-in-Use

There are several rules-in-use that could be expected to impact government-nonprofit relations. First, the electoral environment at the local level helps determine the set of informal rules that governs the relationship between government actors and nonprofits. Without political competition, local government officials have a monopoly on power similar to that which existed under one-party rule. Within such an environment, officials cannot be expected to surrender voluntarily the political power that could not be taken from them in the electoral arena. As noted in chapter 3, political conditions in Nuevo Laredo, unlike those at the other three sites, continue to resemble one-party rule. In this border city and throughout the state, PRI candidates selected behind closed doors continue to win elections by large margins. Because officials in Nuevo Laredo and Tamaulipas face no viable opposition, one could expect to find fewer and smaller political openings for civil society organizations.

Another rule-in-use that could be expected to impact government-nonprofit relations is decentralization. Since 1983, Mexico has embarked on a process of transferring public administration from the federal to state and municipal government. Advocates of decentralization argue that it brings the policy process closer to citizens, facilitates citizen access to the policy arena, and creates policies more in line with citizen needs and demands (Ostrom, Parks, and Whitaker 1973; Peterson 1997). In his study of the border state of Sonora, Stephen Mumme (2000a, 123), concludes that, "in the matter of process, it is clear that decentralization is a highly complex course of action that is opening new opportunities for local-level engagement and initiative in public policy." One would thus expect there to be a larger political openings for nonprofits and concerned citizens in government agencies at the local than at the state or federal level.

On the other hand, one cannot assume that local government actors will be any more democratically inclined than their federal predecessors. Andrew Selee (2006) concludes that, even though decentralization has increased the political power of municipalities, including that of Tijuana, local governments are not responsive to their citizens. Selee points out that, at the municipal level, voters only directly elect their mayor. Candidates for city council are presented on a list drawn up by the political parties. A vote for the municipal president is also a vote for the mayor's party list. The rules allotting seats ensure that the victorious mayor is guaranteed a supermajority on the council. Moreover, city council meetings are typically not open to the public. These and other institutional rules prevent a more responsive government at the local level (Selee 2006). Given these two opposing viewpoints, this study compares the relative openness of federal, state, and municipal agencies within the policy arena.

International agreements could also be expected to impact political opportunities in public administration. The BECC, the CEC, and the Border 2012 program all offer mechanisms for citizen participation and oversight. They allow citizens the opportunity to voice their opinions in public meetings and to file formal complaints about environmental abuses; they establish task forces on environmental issues and provide funding for civil society initiatives. Although critical of public participation in the BECC, María Carmen de Mello Lemos and Antonio Luna (1999, 58) conclude that the BECC's success in creating opportunities for public participation "represents a significant departure from traditional patterns of policymaking in Mexico." Consequently, this study explores the extent to which binational institutions and programs create political opportunities for the nonprofit sector at the four research sites.

In summary, chapter 7 puts forth several hypotheses to explain the presence, absence, and nature of political opportunities. It then examines the impacts of the physical attributes of the policy problem, the attributes of the community, including the strength and nature of associational life and variation among administrations, and the rules-in-use, including informal rules created by continued one-party rule, decentralization, and international agreements.

Methodology

Within public administration, the creation of committees for public participation is perhaps the easiest method to include citizens and organizations in the policy process. For example, the municipal environmental agency in Nogales, Sonora, had convened three separate citizen committees on environmental education, reforestation, and the detection of contaminants. Committees take a variety of forms, but the most salient distinction is between committees open to whoever wishes to participate and those restricted to a few civil society representatives. Other important political opportunities include access to information, official complaint mechanisms, legal recourse in the courts, and government grant competitions for nonprofit organizations. Government actors might also support the third sector by donating in-kind services or offering human and political resources to civil society–led projects.

The following analysis first describes and then seeks to explain variation in these different political opportunities across thirty-five government agencies operating in water-related policy arenas at the four research sites. Because federal agencies extend over all four of the research sites, these agencies are divided into separate observations. For example, the Federal

Attorney General's Office for Environmental Protection (PROFEPA) has state-level delegations in each of the four cities, and different delegations provide different opportunities nonprofit organizations. Furthermore, many government agencies are responsible for diverse aspects of water-related problems and provide different opportunities across these distinct policy concerns. In Tijuana, for example, the water utility is active both in providing water and sewer services, where the agency has created political opportunities for civil society participation, and in offering environmental education, where it has little or no interaction with the third sector. Dividing the thirty-five government agencies across different cities and different aspects of water-related policy arenas creates seventy-four observations.[2]

Findings

In the 74 observations, the study found 18 open committees and 11 restricted-participation committees; 14 government agencies with citizen complaint procedures; 23 instances of low-level government cooperation or support for a civil society organization; 10 instances of government participation and official membership in a civil society–led effort; and 16 instances of no government–civil society relations. Although government agencies have clearly created numerous opportunities for public participation, these opportunities have considerable limitations. The following descriptive analysis examines the relations between government and nonprofits with regard to water-related public problems and the opportunities afforded civil society organizations to hold officials accountable and impact public policy. Because clientelism has historically been the dominant informal rule governing nonprofit-government relations, the analysis begins by examining its persistence.

Transitioning Away from Clientelism

Very few of the seventy-two organizations examined in the main part of this study maintain a clientelistic relationship with political patrons. Nonetheless, as discussed at length in chapter 3, the study found clear evidence of clientelism in Nuevo Laredo. ACOPO, Lideres Unidos, and Frente Unido Nacional (FUN) all tie public goods and services in the low-income communities where they operate to partisan politics. On the other hand, in Tijuana and Ciudad Juárez, where clientelism, though still present, has been reduced significantly, many low-income communities continue without services. Indeed, there are a higher percentage and number of residents without sewer infrastructure in Tijuana than at the other research sites. The following discussion explores the process of political change and continuity in these two cities.

Although the PRI remained unchallenged in much of Mexico during the 1980s and 1990s, opposition parties were winning elections in Ciudad Juárez and Tijuana at that time. Nonetheless, when PAN administrations came to power in Ciudad Juárez in 1983 and again in 1992, they still faced a dense corporatist network that was loyal to their principal political opponent, the PRI. In addition to priista organizations like ACOPO, Ciudad Juárez was also home to the Comité de Defensa Popular (CDP; Popular Defense Committee), a radical social movement that invaded private property and established settlements for low-income residents. Although the CDP was originally not dependent on the PRI, it made use of the same clientelistic techniques as that party and would unofficially join the corporatist system through the PRI-dependent Workers Party (PT; Lau and Quintana Silveyra 1991; Padilla Delgado 2000).

Having spent decades as an opposition party denouncing the clientelism of its rivals, the PAN was not about to collaborate with the old priista networks of community leaders. Instead, in 1983, the incoming *panista* administration of Francisco Barrio Terrazas created hundreds of ostensibly democratic, formally established neighborhood committees (*comités de vecinos*) in each of Ciudad Juárez's colonias (a policy later replicated in Tijuana). Although the PAN was removed from office in 1986 in what were widely considered to be fraudulent elections, the committees were reinstituted in 1992, when PAN candidate Francisco Villarreal Torres won the municipal elections.

According to a 1994 municipal regulation, the neighborhood committee represents a colonia (typically, from 35 to 500 families) and serves as "an organ of collaboration and citizen participation that has as its objective to solicit and assist in the realization of public works and services for the common good, as well as to participate and propose solutions to obtain the common good" (H. Ayuntamiento de Ciudad Juárez 1994, 3).

Each committee is established and coordinated by the social development office of the municipal government, which oversees the confidential, democratic election of an executive committee (*mesa directiva*), made up of a president, secretary, treasurer, and eight subcommittee chairpersons (*vocales*), dedicated to public security, sports, culture, health, education, public works and services, ecology, and attention to youth. Each executive committee officer is to serve a two-year term and can be reelected, although the president can be reelected only once. Neither executive nor neighborhood committee members can receive any remuneration for their work. According to the 1994 regulation, each neighborhood committee is supposed to convene at least once every two months, with a quorum of at least half the number of residents who attended the initial meeting and with at least two days' advance notice. Neighborhood committees are expressly forbidden to engage in political party or religious activities, and executive committee members doing so must step down (H. Ayuntamiento de Ciudad Juárez 1994).

The regulation's provisions outline a comprehensive array of responsibilities. Thus the security subcommittee chairperson is charged with organizing citizen security groups; the education subcommittee chairperson, with determining the number of children above fifteen years of age who have not attended primary school and with helping authorities place them in educational programs; the health subcommittee chairperson, with organizing groups of health promoters; and the public works and services subcommittee chairperson, with soliciting water, sewer, pavement, public lighting, and other public services.

According to a former official in Barrio's administration, the neighborhood committees were designed to differ from previous PRI clientelistic organizations in two important respects. First, they were to have no links to any party. And second, they were to address only community-wide and never individual concerns, a measure that sought to exclude "traditional leaders," who had a reputation for exploiting both government and community for personal gain. Administration officials hoped to meet these requirements through the creation of a 10-person board of directors, elections for community leadership, guidelines on meetings, term limits for officers, and leadership courses.

Despite their well-thought-out formal design, the committees did not provoke what Jonathan Fox (1994) has called a "transition from clientelism to citizenship." Despite the democratic rhetoric surrounding them, in practice, the neighborhood committees were used to undermine the political base of the traditional governing party and of the powerful Popular Defense Committee (CDP) and even promote the political ambitions of individual politicians (Padilla 2000).

To illustrate, the colonia Nueve de Septiembre, established by land invasion under the leadership of the CDP, lacked basic public services and property rights. CDP leaders had been trying to obtain services for the community since its founding, but without success. To undermine the radical group, the PAN government helped established a new neighborhood committee under the leadership of María del Carmen Rodríguez, which was to be an ally to the administration and a rival to the CDP leadership. The administration worked with Rodríguez and her committee to install the infrastructure for water, sewer, and electricity. The approach was successful, and today Rodríguez brags that it was her committee and not the CDP that brought services to the community. Over a decade later, Rodríguez remains a strong supporter of the PAN and still maintains her leadership position in the neighborhood committee (despite rules prohibiting continued reelection).

In addition to challenging groups loyal to the PRI, the PAN administration also turned a deaf ear to independent nonprofit organizations such as the Popular Independent Organization (OPI). Even though the OPI had been active in several of Ciudad Juárez's western neighborhoods since its emergence in the 1980s, the PAN administrations insisted that only the official neighborhood committees had the right to articulate the community's interest.

Rather than create a new democratic neighborhood association, the PAN administrations had created a new clientelistic network of community organizations. Of particular importance in this process was PAN militant Ramón Galindo Noriega. After losing his party's nomination for municipal president in 1992 to Francisco Villarreal, Galindo was appointed to lead the social development agency responsible for the committees and social welfare issues in low-income neighborhoods. Galindo subsequently used the neighborhood committees to build a base of political support that allowed him to win both the election for municipal president in 1995 and his party's nomination for governor in 1998 (Padilla 2000).

The formal institutional rules of the PAN neighborhood committees were designed to prevent political manipulation by colonia leaders, but not by PAN officials, who not surprisingly proceeded to use the committees for political gain. In fact, Galindo's clientelistic gamble was a successful means to power, both for him and his party. As a result, although there existed electoral competition and opposition party administration in Ciudad Juárez, the city and its panista administration, whether by choice or by necessity, continued to operate within the confines of the informal rules of clientelism.

The above events, however, occurred in the early stages of Mexico's transition to democracy. More than two decades since Barrio was first elected municipal president in Ciudad Juárez, and six years after Fox's victory at the federal level, scholars generally credit PAN administrations for having challenged the political culture of clientelism (Espinoza Valle 2000; Selee 2006). In Tijuana, for example, Selee (2006) finds little evidence of partisan involvement in Tijuana's neighborhood committees. Nonetheless, the following discussion reveals both change and continuity in the colonias.

At the time of the research, municipal authorities claimed that there were 469 neighborhood committees operating in Ciudad Juárez and 304 in Tijuana. A Tijuana survey of 127 neighborhood committee leaders offers a sense of what types of individual are participating in current committees. Of the 127 leaders surveyed, 57 percent were women, most of them housewives, whose average education level was just beyond secondary (middle) school. The leaders were between the ages of 27 and 77, with an average age of 46, and had lived in Tijuana on average for more than 26 years, a relatively long time, given that 60 percent of the city's residents were born elsewhere.

Survey responses reveal that many of the committees function as they were designed: they encourage participation in public affairs, employ democratic methods, and demonstrate independence from partisan politics. Thus 43 percent of the leaders reported that they determined their committees' priorities through voting in assemblies, suggesting that the committees at least have the potential to encourage democratic methods and norms. Indeed, 91 percent agreed that elections were the best way to ensure that government represented the majority (see table 7.1). Moreover, based on interviews, the study found no evidence that the neighborhood committees were still subject to the gross manipulation that they suffered under Galindo's leadership. These findings would suggest that time, opposition party administrations, electoral competition, and the democratic transition have in fact mitigated the worst of clientelism.

More specifically, recent PAN administrations have employed good public policy tools and institutional rules to restrict their own ability to manipulate the neighborhood committees. For example, one of the traditional tasks of neighborhood organizations in Mexico has been to collect community contributions to government infrastructure programs. Typically, government requires a certain percentage of the costs from the community before initiating a project. Thus, if the water utility was going to introduce water connections into a community, then the neighborhood associations would have the task of raising a small portion of the total cost, a function still performed by neighborhood organizations in Nuevo Laredo. This financial role creates considerable opportunity for corruption and mismanagement, however, whether funds are collected by neighborhood organizations or by government itself.

Because of economic hardship, such collection is a long-term process. Earlier payers would surrender their money and then wait long periods before projects would be initiated. In two cases reported by interview respondents, individuals paid into a fund to supply services to the community. When, however, a new administration canceled the projects, and the respondents tried to get their money back, they had great difficulty in doing so or found that the money was no longer available. Such cases, combined with a widespread perception of corruption, have created a lack of confidence in both community leaders and governments to handle scarce personal funds.

To address this problem, PAN administrations in Tijuana and Ciudad Juárez worked out an arrangement with local private banks whereby individuals could deposit money into a personal savings account flagged for a given infrastructure project. Local administrations could see how much individuals had deposited into the account but could not access the funds until each citizen signed a release. This institutional innovation avoids the

Table 7.1 Attitudinal survey responses of Tijuana neighborhood committee leaders, 2003[a]

Survey statement	Strongly disagree (percent)	Disagree (percent)	Somewhat disagree (percent)	Neither agree nor disagree (percent)	Somewhat agree (percent)	Agree (percent)	Strongly agree (percent)
Elections are the best method to select a government that decides for the majority.	6.6	0.8	0.0	0.8	5.7	36.9	49.2
One of the problems with people is that they disobey authority.	12.4	14.2	8.8	6.2	17.7	23.9	16.8
Cooperation with other people almost never works.	11.0	28.8	11.0	4.2	19.5	15.3	10.2
It does not matter whom you vote for, things will remain the same.	8.4	27.7	7.6	8.4	12.6	17.6	17.6

Source: Comisión de Planeación del Desarrollo Municipal (COPLADEM)
[a]Total of 127 respondents.

problems of corruption, but more important, it avoids the perception and fear of such behavior.

In another important innovation, municipal authorities in the two cities have convened councils with citizen participation to approve urban infrastructure projects. Having to defend their projects to a committee, administrations are less likely to propose infrastructure extension for merely partisan reasons. During the PAN administration of Guadalupe Osuna Millán (1995–1998) in Tijuana, a municipal regulation was passed that created elected delegation subcommittees. Tijuana is divided into delegation districts; within each, residents elect thirteen citizen counselors to a delegation subcommittee. These thirteen, along with the three government officials, would determine infrastructure expenditures for small and medium-size projects (Selee 2006). In addition, the independent planning institute IMPLAN (IMIP in Ciudad Juárez) would participate in project selection and design.

Thus institutional mechanisms created by more recent PAN administrations have reduced clientelism and the ability of political patrons to use clientelistic tactics, although these institutional measures are often highly subject to discretionary decisions made by a given administration. Increased electoral stakes, a change in administration, or election-year politics can easily lead to a return to political and financial manipulation. In 2001, the state electoral agency nullified the municipal elections in Ciudad Juárez after it found the PAN candidate Jesús Delgado Muñoz guilty of campaigning during restricted hours leading up to the election. The PRI–controlled state legislature appointed a priista interim administration to govern for nine months until new elections could be held. In interviews, PAN officials and nonpartisan civil society observers of local politics contend that the interim administration took advantage of its brief time in power to create new neighborhood committees and direct funding toward them, much as Galindo had done in the 1990s.[3]

Although the study found no evidence to suggest that recent PAN administrations have exploited the committees as Galindo once did, panista administrations are certainly not viewed as being entirely above partisan benefit. Neighborhood committee respondents in Ciudad Juárez and Tijuana were asked if being a member of the PAN facilitated access to the government. Though most disagreed, 21 of 45 (47 percent) did not; many of these took such favoritism as a given. Although this statistic may reflect perceived rather than actual partiality, it nonetheless indicates a lack of trust in government-promoted forms of collective action. Moreover, in interviews with members of the two cities' other nonprofit organizations, the neighborhood committees were frequently dismissed as partisan. From the perspective of the average citizen, evidence that political opportunists have manipulated community organizations in the past is sufficient cause to believe they are controlling such organizations in the present. Given Mexico's history, it appears to be very difficult for a government-created citizen association to be seen as autonomous. This conclusion seems to explain the experience of at least some of the interviewed neighborhood committee members. One committee president in Tijuana, for example, complained that a previous committee was unpopular and ineffective; as a result, he has spent over six years trying, with only limited success, to earn the trust and confidence of the community.

Perhaps the largest threat to the autonomy of the neighborhood committees is their manipulation, not to gain votes, but to realize administrative objectives. Thus, if an administration initiates a new program, city officials report, the committees are expected to disseminate information about the initiative and mobilize participation. In the case of a cost-sharing infrastructure extension program, for example, it is cheaper for government officials to have volunteer neighborhood committee members, rather than salaried government bureaucrats, going door-to-door urging neighborhood residents to pay their share of the project.

Survey responses in Tijuana suggest that neighborhood committees are overly dependent on municipal administration, have quite limited contact with other levels of government, conduct few self-help activities, and have little interaction with autonomous civil society organizations. Thus 91 percent of respondents in the Tijuana survey reported that they engaged primarily with municipal authorities; 96 percent, that they received their information about government programs from the municipality (see table 7.2). In addition, 79 percent reported that they worked with the authorities to find solutions to their problems, whereas only 11 percent found solutions independent of government. Furthermore, despite the presence of a strong local and foreign nonprofit presence in the community, only 21 percent had contact with other nonprofit organizations.

Table 7.2 Selected survey responses from Tijuana neighborhood committee leaders, 2003[a]

Question	Answer 1	(%)	Answer 2	(%)	Answer 3	(%)	Answer 4	(%)
How does the executive committee respond to the needs of the community?	Solicit government for public works and improvements in the community	61	Hold an assembly to discuss problems	32	Disseminate agreements about public works and programs in the colonia	7	—	—
Does the neighborhood committee have problems with unity or communication?	Lack of unity with the community	41	Lack of unity within the executive committee	35	Lack of dialogue with government	24	—	—
How regularly does the committee meet?	Once a week	7	Every two weeks	11	Once a month	25	Only when necessary	57
Whom does the neighborhood committee approach to request support?	Municipal delegation	84	Social development	7	Social development of the state government	6	Other	3
Who provides you with information about support programs for the community?	Municipal delegation	82	Social promoter	14	News media	3	Neighbors	1
What method of action does the executive committee use?	Protest in front of the appropriate government agency	10	Address problems on the committee's own, without intervention of the government	11	Involve the authorities in the solution of problems	79	—	—

Source: Comisión de Planeación del Desarrollo Municipal (COPLADEM)

Committee leadership responses suggest that committees have closer ties to the municipality than to their own members. When asked how the leadership responds to problems in the community, 63 percent of the respondents in Tijuana stated that they interacted with the government to find a solution, whereas only 32 percent said that they convened a meeting to discuss these problems. When asked if there were communication failures related to the neighborhood committees, 35 percent said that there was a lack of unity among the leadership, 41 percent a lack of unity among the community, and only 24 percent said that there was a lack of dialogue with the government. As argued in chapter 4, the network ties of successful civil society organizations to other associations, U.S. nonprofits, foundations, and universities increased the opportunities available to these organizations. In the case of the neighborhood committees, overdependence on the municipality and the lack of external ties could be expected to undermine the autonomy of the committees and the opportunities available to them.

With respect to attitudes, there is also cause for concern. More than half (59 percent) of the 127 respondents in the Tijuana survey agreed from somewhat to very much with the statement that one of the problems with people is that they disobey authority (see table 7.2). Moreover, 44 percent agreed from somewhat to very much with the statement that cooperation with other people almost never works. These are hardly encouraging responses from people tasked with promoting autonomous and democratic participation in public affairs.

Although using citizen committees to mobilize participation in administrative programs is certainly a marked improvement over using them to gain votes, it falls short of encouraging democratic citizenship. "A critical analysis," writes Philip Selznick (1966, 220), "cannot overlook that pattern which simply transforms an unorganized citizenry into a reliable instrument for the achievement of administrative goals, and calls it 'democracy.'"

That said, other models do exist for governments to promote citizen participation in the public arena in low-income areas. Governments can simply fund preexisting civil society organizations through competitive granting. In fact, Tijuana and Ciudad Juárez both have numerous organizations working at the grassroots level to help residents identify problems in their communities and develop strategies to address them. Ciudad Juárez's planning institute IMIP has also developed a program called "micro planning," in which it partners with nonprofit organizations and uses its staff of social scientists and engineers to achieve the same objective.

In summary, localities such as Tijuana and Ciudad Juárez, which have experienced competitive elections and opposition party administrations over an extended period, have not witnessed a proliferation of clientelistic organizations such as Nuevo Laredo's ACOPO, Lideres Unidos, and Frente Unido Nacional. Institutional rules that constrain opportunism among community leaders and government officials have produced a transition away from clientelism. Nonetheless, the neighborhood committees fall far short of political autonomy. Restrictions to limit government manipulation can easily be withdrawn or ignored. Moreover, having strong ties to the municipal administration and few ties to civil society creates overdependence on the municipal government and limits the opportunities available to neighborhood committees. Thus the committees are best viewed as tools to mobilize support for administrative programs, a limited means to solve public problems, and an unlikely mechanism to hold government officials accountable.

Public Participation Committees: Opportunities, Window Dressing, or Co-Opted Spaces?

Beyond the neighborhood committees, the study found an impressive 29 public participation committees within various government agencies: 18 open committees and 11 restricted in their membership. These committees vary in number and kinds of participants, appointment and decision-making rules, how agendas are determined, how meetings are structured and how often held, and how committed government officials are to public participation, among other factors. From this array of different committees, there emerge four general types. These are detailed below.

The first type contains committees established to provide information to citizens and gain their support for certain policies. Within this type, there is a continuum from mere propaganda machines to committees that genuinely engage citizens and provide them with complete and reliable information. This type is perhaps best exemplified by the public participation committees required to obtain certification from the Border Environment Cooperation Commission for water, sewer, and other infrastructure projects. The BECC requires that a sponsor agency (such as a water utility) convene a citizen steering committee, which then leads a public participation program to inform citizens about the technical and financial elements of the project and solicit their support (BECC n.d.). For the sponsor to obtain certification, the steering committee must present the BECC board of directors a report on the public participation process with some evidence that the public generally accepts the proposed project. Seeking public support through this process is a smart strategy: BECC–certified projects such as the construction of a wastewater treatment plant, extension of water or sewer lines, or rehabilitation of existing infrastructure, often entail a substantial hike in user fees, although these have traditionally been highly subsidized.

Citizens at a BECC–required public meeting are able to express their concerns freely and offer suggestions about ways to improve the proposed project or even about alternative projects. Nonetheless, as interviewed BECC officials admit, because a project is already fully developed and can only be adjusted at the margins by the time the public meetings are held, the meetings are really an opportunity for public officials and members of the citizen steering committee to provide information, answer questions, and reassure concerned citizens about the proposal. The BECC process, if adequately applied, does provide citizens with detailed technical and financial information about both the costs and the benefits of a proposed project. The process also allows citizens to challenge government officials in public, creating incentives for officials to ensure that project proposals are thoroughly developed. In addition, as BECC personnel are quick to point out, when a project generates substantial public opposition, the BECC board of directors may reject it, as they did a proposed project in Tecate, Baja California, in 2002. Unfortunately, however, the BECC process, despite oversight by the BECC itself, is highly dependent on the actions of the project sponsor. Chapter 3 details some of the problems with implementing public participation in Nuevo Laredo. The city provided only two days of poorly advertised notice for public meetings, despite a thirty-day advance notice requirement. Written material on the project was not made available to the public, as required by BECC criteria. Although public meetings were well attended, the vast majority of attendees were city and utility personnel, resulting in a complete absence of dissent despite a proposed increase to user fees of between 30 and 40 percent.

By contrast, in 2004, Nogales, Sonora, implemented an exemplary public participation program using the same BECC guidelines. The city contracted with a local nonprofit organization to coordinate public participation and citizen oversight of the project. A resident of Nogales, María Josefina Guerrero is the driving force between more than one civil society organization. As a former member of the BECC's advisory committee, Guerrero had helped write a manual on public participation for BECC certification. When Nogales's mayor became interested in seeking BECC certification for a street-paving project, Guerrero was an obvious candidate to lead the public participation. A citizen steering committee was established, which, along with the municipal government, held dozens of informational meetings throughout the city to explain the project and answer questions. University students were brought on to conduct opinion surveys. The informational meetings and two large citywide meetings were broadly publicized and well attended. Most important, the citizen steering committee committed itself to monitor the implementation of the project rather than just support the public participation process.[4]

In summary, although forms of public participation like the BECC process allow residents to voice their opinions, at their core, they seek to gain citizen support for government programs through increased diffusion of information. Comparing the Nuevo Laredo and Nogales experiences makes it clear that the BECC process is subject to those responsible for its implementation. When officials are committed to informing citizens and winning their support through conviction, as in Nogales, this form of public participation can be very effective. On the other hand, when officials are uncommitted to implementing such a program, the BECC process is merely window dressing.

A second type of government-sponsored public committee offers government officials a means to mobilize citizens to support government programs. Such committees aim to ensure more effective implementation of government policy, rather than to enable citizens to impact policy decisions or to hold officials accountable. Ciudad Juárez and Tijuana's neighborhood committees are a good example of such public participation committees. Through the committees, the municipal administration can disseminate information and facilitate citizen participation in government programs. To offer an additional example, in the state of Tamaulipas in the early 2000s, the PROFEPA delegation based there recognized that it lacked sufficient manpower to realize its mandate. As a result, the delegation created Comités Regionales de Vigilancia y Protección al Medio Ambiente (COREVAs; Regional Committees for the Monitoring and Protection of the Environment), which sought to involve citizens as the eyes and ears of the delegation in monitoring potential sources of contamination. The PROFEPA provided training workshops and certified members of the COREVAs as official environmental monitors. Such committees can encourage coproduction, result in more effective provision of public goods and services, and improve implementation of government policy. On the other hand, citizens attempting to use these committees to impact policy or hold officials accountable become frustrated when they discover, often after a considerable investment of time, that the committees will not allow them to do either.

A third type of committee is designed to listen to citizens, obtain input into government projects and policy, and offer some oversight. By institutional design, however, this type offers government officials considerable discretion. Within it, as within the first type, committees can be placed along a continuum depending on the officials who lead them, from mere outlets for voicing opinions to important tools enabling citizens to impact policy.

The Nuevo Laredo citizen transparency commission, made up of the city's chief financial officer and eight citizens selected by the Citizen Coordinating Council (Consejo Coordinador Ciudadano), is a committee of this third type. The commission is charged with helping identify shortcomings in the availability of information and offering proposals on how to improve transparency as part of Nuevo Laredo's annual transparency plan.

Other committees of this type can be found within Baja California's Comité de Planeación para el Desarrollo del Estado (Planning Committee for State Development), which has convened both municipal and state-wide committees on a number of topics related to water concerns, including protecting natural resources, water and sewer infrastructure, and public health. Thus, with representatives from 2 federal, 7 state, and 8 municipal agencies, 4 representatives from Baja California's universities, and 5 from local chapters of the Association of Architects, the Special Subcommittee on Potable Water, Sewer, and Sanitation is charged with overseeing the development of a state water and sewer plan within the confines of preexisting federal, state, and municipal planning.

In these committees, government officials have considerable discretion as to whether concerns raised by participating citizens may impact policy. As a result, the effectiveness of the committee depends considerably on the officials responsible. Not surprisingly, interviews with members of civil society reveal considerable frustration with this arrangement. One citizen who has participated extensively on a number of state and municipal environmental committees noted that government officials are perfectly willing to have public input and participation so long as they can control what comes of them. Drawing a clear distinction between "administration" and "authority," he went on to explain that, though willing to allow citizen committees to administer the policy decisions of the government, the officials were unwilling to surrender any actual authority to alter or reject their decisions—and even more unwilling to allow citizen committees to make policy decisions of their own.

A fourth and final type of committee is similar to the third type; however, institutional rules give citizen representatives important decision-making power and oversight authority. The best examples of this type are the administrative councils created by the water utilities in Tijuana, Ciudad Juárez, and Nuevo Laredo. Each of these councils has been afforded considerable oversight authority. In Ciudad Juárez, for example, the council has the power to oversee the utility's budget, reject appointments to leadership positions, and rule on tariff increases. Although the council is primarily made up of government officials, three citizens also participate. The council's clear mandate and voting procedures offer citizen representatives, albeit with a minority vote, an opportunity to impact policy and hold officials accountable. On all three councils, however, citizen membership is restricted to representatives from the business community, such as from the chambers of commerce, which has given rise to complaints from many of the civil society actors interviewed.

In summary, a first type of public participation committee allows for better diffusion of information and seeks to win citizen support for government programs. Committees of this first type can lead to greater transparency, a more educated citizenry, and backdoor accountability, although they can also result in co-option. A second type seeks to ensure more effective implementation of government programs. A third allows citizens to voice their opinions but grants them authority only at the discretion of government officials. Committees of this type can result either in citizen impact and official accountability or in co-option. A fourth type of committee gives citizen members a genuine opportunity to impact policy and hold officials accountable, although, in the few cases studied here, citizen members were drawn from the business community and had only a minority vote.

Most public participation committees of whatever type do not offer citizens the opportunity to effectively monitor government officials, hold them accountable, or impact policy decisions. Nonetheless, as this chapter will argue, even the limited political openings afforded by some of these committees can be expanded and new opportunities created.

Transparency

To carry out their respective missions, nonprofit organizations are highly dependent on government for access to information, about government expenditures, for example, to ensure appropriate use of the tax revenues or about water quality to monitor levels of contamination. In 2002, the Federal Transparency Law (Ley de Transparencia y Acceso a la Información Pública) went into effect, guaranteeing the Mexican public the right to information produced by the federal government.[5] The law includes several features to ensure effective implementation: most important, it established the Instituto Federal de Acceso a la Información Pública (IFAI; Federal Institute for Access to Information), which serves as advocate for those requesting access to public information (IFAI 2004).

In 2005, the Mexican federal government received nearly 50,000 requests for information, some 2,700 of which were brought before the IFAI (SISI 2006). Of the 48 members of nonprofit organizations who responded to questions about the law, only 15 have attempted to use the federal law to obtain information. Of those, only 8 have received the requested information. These numbers suggest that (1) many members of civil society are not trying or do not know how to access newly available information and (2) that there are problems in the implementation of the law. In fact, making information available to the public requires an entire restructuring of how information is collected and stored.

Those who reported attempting to access information requested many different types of information, about the quality of tap water, about potentially dangerous emissions from industrial parks, about grants awarded by the federal government, to name just three. Of those who have *not* tried to use the law, some reported no informational needs. For example, many organizations with strong ties to government officials stated that, even without legislation, they were able to obtain the information they needed through personal contacts. Others, however, doubted that the law represented a genuine opportunity to access information. One respondent stated, "They're only going to give [you] the information they want to. To get the information you really want will take a huge investment of time that won't be worth it." Another offered, "I've tried to obtain information, but the transparency laws in Mexico at all three levels [of government] don't work. They were created to give the government the image that it's honest and that there's no corruption. [But] it's all a sham." Clearly, some organizations are not requesting information because they lack confidence in the law and the government. The fact that several groups have been unable to obtain requested information only strengthens their view.

Others, however, accept individual responsibility for not taking advantage of the reform. Many of the respondents expressed uncertainty about the relatively new legislation: how to use it, who to ask for information, and what kind of information is available. In Tijuana, Proyecto Fronterizo de Educación Ambiental (PFEA) and a network of environmental organizations obtained a grant to identify how the law could be used to better protect the environment. Laura Silvan of PFEA argues that this effort seeks to promote a culture of asking for information, that any law on the scale of the transparency law is going to have implementation problems, and that it is therefore necessary to regularly request information to help work out the kinks in the system. Recognizing uncertainty about the law, IFAI has developed an educational workshop to teach organizations and interested individuals how to make use of the legislation. In 2004, PFEA hosted IFAI officials for a two-day workshop for Baja California's civil society.

Another potential opportunity to obtain information is through Mexico's Registro de Emisiones y Transferencia de Contaminantes (RETC; Pollutant Release Transfer Registry), which, like the U.S. Toxics Release Inventory, aims to collect and make public information on pollution, specifically, 178 different types of pollutants and their emission into the air, soil, and water. The RETC has the potential to be a powerful tool for organizations and citizens to obtain information about environmental conditions. Though signed into law before the general transparency legislation, the RETC has not yet been fully enforced. In principle, the delegations of the Secretariat for the Environment and Natural Resources (SEMARNAT) "are responsible for receiving the manifests from businesses in each state," the Commission for Environmental Cooperation (CEC 2003, 125) reported. "In practice, [however,] they do not have the control capacity at the service counters to ensure that forms are properly filled out, nor to capture and analyze data in a timely manner in order to prepare and release interpretations." A 2003 conference panel on the RETC raised similar concerns about the quality of emissions measurement and problems in verifying industry-reported emissions (Innovative Mexican Regulations 2003). The environmental authority SEMARNAT has taken steps to improve the implementation of the law, including the 2004 passage of implementing legislation, yet significant limitations remain.

Another obstacle to accessing information is that the Federal Transparency Law applies only to information produced by the federal government. Although, by 2007, all thirty-one states and the federal district had passed transparency legislation, many had not passed implementing legislation. Moreover, at the time of the research, none of the states of the four research sites had such transparency laws.[6] The lack of access to information at the municipal and state level has been a problem for the study's civil society organizations. For example, in Ciudad Juárez, between the panista administration of 2002–2004 and the priista administration of 2005–2007, a great deal of recorded information simply vanished. One organization reported that years of complaints, petitions, and other paperwork submitted to the municipal government had apparently disappeared. Another nonprofit stated that legal documentation granting it rights to operate a community center had also been lost. Interview respondents contend that this was not an uncommon occurrence between administrations and particularly between administrations of a different party.

Thus, although legal openings exist to access federal information, access to state and local documentation is more restricted. This lack of access poses a significant obstacle to associational life: states and municipalities produce a large amount of useful information. For example, they monitor the quality of drinking water. Although water utilities from all four cities claim that their tap water is safe to drink, there are no public data to support this claim. Moreover, when interviewed, Chihuahuan state health officials revealed that, even when state authorities detect contamination in municipal water, there is no policy to alert potentially affected consumers. In Nogales, Sonora, the Unión de Usuarios (Union of Users) has protested increases in user fees by demanding that the city provide data attesting that the water is safe to drink. It remains to be seen if recent legislation will address these concerns.

In summary, though the federal transparency law is an important opportunity for civil society organizations, significant limitations exist in access to information and in the implementation of right-to-know legislation. In response to these limitations, many organizations recognize that they need to do more to test existing laws and increase transparency. Others, however, remain skeptical and continue operating without government information.

Formal Complaints

Another tool for citizens and organizations in water-related policy arenas is the formal complaint. Mexican law allows citizens and civil society organizations to file formal allegations of pollution or official misconduct. Allegations of pollution can be reported to environmental authorities at the municipal, state, and federal level. An environmental complaint filed with the PROFEPA initiates an obligatory investigation with clearly prescribed procedures certified by ISO-9001, a rigorous international standard. Complaint mechanisms at the municipal and state levels generally lack the formalized procedures of the PROFEPA. Complaints against public officials can be made to a variety of agencies within all three levels of government. Complaints against the water utility, for example, can be filed with the Procuraduría Federal del Consumador (PROFECO; Federal Consumer Protection Agency).

Of 48 civil society respondents active in water-related policy arenas, 14 have filed a formal complaint with a government agency; of these, 8 organizations have reported cases of environmental contamination. As with the transparency legislation, however, several respondents argued that formal complaints do not bear fruit and thus are not worth the time invested. Thus one respondent stated that he had filed complaints about a commercial operation causing contamination problems in an area zoned residential. Even though the municipal government sent personnel out to the site on several different occasions, and even though the zoning violation was clear, no action was ever taken against the operation. Another respondent reported that, because he believed its local delegation to be corrupt, he chose to file a complaint with the PROFEPA in Mexico City rather than in Ciudad Juárez. As a result of these concerns, many organizations have preferred to make their complaints public through statements in the newspapers and over the radio rather than through formal paperwork. This may explain why formal complaints against industrial contamination are few despite a common belief that pollution is widespread. In 2003, the PROFEPA delegation in Ciudad Juárez reported receiving a mere 24 industrial contamination complaints for the entire state of Chihuahua.

As in the case of requesting information, interviews uncovered uncertainty about the reporting process, including how to submit a complaint, which level of government has jurisdiction over different types of pollution, and which agency to approach. This uncertainty suggests that, like transparency laws, complaint procedures represent a limited political opportunity for the most part avoided by a generally distrustful civil society.

Where the Mexican government has failed to enforce its environmental laws and prosecute violations, citizens also have the option to file a complaint with the tri-national Commission for Environmental Cooperation (CEC; Comisión de Cooperación Ambiental). By the end of the research period, only one complaint had been submitted to the CEC across the four sites, against the closed-down lead smelter Metales y Derivados in Tijuana. In that case, although the CEC did issue a "factual record" that supported the claims against the Mexican government, the commission's findings do not obligate a member government to respond. In late 2004, six years after the CEC submission and four years after the finding, the Mexican government finally began a cleanup of the site. Although the CEC process led to an eventual response, the long delay has been discouraging for organizations in the region.

Only one organization in the study reported using the court system to pursue a policy concern. In 2005, after federal and state governments failed to release information regarding train cargo that was passing through the center of Nogales, Sonora, the court ruled in favor of the plaintiff Unión de Usuarios (Service Users Union). Admittedly, filing a complaint through the CEC or the courts is a lengthy and sometimes expensive process that may not result in a favorable outcome, and even if it does, executive action is not necessarily guaranteed. This is especially the case with CEC findings, but even possible with judicial rulings. The courts have only recently emerged from decades of corruption and subordination to the executive branch.

Government Cooperation and Funding

Another form of government-nonprofit interaction is government cooperation with, or financial support for, civil society initiatives. Of 74 observations, there are 23 instances of government cooperation or support. Cooperation between a nonprofit organization and a government agency involve a variety of activities. For example, in Tijuana, the Bio-Regional Environmental Education Project (PROBEA) works with the public school system to prepare teachers in environmental education. In Nuevo Laredo, federal, state, and municipal authorities assist in the Rio Grande river celebration and cleanup promoted by the Centro Internacional de Estudios del Río Bravo (CIERB; Río Bravo International Studies Center). In Nogales, Sonora, the Asociación de Profesionales en Seguridad Ambiental (APSA; Environmental Security Professionals Association) collaborates with regulatory authorities to provide workshops on environmental legislation for their member businesses. In these cases, government actors provide in-kind or political resources to support civil society efforts.

Mexico's recently passed Law to Strengthen the Social Development of

Civil Organizations (Ley de Fomento a Actividades de Desarrollo Social Realizadas por Organizaciones Civiles) commits the federal government to providing financial support for the nonprofit sector. Of the 48 reporting nonprofits examined in this study, 17 (35 percent) received some government funding, most in the form of grants from the federal government, administered through the Secretariat of Social Development (SEDESOL). In addition, the Fox administration developed a matching grants program for nonprofit organizations, under which the federal government would match state and municipal contributions. At the time of research, only Tijuana and Baja California had participated in the federal matching program. To disburse the grant funds, Tijuana's social development agency, Municipal Social Development (DESOM), convened a Consejo Municipal de Organismos de la Sociedad Civil (Municipal Council of Civil Society Organizations), made up of thirteen members of civil society, which receives proposals and determines what organizations to support with matching grant funds.[7]

In rare cases, a municipal or state government, acting on its own, has extended discretionary financial support to a civil society effort or contracted a nonprofit organization. Thus, in Ciudad Juárez, the municipal government has funded the citizen-led planning effort Plan Estratégico de Juárez and has also contracted Aqua 21 to organize and coordinate civil society input in the creation of a municipal plan for environmental education.

There are, however, ten cases of government-nonprofit cooperation that deserve special attention (see table 7.3). In these cases, government support for civil society organizations went far beyond cooperation or financial assistance: government agencies actually joined civil society–led efforts. In doing so, they surrendered substantial decision-making power, agenda-setting authority, and control over financial, human, and political capital to these citizen initiatives. The ten cases are unique because, rather than merely participate on a citizen committee, nonprofit organizations created their own political opportunities.

The most impressive of these cases are to be found in Ciudad Juárez. As described in chapter 6, the Strategic Plan of Juárez has mobilized the community to envision and create a better Ciudad Juárez. The project has attracted the support and participation of the private sector, a large number of nonprofit organizations, the academic community, individual cit-

Table 7.3 Civil society initiatives joined by government agencies

Civil society initiative	City	Promoter	Business participation	Government participation
Strategic Plan of Ciudad Juárez	Ciudad Juárez	Business community	Yes	All levels
Tijuana River Watershed Binational Vision Project	Tijuana	Academic community	Limited	All levels and Border 2012
Rio Grande Park Promoter Group (GPPRB)	Ciudad Juárez	Business community	Yes	All levels
Local Development Forum	Nogales	Foundation	Yes	Municipal and state
Ambos Nogales Revegetation Partnership (ARAN)	Nogales	Academic and business communities	Yes	Municipal
Environmental Education Council for the Californias (EECC)	Tijuana	Academic and environmental communities	No	Border 2012
Paso del Norte Water Task Force	Ciudad Juárez	Academic community	Yes	All levels
Paso del Norte Environmental Health Task Force	Ciudad Juárez	Academic and service provider communities	No	Border 2012
Ecoparques	Ciudad Juárez	Business community	Yes	Municipal and state
Consejo de Desarrollo Económico de Tijuana	Tijuana	Business community	Yes	Municipal and state

izens, and, most important for this discussion, government officials from all three levels of government. To illustrate, 6 of 20 members (nearly one-third) of the organization's advisory council (*grupo promotor*) are representatives of government agencies. Moreover, the municipal president and the governor sit on the 26-person governing council of the organization. The two levels of government have each committed to provide 25 percent of the initiative's budget.[8] This extent of government support is perhaps surprising, given that Strategic Plan is a citizen initiative whose agenda cannot be controlled by either the state or the municipality.

Also in Ciudad Juárez, the Rio Grande Park Promoter Group obtained government support to rehabilitate Tortoise Park along the banks of the Rio Grande. The Mexican section of the Boundary and Water Commission, the Comisión Internacional de Límites y Aguas International (CILA), gave approval for the construction of the park in the federally controlled area along the river. In addition, the municipal planning institute developed the designs for the reconstruction, and the municipality paid for the majority of the renovation.

To offer another example, representatives from Ciudad Juárez's water utility and planning institution have participated in the citizen-led Paso del Norte Water Task Force, an effort to address the overexploitation of water resources in the El Paso–Las Cruces–Ciudad Juárez region. Although the task force was promoted by nonprofit organizations, it succeeded in standardizing information exchange between public water utilities in the region.

The incorporation of government officials and agencies into civil society initiatives is not, however, unique to Ciudad Juárez. In Nogales, Sonora, the municipal government has joined the Ambos Nogales Revegetation Partnership, an effort promoted by the business and academic communities to reforest the Ambos Nogales area. In Tijuana, government officials from both sides of the border participate in a binational effort promoted primarily by the academic community to address environmental concerns in the Tijuana River watershed.

In summary, the study found considerable interaction between non-profits and government — through openings to participate on citizen committees, mechanisms to access information, complaint procedures, and opportunities to obtain political, in-kind, and financial support. At the same time, it found significant obstacles to more effective forms of interaction on both sides. In the case of water politics in low-income communities, there is a tendency for government agencies interacting with nonprofits to be clientelistic. In addition, citizen committees generally lack power and those which do have power are biased toward the business community. Transparency laws and complaint procedures suffer from problems in implementation. Despite these obstacles, however, spaces for civil society are significant enough across the four sites to represent important political opportunities worth taking and expanding. By soliciting more information through the federal transparency law, organizations can work out problems in the implementation of the law. Furthermore, by investing the time in participating on citizen committees, members of civil society can identify strategies to use such committees to ensure accountability or impact policy.

Herein lays the dilemma. The nonprofit sector, limited in size and resources, is on the whole unaware or distrustful of the political opportunities available to it. Its unawareness and distrust appear to reinforce a common view that these opportunities are too limited to warrant investing time and energy in them. Although there is some truth to this view, by not seizing what limited opportunities there are, civil society organizations will only ensure that they remain limited.

Explaining Political Opportunities

Given the importance of political opportunities, this section seeks to offer insight into their presence or absence, their nature, and how they can be actively created by nonprofit organizations. In the theoretical discussion of this chapter, factors were proposed to explain variation in political opportunities. The following analysis considers the impacts of the physical attributes of water problems, the attributes of the community, and the rules-in-use on relations between nonprofit organizations and government agencies.

Physical Attributes

The physical nature of policy problems they address sets the stage for nonprofit-government interactions. Thus, for example, collecting and publicizing information about industrial emissions have run into problems in implementation largely because of the physical nature of the policy problem. Collecting and verifying emissions data are complicated, technical processes. To this must be added an even more challenging obstacle: obtaining sensitive information from the industrial community. Considering the government's lack of resources, and perhaps even lack of will, it is not surprising that officials have been unable to collect reliable data about emissions despite the RETC law.

Thus, too, as discussed above, the physical nature of providing essential water and sewer services creates conditions favorable to clientelism in low-income areas without services. Political opportunists, such as Ramón Galindo in Ciudad Juárez, know that they can convert promises into votes in communities desperate for services. Although the PAN attempted to use rules governing neighborhood committees to reduce clientelism, these rules were easily circumvented. A second generation of formal institutional rules, including innovative payment procedures, infrastructure approval committees, and scientific planning, has reduced the worst clientelistic abuses of the past. Nevertheless, the neighborhood committees are still highly dependent on the municipal government. Thus, even though the rules-in-use can mitigate its impact, the physical nature of providing water and sewer services still sets the stage for cross-sector interactions in this policy arena.

Attributes of the Community

The study found that strong coalitions led by elite actors were able to expand political opportunities or create new ones, even where such opportunities were limited or nonexistent. In the cases of the Plan Estratégico de Juárez, the Rio Grande Park Promoter Group (GPPRP), the Paso del Norte Water Task Force, the Asociación de Reforestación de Ambos Nogales Ambos (ARAN; Nogales Revegetation Partnership), and others, government officials willingly surrendered control over resources and decision-making authority to citizen-led efforts. In the ten cases listed in table 7.4, government actors joined civil society initiatives as an equal or lesser, rather than dominant, partner. These cases represent a marked departure from existing public participation committees, where government officials exercise considerable discretion. Interestingly, as table 7.4 shows, almost all the groups and coalitions that have gained government support were either initiated by or had attracted the participation of the business community.

Indeed, evidence suggests that government officials are more willing to cooperate with members of the business community and even academics than they are with other elements of the nonprofit sector. Membership in several of the restricted-participation committees is limited to representatives of business chambers, professional associations, and academic institutions. As discussed above, at all three sites where the water utilities have administrative councils (Tijuana, Ciudad Juárez, and Nuevo Laredo), participation is completely restricted to representatives of business associations, a matter of particular importance, given that the administrative councils exercise greater authority than any other citizen committees in the study.

In these restricted cases, some interview respondents have argued that it makes practical sense for a water utility to enlist the participation of representatives of the Association of Engineers and an environmental agency to involve representatives of chemical or biological professional associations. On the other hand, other respondents have contended that these appointees can suffer a conflict of interest. In Nuevo Laredo, for example, critics questioned the appointment of several contractors of the water utility to serve as citizen representatives on a citizen public participation committee. Still others argue that participation amounts to a stepping-stone to public office or a means to obtain government contracts. In fact, the president of the Nuevo Laredo public participation committee was appointed to public office in the following administration. The findings of this study lend support to the thesis that government officials are more willing to create political opportunities for elite actors, particularly members of the business community, than for the rest of the citizenry and the nonprofit sector.

Nonprofit-government relations hinge not only on the nature of associational life but also on the nature of public officials. As noted repeatedly above, the degree to which a public participation committee offers genuine political opportunity depends considerably on the discretion of the government officials who preside over that committee. Despite the advances made in nonprofit-government relations, the study found public officials who remained deeply suspicious of citizen initiatives and who appeared to subscribe to a more traditional view of paternalistic government. For example, one official interviewed for this study questioned the entire premise behind public participation, arguing that he did not need citizen input and public meetings to know that people wanted water and sewer services. The official severely criticized the public participation criteria required by the BECC and argued that they amounted to forcing Mexicans to eat hamburgers when they would rather eat tacos. Thus gradual but irreversible democratic reform of public administration over time cannot be assumed. Rather, achievements under one administration can be rolled back under the next.

By way of example, consider the case of Chihuahua. During the state administration of Francisco Barrio Terrazas (1992–1998), the panista government took three important steps (of concern to this study) supportive of civil society. First, in 1995, the Instituto Municipal de Investigación y Planeación (IMIP; Municipal Institute for Research and Planning) was created in Ciudad Juárez and charged both with generating reliable technical information and with promoting long-term, rational urban planning. IMIP has been an important point of contact for nonprofit organizations: it has served as a meeting place and central source of information for nonprofit efforts, and it has integrated nonprofit organizations into its micro planning.

Second, the Fundación del Empresariado Chihuahuense A.C. (FECHAC; Chihuahuan Business Foundation), an important source of funds, information, and capacity-building activities for Chihuahua's nonprofit organizations, was given responsibility for administering revenues from a voluntary tax on state businesses during the Barrios administration. Because of this fund, from 1994 to 2002, the FECHAC distributed 96.5 million pesos (roughly 8.8 million dollars at the 2004 exchange rate) to nonprofit organizations and social development work in Ciudad Juárez alone (FECHAC 2002).

Third and most directly related to water issues, the state water utility worked with interested citizens to form Aqua 21, charged with conducting environmental education in Ciudad Juárez on behalf of the city's Junta Municipal de Agua y Saneamiento (JMAS; Municipal Board of Water and

Sanitation). Although formally independent of the utility, Aqua 21 received funds, in-kind services, and office space from it and worked closely with the utility to promote environmental education, public health, and water conservation in the Ciudad Juárez community.

In 1998, the PAN lost the governorship to the PRI candidate Patricio Martínez García. Martínez and officials within his administration treated the IMIP, FECHAC, and Aqua 21 as PAN rather than civil society initiatives and acted to undermine each. When one of its infrastructure projects ran afoul of the IMIP's master plans, the Martínez administration attempted to disband the institute. Fortunately, strong protests from civil society organizations kept this from happening.[9] In 2004, the administration sought to restructure the FECHAC to give government officials equal representation on the foundation's governing board, which was primarily made up of businessmen and -women. When foundation members argued that the business community had a right to determine the use of a voluntary tax, the Martínez administration countered that government officials should have greater oversight of tax revenue. Again, public opposition forced the administration to back down, and a compromise arrangement was reached. Finally, when the water utility refused to work with Aqua 21 unless it changed its leadership, Aqua 21 declined and began to operate independently of the utility.

To some extent, these actions of the Martínez administration can be seen as attempts to reverse PAN policies rather than as attacks on civil society. That the FECHAC's former president attempted to enter partisan politics under the PAN banner supports this view. Other actions, however, suggest that there was a general distrust of civil society organizations in the Martínez administration. Thus, despite the popularity of a federal matching grants program established to fund civil society organizations, the state withdrew, sacrificing the federal matching funds. Moreover, in late 2003, PRI state legislators submitted a bill that would have subjected many civil society organizations to a governing council, to be funded by a small tax on their revenues. The council would have been charged with approving the organizations' budgets and activities; most important, it would have had the power both to approve the creation of organizations and to order their disbanding.[10] Not surprisingly, interview respondents often complained that the Martínez administration represented a threat to autonomous associational life.

The Rules-in-Use

The first set of rules-in-use that could be expected to impact government-nonprofit relations are the informal rules produced by the continuation of one-party politics. All four of the sites, regardless of the party in power or the competitiveness of the elections, offer some opportunities to nonprofit organizations and citizens. Even in Nuevo Laredo, where the lack of electoral competition and the continuation of PRI dominance appear to restrict civil society organization growth, there are still opportunities to access the policy process.

On the other hand, the nature of its limited political opportunities continues to make Nuevo Laredo stand apart from the other three sites. To concerns about the persistence of clientelism and the failure to observe BECC guidelines for public participation, both discussed at length in chapter 3, must be added concerns about Nuevo Laredo's Consejo Coordinador Ciudadano (CCC; Citizen Coordinating Council), the official point of contact between the municipal government and the city's associational life. Although, to some extent, the CCC represents an important opportunity for public participation, it is housed within the municipal government; citizens unaffiliated with associations cannot participate in the council; and those associations must be more than five years old. In practice, these rules largely restrict participation to the city's many business and professional associations. Clearly, one-party rule in Nuevo Laredo has shaped the opportunities available to associational life and limited the ability of concerned citizens to participate effectively in the public policy process.

The study also found evidence that government agencies at the municipal level are more likely than those at the state or federal level to offer political opportunities to nonprofit organizations, although the quality of such opportunities often appears to be higher at the federal level. Table 7.4 presents a cross-tabulation of municipal, state, and federal agencies and participation of residents from the research sites on a public participation committee. All else being equal, the cross-tabulation and correlation suggest that citizen participation at the four sites is more likely to occur in conjunction with municipal agencies than federal and state agencies. Logistically, it is simply much easier for a municipal agency to incorporate local civil society participation. A comparison of citizen committees within Mexico's environmental agencies is illustrative.

In 1995, SEMARNAT created the Consejos Consultivos para del Desarrollo Sustentable (Sustainable Development Advisory Councils) to develop environmental policy recommendations for the agency. The councils include a national council of ninety-seven members representing diverse sectors from across the country. In addition, regional councils operate in each of the SEMARNAT's five geographical regions. In the northwest region, which includes Tijuana and Nogales, the council has over twenty members from universities, nonprofits, private businesses, and government. According to SEMARNAT, the various councils made 343 recommendations over the period 2002–2004; of these, the agency has acted on 195 (57 percent).

Unfortunately, because the councils operate at the regional and national levels, smaller cities such as Nuevo Laredo and Nogales do not have citizen representatives on the councils; even large cities such as Tijuana and Ciudad Juárez have only one representative. Despite this limitation, SEMARNAT's councils were generally well regarded by many interviewed members of civil society. This problem of scale repeats itself in the state government. In Baja California and Tamaulipas, the state environmental agencies also have public participation committees at the state level, but again, Tijuana has only one citizen member on the committee and Nuevo Laredo has none. The conclusion is not that state or federal authorities are somehow opposed to public participation, but that the size of their respective jurisdictions makes it impossible to convene open committees for the entire state or region. At the municipal level, however, public participation is simply much easier. For example, in Nogales, Sonora, a small municipal environmental agency convened three separate committees on reforestation, the detection of contaminants, and environmental education. These committees were open to the public and attracted dozens of attendees.

Federal and state authorities are able to successfully incorporate greater local participation given a sufficient degree of decentralization of author-

Table 7.4 Presence or absence of public participation committee[a]

| | Level of government | | | | | | | |
| | Municipal | | State | | Federal | | Total | |
	No.	Percent	No.	Percent	No.	Percent	No.	Percent
Present	17	53	9	37.5	3	18	29	40
Absent	15	47	15	62.5	14	82	44	60
Total	32	100	24	100	17	100	73	100

[a]Kendall's Tau-b association = .266, significant at a .05 level.

ity, which can occur in distinct forms: "devolution" implies the transfer of authority from federal to state and municipal government, whereas "deconcentration" refers to the transfer of authority to lower levels within the bureaucratic hierarchy. As addressed above, the state water utilities in Tijuana and Ciudad Juárez both have powerful administrative councils made up of government officials and civil society representatives. Nogales, however, lacks such a local administrative council. The difference appears to be explained by deconcentration. Although Tijuana and Ciudad Juárez's water utilities are owned by the state, they are administered by deconcentrated local agencies with considerable autonomy. At the time of research, however, Nogales's water utility Comisión de Agua Potable y Alcantarillado del Estado (COAPAES; State Commission for Potable Water and Sewer) remained under the control of a centralized state agency in the capital. Thus, at a time when Tijuana and Ciudad Juárez had local councils with citizen representatives, COAPAES had only a statewide oversight committee based in the state capital.

Despite the importance of devolution and deconcentration, there is some evidence that suggests the quality of political opportunities might be greater at the federal level. At the time of research, transparency legislation existed only in the federal government. In addition, with the exception of Baja California, only the federal government had passed a law committing support for civil society efforts. To offer another example, the Federal Attorney General's Office for Environmental Protection (PROFEPA) is the only environmental agency with a clearly laid out procedure, certified by ISO-9001, to respond to citizen complaints of environmental contamination. These and other examples suggest that, even though it is logistically much easier for municipal authorities to institute public participation programs, the federal government is actually more sophisticated in doing so.

Opportunities have also been expanded by international agreements. The Border 2012 program, for example, provides important political opportunities in two respects. First, the program allows for public participation opportunities in policy arenas where no openings previously existed. For example, at the time of research the Mexican section of the International Boundary and Water Commission (CILA) and the Comisión Nacional de Agua (CONAGUA; National Water Commission) offered minimal opportunities for civil society organizations to participate in water issues at any of the four research sites.[11] However, the Border 2012 program has created binational water task forces in each of the four binational regions. These task forces offer nonprofits the chance to access local, state, and federal officials about regional issues all within the same task force.

Second, the Border 2012 program has embraced already existing citizen initiatives that had not previously earned the support of government agencies. For example, rather than create new working groups, the program tapped already existing nonprofit initiatives such as the Paso del Norte Water Task Force, the Paso del Norte Environmental Health Task Force, the Tijuana River Binational Vision Project, and the Environmental Education Council for the Californias (EECC; Consejo de Educación Ambiental de las Californias) to serve as official binational task forces. The EECC, for example, was formed in 1998 with significant participation from both sides of the border. The council seeks to promote a culture of environmental sustainability in the binational region of the Californias through environmental education. In early 2003, the EECC had attracted the participation of individual government officials but not of government agencies as institutions. In 2003, however, the Border 2012 program, led by the SEMARNAT and the EPA, selected the EECC to be the official Border 2012 environmental education task force in the San Diego–Tijuana region. As part of the Border 2012 program, the initiative attracted more widespread governmental participation and obtained greater financial resources for its organizational efforts. On the other hand, Border 2012 task forces have not escaped criticism. Some interview respondents complained that key government officials did not attend task force meetings; that available grant funding was minimal; that meetings were more talk than action; and that the various task forces differed considerably in their effectiveness.

Beyond the Border 2012 program, other binational arrangements have also had a positive impact on opportunities available to nonprofits, although each arrangement also has its detractors. The Commission for Environmental Cooperation offers recourse when governments fail to address citizens' environmental concerns. The commission's "factual records" are slow in coming, however, and do not obligate a member government to respond. The public participation required in the certification process of the Border Environment Cooperation Commission (BECC) represents another opportunity, but, as the Nuevo Laredo case illustrates, local officials may choose to meet only minimal criteria to obtain certification. Based in Ciudad Juárez, the BECC does not have the mandate to enforce all public participation requirements in its municipality, let alone elsewhere in the border region. Moreover, public participation is only one of many rigorous criteria that must come into alignment in what has been criticized as an already lengthy process. Although in specific instances, binational programs have created important opportunities for nonprofit organizations, being largely at the discretion of government officials, the proper implementation of transnationally promoted public participation initiatives along the length of the border cannot be assured.

Conclusions

Like the third sector's other borders, the boundary between nonprofits and government has major implications for the future of the sector and its capacity to successfully address public problems. Although civil society is often celebrated for its ability to check the power of the state (Arato 1981) and overcome government failures (Douglas 1983; Hansmann 1987; Weisbrod 1988), the third sector's dependence on government cannot be easily overstated. Indeed, the paradox of what Michael Walzer (2003) calls "the civil society argument" is precisely the sector's dependence on the state.

Fortunately, the considerable economic, electoral, and administrative changes that Mexico has undergone in recent decades have created unprecedented opportunities for nonprofits to engage government without surrendering their autonomy. This study finds a number of mechanisms for civil society organizations to influence public policy, including citizen committees, access to information, complaint proceedings and judicial recourse, and cooperation and collaboration with government agencies. Nonetheless, within this environment of political change, there are also clear instances of continuity, which are preventing more effective interaction on the part of both government and civil society. Mechanisms for public participation lack power and are biased toward elites; transparency laws and complaint procedures are relatively new and suffer problems in implementation; and judicial mechanisms are slow, expensive, and uncertain. Although some actors are taking advantage of newly available political opportunities, this chapter suggests that civil society as a whole is largely unaware of the extent, but deeply aware of the limitations, of available opportunities and generally distrustful of government. As a result, government actors have created only small opportunities, and civil society has failed to exploit and expand them.

Accountable government, autonomous associations, and cross-sector solutions to policy problems will require overcoming the remaining legacies of one-party rule and completely rewriting the informal rules that govern relations between government and civil society. Decentralization may have made committees more likely and binational agreements may have created more opportunities, but the most impressive political openings were created by broad-based, multi-sector coalitions including civil society organizations, academics, members of the business community and, of course, government officials. Although obstacles remain to altering the informal rules of Mexican politics, efforts such as the Strategic Plan of Juárez, the Rio Grande Park Promoter Group, the Paso del Norte Water Task Force, and the Ambos Nogales Revegetation Partnership represent the third sector's current best hopes to autonomously engage government in solving public problems.

8 Networks and the Art of Association

Bringing in Civil Society

This book has sought to understand the emergence and growth of civil society organizations that address water-related public problems in the Mexican border cities of Tijuana, Nogales, Ciudad Juárez, and Nuevo Laredo. It builds on a large literature that has found such organizations to be fundamental both to democratic transitions (Adler and Steinberg 2000; Bernhard 1993; Diamond 1999; Gill 2000; Glenn 2001; Linz and Stepan 1996; Olvera Rivera 2001) and to the day-to-day functioning of a democracy (Almond and Verba 1963; Barber 1996; Esman and Uphoff 1984; Ewig 1999; Putnam 1993). The research of this study was intended to find ways to strengthen democracy and in particular self-governance and the capacity of private individuals to collectively solve public problems.

Unfortunately, however, the development model that emerged in Mexico and many countries throughout the developing world left out autonomous citizen engagement in public affairs. Instead, scholars and practitioners alike came to believe that state-coordinated development could overcome the limitations of both individual citizens and the global marketplace (Cardoso and Faletto 1979; Frank 1967; Stepan 1978). Throughout most of the twentieth century, the Mexican state absorbed responsibility for all things public, and, in so doing, it failed to appreciate the need for citizens to participate in their own self-governance (Ostrom 1990), the quasi-voluntary nature of so many public policies (Levi 1988), and the importance of local knowledge to development (Ostrom, Schroeder, and Wynne 1993). "Must the public administration cope with every industrial undertaking beyond the competence of one individual?" Tocqueville (1969, 515) asked rhetorically. "Must the head of the government leave the helm of state to guide the plow?" The Mexican and other developing states seemed to have answered yes.

Although the pendulum continues to swing between market- and state-driven models of development, recognizing the importance of civil society and its organizations offers a potential middle road, an arena where the market's excesses of short-term, pecuniary self-interest can be de-emphasized in favor of long-term, enlightened self-interest. Moreover, an autonomous set of civil society organizations has the potential to check the power of the state and ensure its accountability. Most important, through association, individuals can collectively address their interdependencies and find solutions to the public problems that affect them. Thus the third sector has the potential to overcome the limits of both the market and government (Douglas 1983; Hansmann 1987; Weisbrod 1988).

In fact, nonprofit organizational efforts have unquestionably filled gaps left by market and government failures. Given the peculiar tendency for local government in Mexico to completely reinvent itself every three years with the inauguration of a new municipal president, civil society and its organizations have emerged as one of the few mechanisms to ensure continuity between administrations. Traditionally, the shortsighted nature of partisan politics has not favored actions to protect the environment, but associational life has played a key role in promoting long-term planning and taking actions that protect water resources. Both in collaboration with government and independently, nonprofit organizations have led initiatives in watershed management, urban planning, reforestation, and the creation of parks and protected areas.

Civil society organizations have also been particularly effective in the area of education. Environmental and water resource problems cannot be solved by technological innovation or good public policy alone; their solutions are highly dependent on the millions of daily decisions that citizens make. Nonprofit organizations have responded to this challenge by acting as norm entrepreneurs: contesting old ideas, introducing new ones, and facilitating their adoption. As such, organizations across the four cities studied are not only developing techniques to purify drinking water, conserve water resources, and protect the environment; they are also building norms of environmental awareness and conscientious conservation.

Of course, civil society organizations offer no simple panacea, and many students of the third sector add the problem of "voluntary failure" to market and government failures (Salamon 1987). Indeed, this study has identified the sector's considerable limitations. Without paid employees, office space, regular sources of income, and programmatic activities, many organizations can only respond to, rather than prevent, the crises that affect their constituents. Or, as one interview respondent complained, "All we can do is put out fires."

The limitations of citizen-led initiatives can be seen most clearly in their efforts to secure water and sewer services for low-income communities. Associational life in these communities has tended toward clientelistic or politically contentious strategies to convince government patrons to introduce water and sewer infrastructure. A willingness to be co-opted for material gain has undermined government accountability and hindered the professional development of water utilities. On the other hand, several civil society organizations such as Ciudad Juárez's Organización Popular Independiente (OPI) have advocated on behalf of low-income communities without sacrificing their autonomy. Centro de Mujeres Tonantzin has created and promoted low-cost, sanitary eco-baños, or bathrooms that do not require water and sewer connections. Moreover, a host of organizations have trained community health promoters to teach how to purify drinking water and use sanitary practices.

The limitations of civil society efforts can also be seen in attempts to solve two of the most salient public problems along the border, the over-exploitation of water resources in the region and shortfalls in wastewater treatment. Although binational civil society initiatives have met with only limited success, perhaps because of the great expense and complexity of large-scale solutions, by convening key water users in the region, the Paso del Norte Water Task Force hopes to facilitate the development of water markets and lead government toward sustainable water use. By constructing Ecoparque in Tijuana, a civil society initiative sought to demonstrate that an alternative wastewater treatment model could be effective at not only making up shortfalls in treatment but also revegetating the city's erosion-prone hillsides. By monitoring the quality of ocean water near Tijuana's wastewater treatment plant, the binational coalition JaJan has developed data that can be used to hold government officials accountable for the quality of the plant's effluent.

Recognizing the limitations and advances of the third sector, this study is not a call to move away from both market- and state-dominated models of development and to embark on an entirely new path. Rather, as James Austin and colleagues (2004a, 7) state: "There is a growing recognition that the increasing complexity of social and economic problems transcends the capacity of any single sector." The potential complementarity of the many sectors is evidenced repeatedly in this analysis by the multisector coalitions that have arisen across the four sites to address a diversity of public problems. Their achievements are not based solely on the often-inadequate incentives of the market or the ballot box. Instead, coalitions such as the Strategic Plan of Juárez, the Paso del Norte Water Task Force, the Rio Grande Park Promoter Group (GPPRB), and the Ambos Nogales Revegetation Partnership (ARAN) bring together complementary resources, foster enlightened self-interest, increase government accountability, and offer a potential mechanism to solve complex public problems.

Overcoming Legacies

Unfortunately, however, these collective efforts are relatively new in the four cities studied. Opportunities for public participation and associational life in the decades following the Mexican Revolution came to be dominated by the Institutional Revolutionary Party (PRI; Chalmers and Piester 1995; Fehrenbach 1995; Verduzco 2003; Wiarda 1973). As it evolved in Mexico, the PRI was able to build on the labor movement in some regions, agricultural organizations in others, and indigenous institutions in still others. Throughout the country, evidence suggests that potential public entrepreneurs frequently came to the conclusion that their goals could best be achieved by engaging the services of political brokers and by participating in the PRI system. Although civil society preserved at least some of its autonomy, the extensive intermixing of political and societal realms undermined the independence of nonprofit organizations and limited the development, effectiveness, and legitimacy of the third sector.

Today, however, Mexico has competitive elections at all three levels of government, the bureaucracy is increasingly decentralized, access to information produced by the federal government is guaranteed by law, and there is a recognized right to participate in and oversee the functioning of public administration. These factors are generally considered to be a winning formula for fostering democratic governance. Under such conditions, there should be unprecedented opportunities for the development of autonomous, problem-oriented nonprofit organizations. On the other hand, persistent informal rules and expectations have prevented more dramatic political and social changes. This study suggests that the informal constraints of clientelism, co-option, and cynicism that developed during one-party rule have not disappeared, although they are by no means deterministic.

Writing in 1985, Mark Grannovetter argued that scholars could overcome the errors of over- and under-socialized theorization by focusing on the social networks in which actors were embedded. Indeed, following Grannovetter, I contend that we must examine the networks of civil society organizations if we are to understand their nature, their potential overdependence on patrons, their likely access to diverse human and financial resources, and their prospective ability to address dependencies. Nonprofits that have ties only to government and political parties cannot escape the informal rules of clientelism. Without exposure to new norms of independence and professionalism and without access to alternative resources, dependence on political patrons will remain the dominant strategy to realize their organizational goals. In contrast, nonprofits that are able to develop links to already existing social infrastructure where norms of independence and professionalism predominate will find informal incentives, knowledge, and resources that facilitate alternate paths. Developing a dense and diverse network of ties proves to be essential to the art of association.

Networks are not formed in a vacuum, however. Key contextual factors and the actions and decisions of different network actors come into play. This study found that it is harder to introduce new norms of autonomy, professionalism, and philanthropy in cities such as Nuevo Laredo, where the PRI's control of local politics remains unchallenged. As a result, Nuevo Laredo's nonprofit sector has fewer civil society organizations, more groups tied to political parties, and more limited political opportunities in public administration.

On the other hand, the study also found that cities such as Tijuana and Ciudad Juárez have not only benefited from an end to one-party rule but are also home to norm entrepreneurs who have actively promoted new informal rules of independence, professionalization, and philanthropy. Because of increased political opportunity and efforts to introduce norms friendly to associational life, Tijuana and Ciudad Juárez offer a radically different environment to potential public entrepreneurs.

Moreover, Tijuana and Ciudad Juárez are also home to an extensive social infrastructure of new ideas and human, financial, and organizational resources. The Church, the foreign nonprofit community, universities, and preexisting civil society organizations and networks have played a major role in incubating organizational efforts. For example, in Ciudad Juárez, several organizations emerged out of Church-affiliated groups and religious social movement networks. Across all four sites, a number of associations have developed as coalitions of already existing groups. In Tijuana, which borders a large nonprofit community in San Diego, U.S. organizations have been important for the growth of the sector. Within the networks of preexisting social infrastructure, public entrepreneurs have found information and know-how, access to potential volunteers and supporters, and a broad array of resources.

The importance of social infrastructure has both positive and negative implications for the development of civil society organizations in Mexico. On the one hand, social infrastructure has illuminated an alterative path to address public concerns and has incubated numerous organizational efforts. On the other hand, even though the importance of social infrastructure might bode well for cities with an activist Church, a history of autonomous social movements, research institutions, foundations, or geographical proximity to a large nonprofit sector in the United States, most Mexican cities lack such advantages. Absent such infrastructure, public entrepreneurs in smaller cities such as Nuevo Laredo and Nogales have reduced opportunities to connect to social networks where alternative norms, human capital, and financial resources can be found.

Unless greater efforts are made to promote philanthropic and voluntary norms throughout society more generally, such cities will likely be left with only a small nonprofit community dominated by parochial associations. Even in cities such as Tijuana and Ciudad Juárez, there is reason for only tempered optimism. Throughout Mexican history, there have always been networks dominated by norms friendly to autonomous associational life (Forment 2003); the challenge is how to diffuse these norms. Although the evidence in this study suggests that civil society networks have expanded and grown more numerous, the informal rules that challenge cynicism and clientelism have not permeated society generally. As Kathleen Staudt and Irasema Coronado (2002, 20) write: "Ultimately, though, personal relationships ('strong ties') must grow and expand into weaker ties that connect to larger networks and organizations if the border is to develop into a region with equal opportunity and social justice."

This study found that existing network ties between the nonprofit sector and the business community are generally unable to attract significant human or financial resources to the sector. Although the business community does participate in water-related policy arenas through professional organizations, such as the Association of Engineers and chambers of commerce, contributions of volunteer time, in-kind services, and funds to civil society organizations remain very limited. This gap between the business community and the nonprofit sector exists despite a legal environment that should theoretically create incentives for volunteerism and philanthropic giving. Although legal requirements mandate that civil associations (ACs) have a governing board (which should link such groups to the for-profit sector), most nonprofit organizations do not maintain an active board, and few use the board as a means to obtain resources. Moreover, the study found that, although organizations authorized to offer tax-deductible receipts for contributions do have greater ties to the for-profit sector, only fourteen of these organizations are addressing water-related problems across the four sites.

Recognizing these challenges, this study has identified several promising ways that network ties to the for-profit sector could be developed and strengthened. Institutionalizing and professionalizing civil society organizations, developing active, effective boards of directors, incorporating as authorized donees (DAs), increasing transparency, clearly avoiding partisanship, and improving administrative capacity would all improve for-profit confidence in the third sector, making it more likely that the business community would both cooperate with and invest time and resources in nonprofits.

But change cannot come solely from within the nonprofit sector itself. Instead, norms friendly to associational life have to be diffused beyond the nonprofit community. Fortunately, in Tijuana, Nogales, and Ciudad

Juárez, norm entrepreneurs are working to create local community foundations and promote a culture of philanthropy in the region. Community foundations, if further strengthened, could bridge two sectors that have traditionally operated apart from one another.

Multi-sector coalitions represent a final promising way to strengthen ties across the nonprofit–for-profit divide. Such coalitions allow for effective cooperation between the sectors with limited risk to each group. Through them, members of civil society are reforesting desert regions, developing and implementing strategic plans, building parks, and studying alternatives for long-term water supply.

Solving Public Problems

Although the development of autonomous civil society organizations is a goal in and of itself, the concern throughout this study has been the role played by these organizations in addressing water-related public problems in the border region. Network ties to the business community and social infrastructure are important for the development of the nonprofit sector, yet they are perhaps more important for the resolution of public problems. Dense networks of ties that connect diverse actors bring complementary resources to bear on public problems and serve as a means to address interdependence between actors.

In the border region, few water-related problems are confined to one country; rather, it is almost always the case that a problem affecting one side of the border also affects the other. However important a means to obtain resources for Mexico's growing body of civil society organizations, binational ties are an even more important means to resolve binational water-related problems. Fortunately, most of the organizations in this study have in fact overcome the challenges of cross-border cooperation. Perhaps surprisingly, the differences in culture and language across the border are more successfully overcome than the differences, or perceived differences, between the nonprofit and for-profit sectors. Cross-border cooperation has been aided by key network actors who bridge the political, linguistic, and cultural divide: Mexican nationals working in U.S. organizations; "professional border crossers," or organizations dedicated to coordinating binational efforts; and individuals committed to the importance of binational cooperation, willing to learn the language on the other side of the border, and disposed to invest time and effort in developing the trust necessary to overcome differences. Thanks to these bridges, there are cross-border efforts to train teachers in environmental education, test ocean waters for contamination, and develop and implement plans to protect the region's watersheds.

Unfortunately, even though cooperation is most desirable in cases of binational dependence, this study found that issues of water supply and wastewater treatment were as likely to produce conflict or no cooperation as they were to produce cooperative ties. Rather than look for solutions on the opposite side of the border, U.S. organizations have tended to follow well-worn paths through U.S. courts, congressional representatives, and the executive branch of government. Despite the presence of important bridges across the divide, as long as binational institutions are weak vis-à-vis domestic institutions, U.S. organizations are likely to continue to prefer domestic strategies to address the most significant binational concerns. The failure of binational civil society cooperation to consistently address these salient issues illustrates one of the sector's weaknesses and highlights its continued dependence on government.

This study therefore also explored relations between nonprofit organizations and government. It found that Mexican public policy has shifted to allow at least some opportunities for participation in the policy process across all four research sites, most notably, citizen committees, access to information, complaint proceedings, judicial recourse, and autonomous cooperation with government agencies.

On the other hand, it also found significant limitations to the effectiveness of these mechanisms and continued reason to worry about the porous border between the nonprofit sector and government. Neighborhood associations in low-income communities are still highly subject to clientelism. Citizen committees are frequently powerless to impact policy or hold officials accountable. There is evidence that suggests that political opportunities are biased toward elite groups, such as business leaders. Although government publications consistently highlight the importance of public participation, the term all too often implies mobilizing citizens to ensure the success of government policies rather than giving citizens decision-making authority or the tools to effectively monitor government officials and hold them accountable. Although there has been considerable political change in the four research sites, there has also been a surprising amount of continuity.

Perhaps more surprising than the limitations of these opportunities is civil society's failure to make effective use of them. Although there are important exceptions, many organizations are not requesting government information, not reporting cases of contamination, not using legal recourse mechanisms, and in some cases not even serving on public participation committees. Where entrepreneurial efforts have rewritten the informal rules of clientelism and co-option, these have often been replaced by norms of distrust and cynicism. Strengthening public participation mechanisms will require not only political will on the part of government officials but also action by existing civil society organizations committed to expanding the available set of opportunities.

Paradoxically, there needs to be both greater cooperation between the nonprofit and government sectors and, at the same time, a clearer definition of the boundary between them. Existing political opportunities can only be expanded through greater nonprofit-government interaction, yet without a clear division between the sectors, the line between cooperation and co-option can be crossed all too easily. Beyond the problems of clientelism, of particular concern is the revolving door between government and the nonprofit sector. Victor Lichtinger Waisman, head of Mexico's environmental agency (SEMARNAT) at the time of research, admits that one of the errors of his administration was to place committed and professional environmentalists from civil society into positions of importance within his agency.[1] SEMARNAT soon discovered that, because a significant portion of Mexico's relatively small environmental community had become part of the government, the agency no longer faced necessary civil society pressure. Nor are government actors entirely to blame for the porous inter-sector border: many civil society leaders have used associational life as a platform to enter into politics. Such a conflict of interest not only impairs the effectiveness of civil society efforts; it also damages the image of associational life and strengthens the informal rules of cynicism and distrust.

In summary, even though political changes paralleling Mexico's democratic transition have created unprecedented opportunities for the growth of civil society organizations, informal rules fostered throughout Mexico's political history still keep concerned citizens from becoming public entrepreneurs. Despite this obstacle, however, norm entrepreneurs are promoting new informal rules of autonomy, professionalism, and philanthropy, which have facilitated the growth of new civil society organizations. Within this context, many new civil society initiatives are helping to find solutions to water-related public problems across the four cities studied. The consolidation of the nonprofit sector, however, requires greater legitimacy, greater support from Mexican society generally, less dependency on preexisting social infrastructure, and a clearer delineation of the essential differences between the nonprofit and government sectors, even as cross-sector cooperation increases.

Generalizing the Arguments

Water-related public problems are perhaps unique; one could imagine different implications for organizations that address health care, education, housing, or social welfare problems. Indeed, throughout this study, I have argued that it is the physical attributes of a policy problem that set the stage for understanding a broad array of phenomena. Thus, for example, the study found that clientelism continues to govern nonprofit-government relations in the introduction of water and sewer infrastructure but not in other policy arenas. On the other hand, the topic of water was selected in part because it impacts a wide variety of policy arenas and attracts a diversity of nonprofit organizations. The study thus has included public health groups that confront water-related health problems, education groups that address environmental education, and community development organizations that deal with basic water and sewer issues. Because the sample of organizations the study has examined here represents a broad array of groups, I would argue that it successfully identifies issues that affect the civil society sector more generally. Thus, even though they have more ties to the business community than environmental groups do, public health organizations also suffer from the deficient culture of philanthropy. Of the five public health organizations in this study, one has no ties to the business community and another receives only in-kind support. Of the remaining three, philanthropic contributions make up only a small minority of their funds, which are primarily provided by fees. In addition, of the five organizations, two are not authorized donees and four receive funds from the United States. Most important, only one of the organizations emerged out of the business community and three developed with the essential help of social infrastructure. Although these five organizations represent a very small sample, they suggest that organizations concerned with public health follow many of the same patterns as other associations in this study. In fact, many nonprofits in Mexico, regardless of their substantive areas of operations, are not authorized donees, have only limited ties to the for-profit sector, are hesitant to engage government, depend on social infrastructure, and receive financial support from abroad. I would therefore expect research in other policy arenas to identify similar trends.

It could be argued that the border region is geographically unique and that the conclusions drawn here cannot be generalized to other regions of Mexico. Obviously, a large portion of this analysis is concerned with aspects specific to the border, such as the potential for cross-border collaboration and the role of the maquiladora industry in funding nonprofit initiatives. It seems improbable that associations in other parts of Mexico would have the same levels of U.S. support as organizations along the border. But the argument employed in this study is not that civil society organizations require the U.S. nonprofit community, but rather, that the growth of civil society organizations has depended on preexisting social infrastructure, of which U.S. organizations are only one part. I would expect this finding to generalize to other regions of Mexico. In fact, scholars have illustrated the important role that Church-based groups, universities, and preexisting organizations have played in supporting both social movements and nonprofit organizations in Mexico City (Eckstein 2001; Verduzco 2003). As such, it is not necessary to receive support from U.S. nonprofit community, per se, but only from social infrastructure more generally.

Nonetheless, because social infrastructure and preexisting social networks are so important to the emergence of civil society organizations, I would expect that the nature of a community's preexisting networks would have an impact on the nature of the resulting nonprofit sector. Clearly, the U.S. nonprofit community has helped influence the agenda of

Mexican associational life in the border region. For example, funding opportunities from the Paso del Norte Health Foundation have drawn several organizations into water-related policy arenas. One would therefore expect that associational life in other parts of Mexico would be similarly influenced by the nature of preexisting forms of organizations. For example, the *zapatista* movement and indigenous traditions in Chiapas should have considerable bearing on the nature of the state's nonprofit community.

I would also expect to find variation in civil society organization presence based on differences in local political environments. Just as the continuity of one-party rule has limited the opportunities available to potential public entrepreneurs in Nuevo Laredo, similar political environments could also be expected to undermine the independence of the third sector. For example, Jonathan Fox (1994) found that clientelism and authoritarianism continued in rural indigenous areas. In Chihuahua's Sierra Tarahumara, for example, the prevalence of illegal logging, drug trafficking, and a lack of electoral competition among the traditionally marginalized Tarahumara Indians does not bode well for autonomous civil society efforts. Yet these differences should not be overstated. Because all of Mexico shares a similar political history, one that fostered informal rules of clientelism, co-option, and cynicism, I would expect to find similar patterns of continuity and change across the country as norm entrepreneurs attempt to rewrite these informal rules with varying degrees of success.

This study also has implications beyond the Mexican context. However different the border region may be from other regions of Mexico, and Mexico from other countries, I would nonetheless expect the general theoretical framework used here to apply to much of the developing and postcommunist world. Although other developing countries do not share Mexico's unique political history, I would expect that dense networks of ties that cross multiple cleavages within a society would permit civil society organizations to avoid overdependence and ensure their autonomy, as well as their access to the information and resources they need to address public problems. On the other hand, limited network ties would give rise to overdependence on particular actors and limit the autonomy of such organizations, as well as their access to the information and resources they need to address public problems.

The establishment of civil society organizations is certainly not a solution to all social ills. Yet democratic development requires that a nation tap into and realize the potential of its citizens. To this end, it would behoove government actors to give back some of their political power to the people. But tapping citizen potential requires much more than public policy incentives. Concerned citizens must take action. In some countries, the path from the individual household to effective civil society participation is well cleared and lined with social infrastructure. In others, clearing and building such infrastructure will depend on the emergence of public entrepreneurs, steeped in the art of association and able to forge diverse networks of ties between the many sectors of their respective societies.

Appendix

Study Participants

Table A.1 Tijuana nonprofit organizations included in the study

Spanish name	English translation	Activities addressing water-related public problems
Cámara Nacional de Comercio	National Chamber of Commerce	Serves on water utility's citizen oversight committee; involved in study on water supply options
Cámara Nacional de Industria de la Transformación (CANACINTRA)	National Chamber of Manufacturing Industry	Serves on several public participation committees
Casa de la Mujer: Grupo Factor X	Women's Home: X Factor Group	Involved in environmental health research and education initiatives
Centro de Enseñanza Técnica y Superior	Center for Technical and Advanced Teaching	Conducts environmental education and water monitoring in Alamar River
Centro de Promoción de Salud, Esperanza, A.C.	Esperanza Health Promotion Center	Trains volunteers (promoters) to offer water-related public health and water conservation education
Colectivo Chilpancingo por Justicia Ambiental	Chilpancingo Collective for Environmental Justice	Opposed industrial contamination from Metales y Derivados industrial site
Colegio de la Frontera Norte (COLEF)	College of the Northern Border	Serves as core participant in Tijuana River Watershed Binational Vision Project; operates Ecoparque
Comité Ciudadano Pro-Restauración del Cañón del Padre A.C.	Padre Canyon Pro-Restoration Citizen Committee	Opposed industrial contamination from Metales y Derivados industrial site
Consejo de Desarrollo Económico de Tijuana A.C.	Tijuana Economic Development Council	Involved in study on Tijuana water supply options
Consejo de Educación Ambiental de las Californias	Environmental Education Council for the Californias	Promotes environmental education as binational coalition
Ecoparque	Ecoparque (park watered by effluent from small-scale wastewater treatment plant)	Serves as environmental education center
Eco-Sol, Educación y Cultura Ecológia, A.C.	Eco-Sol, Environmental Education and Culture	Conducts, promotes environmental education; serves on public participation committees including SEMARNAT sustainable development council

Fundación Esperanza	Esperanza Foundation	Trains volunteers (promoters) to offer education on water-related public health issues, water conservation, and water recycling
Fundación Internacional de la Comunidad, A.C. (FIC)	International Community Foundation	Provides mini-grants for environmental projects
Grupo Ecologista Gaviotas A.C.	Seagulls Ecologist Group	Serves as member of JaJan coalition; conducts water monitoring and environmental education; serves on public participation committees
JaJan	JaJan (Good Water)	Conducts water monitoring and environmental education
Los Niños	The Children	Trains volunteers (promoters) to offer education on water recycling and conservation
Promoción y Docencia A.C.	Promotion and Teaching	Conducts, promotes environmental and water conservation education
Proyecto Bio-Regional de Educación Ambiental, A.C.	Bio-Regional Environmental Education Project	Develops curricula and trains teachers in environmental education
Proyecto Fronterizo de Educación Ambiental, A.C. (PFEA)	Border Environmental Education Project	Conducts, promotes environmental education; serves on several public participation committees; coordinates border nonprofit conference; conducts beach cleanups; acts as information clearinghouse
Tijuana Trabaja	Tijuana Works	Serves on public participation committees; conducts studies on urban issues
Universidad Autónoma de Baja California	Autonomous University of Baja California	Conducts water monitoring; involved in Tijuana River Watershed Binational Vision Project
Visión Binacional para la Cuenca del Río Tijuana	Tijuana River Watershed Binational Vision Project	Works on development of vision for protection of Tijuana River watershed

Table A.2 Nogales nonprofit organizations included in the study

Spanish name	English translation	Activities addressing water-related public problems
Asociación de Maquiladoras de Sonora, A.C.: Comité Ambiental	Sonoran Maquiladora Association: Environmental Committee	Supports, promotes reforestation projects, industry compliance with environmental regulations
Asociación de Profesionales en Seguridad Ambiental, A.C.(APSA)	Association of Environmental Security Professionals	Supports, promotes reforestation projects, industry compliance with environmental regulations
Asociación de Reforestación en Ambos Nogales (ARAN)	Ambos Nogales Revegetation Partnership	Conducts, promotes reforestation of Ambos Nogales area
Borderlinks, A.C.	Borderlinks	Supports, promotes latrine construction, alternative water purification techniques
Cámara Nacional de Comercio, Servicios y Turismo de Nogales	Nogales Chapter of the National Chamber of Commerce, Services, and Tourism	Serves on public participation committees
Cámara Nacional de la Industria de Transformación (CANACINTRA)	National Chamber of the Manufacturing Industry	Serves on public participation committees
Centro de Investigación y Estudios Ambientales, A.C.	Environmental Studies and Research Center	Conducts environmental education and research; serves on public participation committees
Fundación del Empresariado Sonorense, A.C. (FESAC)	Sonoran Business Foundation	Promotes strengthening of civil; leads forum for local development
Grupo Ecologista Independiente de Nogales	Nogales Independent Ecologist Group	Opposes industrial contamination and promotes environmental health
Proyecto COMADRES	COMADRES Project	Opposes industrial contamination and promotes environmental health
Unión de Usuarios de Nogales, A.C.	Nogales Service Users Union	Represents users of public goods and services including water and sewer

Table A.3 Ciudad Juárez nonprofit organizations included in the study

Spanish name	English translation	Activities addressing water-related public problems
Alianza Internacional Ecologista del Bravo	International Environmental Alliance of the Rio Grande	Opposes industrial contamination
Aqua 21, A.C.	Aqua 21	Conducts, promotes environmental education; trains volunteers (promoters) to offer education in water-related public health issues and water conservation
Asociación de Maquiladoras de Ciudad Juárez, A.C.: Comité Ambiental	Maquiladora Association of Ciudad Juárez: Environmental Committee	Helps member industries interpret and comply with environmental legislation
Cámara Nacional de Comercio, Servicios y Turismo de Ciudad Juárez	Ciudad Juárez Chapter of the National Chamber of Commerce, Services, and Tourism	Serves on water utility's citizen oversight committee
Centro de Asesoría y Promoción Juvenil, A.C.	Counseling and Youth Promotion Center	Conducts, promotes water-related public health education; involved in Health Communities program to help communities identify and solve public problems; supports, promotes construction of eco-baños
Centro para el Fortalecimiento de la Sociedad Civil, A.C.	Civil Society Strengthening Center	Holds workshops and provides services to facilitate work of nonprofits
Centro de Mujeres Tonantzin A.C.	Women's Center Tonantzin	Promotes eco-baños and alterative technologies to improve public sanitation and hygiene

Table A.3 (*continued*)

Spanish name	English translation	Activities addressing water-related public problems
Centro Educativo Multicultural Yermo y Parres	Yermo and Parres Multicultural Education Center	Operates wastewater treatment plant whose effluent is used to water soccer fields
Centro de Estudios y Taller Laboral, A.C.	Labor Workshop and Studies Center	Opposes industrial contamination
Centro de Investigación y Solidaridad Obrera (CISO)	Research and Worker Solidarity Center	Opposes industrial contamination
Coalición Binacional contra Tiraderos Tóxicos y Radioactivos / Coordinadora Regional Fronteriza de Organizaciones No Gubernamentales	Binational Coalition against Toxic and Radioactive Waste Dumps / Border Regional Coordinator of Nongovernmental Organizations	Opposes industrial contamination; supports efforts to protect Rio Grande
Coalición de la Cuenca del Río Bravo / Río Grande	Rio Grande / Río Bravo Basin Coalition	Supports efforts to protect Rio Grande basin; created Day of the River / Día del Río celebration
Consejo Ciudadano de Desarrollo Social	Social Development Citizen Council	Promotes social development agenda and good governance in Ciudad Juárez
Desarrollo Juvenil del Norte, A.C.	Northern Youth Development	Conducts, promotes water-related public health education; supports, promotes construction of eco-baños, water purification program
Fundación Margarita Miranda de Mascareñas, A.C.	Margarita Miranda de Mascareñas Foundation	Provides mini-grants for environmental initiatives
Ecoparques	Ecoparques	Works to develop environmentally friendly parks

Spanish Name	English Name	Description
Grupo de Trabajo del Agua en la Región Paso del Norte	Paso del Norte Water Task Force	Facilitates information exchange and develops proposals to address water supply problems in Paso del Norte region
Grupo de Trabajo de Salud Ambiental en la Región Paso del Norte	Paso del Norte Environmental Health Task Force	Promotes environmental health research in Paso del Norte region
Grupo Promotor Parque Río Bravo (GPPRP)	Rio Grande Park Promoter Group	Supports, promotes building green corridor along banks of Rio Grande
Fundación del Empresariado Chihuahuense, A.C. (FECHAC)	Chihuahua Business Foundation	Funds Ciudad Juárez nonprofit community
Organización Popular Independiente (OPI)	Independent Popular Organization	Supports, promotes water-related public health education, construction of eco-baños, and community organizing and development
Plan Estratégico de Juárez, A.C.	Strategic Plan of Juárez	Works to determine "Juárez that we want" and develop plan to achieve that vision
Programa Compañeros, A.C.	Companions Program	Involved in Health Communities program
Promoción Social Kölping, A.C.	Kölping Social Promotion	Supports, promotes environmental education, community-level "micro-planning"
Proyecto del Río	River Project	Promotes water monitoring of and education about Rio Grande
Salud y Desarrollo Comunitario, A.C. (SADEC)	Ciudad Juárez Health and Community Development	Conducts, promotes water-related public health and environmental education and research; involved in environmental protection initiatives
Universidad Autónoma de Ciudad Juárez, Instituto de Ingeniería y Tecnología	Autonomous University of Ciudad Juárez, Engineering and Technology Institute	Serves as core participant on Paso del Norte Water Task Force

Table A.4 Nuevo Laredo nonprofit organizations included in the study

Spanish name	English translation	Participation in water-related public problems
Asociación de Colonias Populares (ACOPO)	Association of Popular Colonias	Acts as intermediary between residents and political leaders to obtain public goods and services for low-income communities
Asociación de Constructores de Nuevo Laredo	Nuevo Laredo Builders Association	Serves on water utility's citizen oversight committee and on steering committee for Border Environmental Cooperation Commission (BECC) certification criteria
Cámara Nacional de la Industria de Transformación (CANACINTRA): Comité de Seguridad, Higiene, y Medio Ambiente	National Chamber for the Manufacuring Industry: Security, Hygiene, and Environment Committee	Helps member industries interpret and comply with environmental legislation; supports, promotes environmental education
Centro Internacional de Estudios del Río Bravo, A.C. (CIERB)	Río Bravo International Studies Center	Leads Day of River / Día del Río environmental education and cleanup initiative; conducts, promotes environmental education
Colegio de Ingenieros de Nuevo Laredo	Association of Engineers of Nuevo Laredo	Serves on water utility's citizen oversight committee
Consejo Coordinador Ciudadano (CCC)	Citizen Coordinating Council	Serves on municipal transparency, water utility's citizen oversight, and BECC steering committees
Consejo de Instituciones de Nuevo Laredo, A.C.	Nuevo Laredo Council of Institutions	Takes part in water-related public issue initiatives generally and engages in government oversight

Comité Regional de Vigilancia y Protección al Medio Ambiente (COREVA)	Regional Committee for the Monitoring and Protection of the Environment	Identifies and reports contamination concerns; promotes water-related research
Frente Unido Nacional	National United Front	Acts as intermediary between residents and political leaders to improve public goods and services in low-income communities
Lideres Unidos	United Leaders	Acts as intermediary between residents and political leaders to obtain public goods and services in low-income communities
Sociedad de Ingenieros, Arquitectos, y Técnicos	Society of Engineers, Architects, and Technicians	Supported municipal government on drainage design project

Table A.5   Mexican government agencies interviewed in Tijuana

Spanish name	English translation	Level of government
Comisión Internacional de Límites y Aguas (CILA)	International Boundary and Water Commission (IBWC)	Federal
Procuraduría Federal de Protección al Ambiente (PROFEPA)	Federal Attorney General's Office for Environmental Protection	Federal
Secretaría de Medio Ambiente y Recursos Naturales (SEMARNAT)	Secretariat for the Environment and Natural Resources	Federal
Comisión Estatal de Servicios Públicos de Tijuana: Planeación	State Public Services Commission of Tijuana: Planning	State
Comisión Estatal de Servicios Públicos de Tijuana: Comercial	State Public Services Commission of Tijuana: Billing	State
Comisión Estatal de Servicios Públicos de Tijuana: Relaciones Públicos	State Public Services Commission of Tijuana: Public Relations	State
Comisión Estatal de Servicios Públicos de Tijuana: Saneamiento	State Public Services Commission of Tijuana: Sanitation	State
Comisión Estatal de Agua	State Water Commission	State
Dirección General de Ecología	Department of Ecology	State
Comité de Planeación para el Desarrollo del Estado	State Development Planning Committee	State
Comité de Planeación del Desarrollo Municipal (COPLADEM)	Committee of Municipal Planning and Development	Municipal
Desarrollo Social Municipal: Comités de Vecinos	Municipal Social Development: Neighborhood Committees	Municipal
Desarrollo Social Municipal: Coordinación de Organismos de la Sociedad Civil	Municipal Social Development: Coordination of Civil Society Organizations	Municipal
Dirección Municipal de Ecología	Municipal Department of Ecology	Municipal
Instituto Municipal de Planeación (IMPLAN)	Municipal Planning Institute	Municipal

Table A.6 Mexican government agencies interviewed in Nogales, Sonora

Spanish name	English translation	Level of government
Comisión Internacional de Límites y Aguas (CILA)	International Boundary and Water Commission (IBWC)	Federal
Oficina Binacional de Salud Fronteriza	Sonora-Arizona Border Public Health Office	State and binational
Centro de Información para la Salud	Center for Health Information	State
Comisión de Agua Potable y Alcantarillado del Estado (COAPAES) de Sonora-Nogales: Comercial	State of Sonora Commission for Potable Water and Sewer: Billing	State
Comisión de Agua Potable y Alcantarillado del Estado de Sonora-Nogales: Cultura de Agua	State of Sonora Commission for Potable Water and Sewer: Water Culture	State
Comisión de Agua Potable y Alcantarillado del Estado de Sonora-Nogales: Obras y Proyectos	State of Sonora Commission for Potable Water and Sewer: Public Works and Projects	State
Comisión de Agua Potable y Alcantarillado del Estado de Sonora-Nogales: Asuntos Internacionales	State of Sonora Commission for Potable Water and Sewer: International Affairs	State
Secretaría de Salud Pública	Secretariat of Public Health	State
Secretaría de Infraestructura Urbano y Ecología (SIUE)	Secretariat of Urban Infrastructure and Ecology	State
Dirección de Control Urbano y Ecología	Department of Urban Control and Ecology	Municipal
Dirección de Desarrollo Social	Department of Social Development	Municipal
Dirección de Planificación y Desarrollo Urbano	Department of Planning and Urban Development	Municipal
Dirección de Infraestructura Urbana y Obras Publicas	Department of Urban Infrastructure and Public Works	Municipal
Dirección de Servicios Públicos	Department of Public Services	Municipal

Table A.7 Mexican government agencies interviewed in Ciudad Juárez

Spanish name	English translation	Level of government
Organización Panamericana de la Salud	Pan-American Health Organization	Transnationa
Comisión de Cooperación Ecológica Fronteriza: Comunicaciones	Border Environment Cooperation Commission (BECC): Communications	Binational
Comisión de Cooperación Ecológica Fronteriza: Operaciones	Border Environment Cooperation Commission: Operations	Binational
Comisión de Cooperación Ecológica Fronteriza: Participación Pública	Border Environment Cooperation Commission: Public Participation	Binational
Comisión de Salud Fronteriza México–Estados Unidos	U.S.–Mexico Border Health Commission	Binational
Comisión Nacional de Agua (CONAGUA)	National Water Commission	Federal
Comisión Internacional de Límites y Aguas (CILA)	International Boundary and Water Commission (IBWC)	Federal
Procuraduría Federal de Protección al Ambiente (PROFEPA)	Federal Attorney General's Office for Environmental Protection	Federal
Secretaría de Educación Pública: Mesa Técnica	Secretariat of Public Education: Technical Working Group	State
Junta Municipal de Agua y Saneamiento: Cultura de Agua	Municipal Water and Sanitation Board: Water Culture	State
Junta Municipal de Agua y Saneamiento: Saneamiento	Municipal Water and Sanitation Board: Sanitation	State
Junta Municipal de Agua y Saneamiento: Área Técnica	Municipal Water and Sanitation Board: Technical Area	State
Junta Municipal de Agua y Saneamiento: Comercial	Municipal Water and Sanitation Board: Billing	State
Secretaría de Salud	Secretariat of Health	State
Secretaría de Salud: Departamento de Salud Ambiental	Secretariat of Health: Department of Environmental Health	State
Dirección de Desarrollo Social	Department of Social Development	Municipal
Dirección de Desarrollo Social: Programa Lunares	Department of Social Development: Extension Program	Municipal
Dirección General de Ecología y Protección Civil	Department of Ecology and Civil Protection	Municipal
Instituto Municipal de Investigación y Planeación (IMIP)	Municipal Institute for Research and Planning	Municipal
Instituto Municipal de Investigación y Planeación: Microplaneación	Municipal Institute for Research and Planning: Microplanning	Municipal
Secretario Técnico del Municipio de Juárez	Technical Secretary of the Municipality of Juárez	Municipal

Table A.8 Mexican government agencies interviewed in Nuevo Laredo

Spanish name	English translation	Level of government
Comisión de Salud Fronteriza México–Estados Unidos	U.S.–Mexico Border Health Commission	Binational
Comisión Internacional de Límites y Aguas (CILA)	International Boundary and Water Commission (IBWC)	Federal
Secretaría de Salud del Estado de Tamaulipas	Secretariat of Health of the State of Tamaulipas	State
Secretaría de Educación, Culture, y Deporte	Secretariat of Education, Culture, and Sports	State
Secretaría de Desarrollo Urbano y Ecología	Secretariat of Urban Development and Ecology	State
Comisión Municipal de Agua Potable y Alcantarillado: Atención a Usuarios	Municipal Commission for Potable Water and Sewer: Customer Service	Municipal
Comisión Municipal de Agua Potable y Alcantarillado: Cultura de Agua	Municipal Commission for Potable Water and Sewer: Water Culture	Municipal
Comisión Municipal de Agua Potable y Alcantarillado: Proyectos y Supervisión	Municipal Commission for Potable Water and Sewer: Projects and Supervision	Municipal
Comisión Municipal de Agua Potable y Alcantarillado: Calidad de Agua	Municipal Commission for Potable Water and Sewer: Water Quality	Municipal
Dirección de Contraloría, Presupuesto y Desarrollo Administrativo	Department of the Comptroller, Budget, and Administrative Development	Municipal
Secretario Particular del Presidente Municipal	Personal Secretary of the Municipal President	Municipal
Subdirección de Desarrollo Social	Office of Social Development	Municipal
Subdirección de Ecología	Office of Ecology	Municipal

Table A.9 U.S. nonprofit organizations included in the study

Tijuana–San Diego region	Ambos Nogales region	Paso del Norte region	Los Dos Laredos region
Aqualink	Border Health Foundation	Audubon Society, El Paso Chapter	Frank M. Tejeda Center
Citizens Revolting against Pollution (CRAP)	Environmental Education Exchange	Center for Civic Engagement	Lamar Bruni Vergara Environmental Science Center
Environmental Education Council for the Californias (EECC)	Friends of the Santa Cruz River	Center for Environmental Resource Management (CERM)	Rio Grande International Study Center
Esperanza International	Platicamos Salud, Mariposa Community Health Center	Rio Grande / Rio Bravo Basin Coalition	Texas Watch
International Community Foundation (ICF)	Project Wet	Environmental Defense	
Pro Peninsula	Santa Cruz River: Its People and Environment	Frank M. Tejeda Center	
Project Mercy	Sonoran Institute	El Paso Interreligious Sponsoring Organization	
Regional Workbench Consortium	University of Arizona, Bureau of Applied Research in Anthropology	Paso del Norte Health Foundation	
San Diego Baykeeper	University of Arizona, Udall Center for Studies in Public Policy	Paso del Norte Watershed Council	
San Diego Dialogue		Southwest Environmental Center	

San Diego Natural History
  Museum
Southwest Consortium for Environ-
  mental Research and Policy
Sierra Club, San Diego Chapter
Surfrider Foundation, San Diego
  Chapter
Southwest Wetlands Interpretive
  Association
Synergos Institute
Tijuana River National
Estuarine Research Reserve
  (TRNERR; quasi-governmental)
University of California, San Diego,
  Center for U.S.–Mexican Studies

Table A.10   Research activities conducted to collect primary source data

Research activity	Number
Members of Mexican civil society interviewed	82 (58)[a]
Leaders of neighborhood associations interviewed	60
Mexican government officials interviewed	63
U.S. nonprofit organizations interviewed	43
Meetings observed	46
U.S. government officials interviewed	18
Total research activities	312 (58)[a]

[a]Numbers in parentheses represent the number of follow-up interviews conducted.

Notes

Chapter 1. A New Choice

1. Clientelism threatens the nonprofit sector in many other countries besides Mexico. Even in the United States, it would be hard to compare the volunteer fire departments of Benjamin Franklin's Philadelphia, formed to address a community problem, with those of Tammany Hall's New York, used to build Tammany's political power. Indeed, the political objectives of the Tammany fire departments prevented them from effectively fulfilling their ostensible purpose.

2. By excluding parochial organizations, Diamond's and my definition of civil society deviates from that of other scholars. Skocpol and Fiorina (1999, 2), for example, define civil society broadly as "the network of ties and groups through which people connect to one another and get drawn into community and political affairs." For review, see Olvera Rivera 2004; Walzer 2003.

3. Often compared geographically to the U.S. county, the municipality is the basic unit of local government in Mexico.

4. By contrast, Carlos Forment, whose meticulous study (Forment 2003) documents numerous associational efforts throughout the country, argues that a diverse associational life was alive and well during the nineteenth century.

5. In fact, major reforms undertaken by the de la Madrid administration did not offer the municipalities any greater share of federal tax revenues. As Rodríguez (1997, 59) writes, "In fiscal terms, the federation strengthened its control over revenues and showed no willingness to increase the amounts transferred to the states and municipalities." The record of the Salinas administration is even more mixed. Although PRONASOL increased local decision making, the program was operated out of Salinas's office and bypassed state and municipal governments. Additional actions by Salinas also threatened lower levels of government. An unprecedented sixteen governors stepped down during his administration, many presumably at the wish of the president (Rodríguez 1997).

6. Civil society actors were far from passive observers during Mexico's democratic transition. Indeed, civil society organizations such as Alianza Cívica (Civic Alliance), a coalition of organizations and individuals formed to monitor Mexico's elections, played a major role in that transition. In the 1994 presidential elections, Alianza Cívica mobilized almost 40,000 citizens to monitor some 2,000 polling places (Olvera Rivera 2001).

7. Despite its hierarchical structure, the Catholic Church is of course a diverse organization. The reforms of Vatican II gave individual bishops greater authority, increasing geographical variation in the Church's responses to citizen initiatives. Religious orders such as the Jesuits further increase the diversity within the Church structure and have been essential supporters of civil society's development.

8. Some scholars use the term "social infrastructure" to speak to a much broader concept. Robert Hall and Charles Jones (1999), for example, use it to include norms and even government policies. Here the focus is on preexisting elements within the third sector that are capable of incubating civil society initiatives. To operationalize social infrastructure, I focus on churches, universities, foreign nonprofit organizations, and preexisting organizations and networks.

Chapter 2. Cities, Policy Problems, and Nonprofits

1. Cities also vary in terms of population. For example, Tijuana and Ciudad Juárez have over 1.3 million residents, whereas Nogales has just under 200,000. As will be discussed in chapter 3, this study attempts to control for population through the creation of a dependent variable entitled "civil society organizational presence." I will argue below that it is not so much population per se that impacts the development of civil society organizations as the presence of social infrastructure.

2. Following the primary research period, electoral conditions changed in Tijuana and Nogales. In 2005, the PRI retook Tijuana after fifteen years of PAN administrations. In Nogales, a PAN candidate for municipal president finally won in 2006.

3. Although the PAN's dominance seemed guaranteed to endure, in the 2004 elections, the PRI upset PAN favorites in Tijuana and Mexicali, the capital of Baja California.

4. The PAN would eventually win the municipality for the first time, in 2006 (after the research period of this study).

5. Water utilities in the four locations include Tijuana's State Comisión Estatal de Servicios Públicos de Tijuana (CESPT; State Commission for Public Services of Tijuana) Nogales's Comisión de Agua Potable y Alcantarillado del Estado (COAPAES; State Commission for Potable Water and Sewer), Ciudad Juárez's Junta Municipal de Agua y Saneamiento (JMAS; Municipal Board of Water and Sanitation), and Nuevo Laredo's (Comisión Municipal de Agua Potable y Alcantarillado (COMAPA; Municipal Commission for Potable Water and Sewer). In 2005, service provision in Nogales was devolved to the municipality and COAPAES became the Organismo Operador Municipal de Agua Potable, Alcantarillado y Saneamiento de Nogales (OOAPASN; Nogales Municipal Water, Sewer, and Sanitation Operator).

6. For example, in Nuevo Laredo the municipal president at the time of research had previously been the head of the water utility. In addition, the head of the water utility at the time was a candidate for his party's nomination for upcoming mayoral elections.

7. City planning became the responsibility of municipal governments after 1983

reforms to Article 115 of the Mexican constitution; however, municipalities are highly constrained by federal and state laws.

8. Planning institutes include the Instituto Municipal de Planeación (IMPLAN; Municipal Planning Institutes) in Tijuana and Nuevo Laredo and the Instituto Municipal de Investigación y Planeación (IMIP; Municipal Research and Planning Institute) in Ciudad Juárez. Tijuana and Baja California also have policy planning agencies that seek to improve interinstitutional cooperation and encourage citizen participation. These include the Comisión de Planeación del Desarrollo Municipal (COPLADEM; Municipal Commission for Planning and Development) and the Comité de Planeación para el Desarrollo del Estado (COPLADE; Planning Committee for State Development).

9. Decreto por el que se reforman, adicionan, y derogan diversas disposiciones de la Ley de Aguas Nacionales. *Diario Oficial*, April 29, 2004.

10. Despite the identification of the cluster and years' worth of tests, no culprit has emerged. It was commonly perceived that trichloroethylene (TCE) and tetrochloroethylene (PCE) plumes in the aquifers under the Nogales Wash were to blame for the clusters; however, epidemiological studies have failed to find a relationship (Sprouse, Cory, and Varady 1996).

11. Specifically, the binational study found hexachloro 1-3 butadiene, hexachloroethane, and 1-4 dichlorobenzene.

12. Representatives of the groups were contacted by phone, e-mail, or in person and asked to participate in the study. Interviews were typically held in person with organization directors, although in several cases a different member of the organization was interviewed. Respondents were asked about the details, history, and activities of their organization, as well as their relationships and cooperation with other nonprofits, U.S. organizations, the for-profit sector, and government. Eighty-two hour-long interviews with organizational representatives through 2003 and 2004 were complemented by follow-up interviews in early 2005 with 58 of the original respondents.

13. Eleven interviews were conducted with neighborhood presidents of Nuevo Laredo's Asociación de Colonias Populares (ACOPO; Association of Popular Colonias). Data on Ciudad Juárez's neighborhood associations were collected by Gustavo Córdova Bojórquez from the Colegio de la Frontera Norte (COLEF; College of the Northern Border) and me. During the month of March 2004, interviews were conducted with twenty-five neighborhood committee leaders in three sectors of Ciudad Juárez. Information on Tijuana's neighborhood associations is the result of a survey of neighborhood committee leaders administered by the Comisión de Planeación del Desarrollo Municipal (COPLADEM; Municipal Commission for Planning and Development), a research arm of the municipal government, in November 2003. I had the opportunity to accompany COPLADEM as they were implementing the survey, which allowed me the chance to have confidential and qualitative interviews with twenty-four community leaders. Of 304 committees that the municipality claims are operating, 127 participated in the survey.

Unfortunately, the survey has severe methodological limitations, chief among which is that it was not anonymous. Because it was administered by the municipality, on which the neighborhood committees are dependent, there were incentives to manipulate responses. In addition, the survey forms were filled out by those committee presidents who attended meetings convened by COPLADEM; thus the survey is not a random sample of the existing committees. Nonetheless, there is still insight that can be gleaned from the responses presented in this study, which are less apt to have been impacted by the survey's methodological flaws. Moreover, respondents faced reduced incentives to falsely report their opinions in the one-on-one interviews I conducted.

14. The interviews typically lasted one hour and were usually conducted with the head of the agency or the head of the branch or regional office most relevant to the study. For example, in each of the cities, several employees from the water utility were interviewed. These included technical personnel and persons responsible for relations with the community, environmental education, and billing, although interviews were at times not conducted if the agency did not maintain an office at the research site. Agency representatives were asked about responses to policy problems, opportunities for public participation, transparency, and interaction with civil society organizations.

The research was conducted during the municipal administrations of José Gonzales Reyes (2001–2004) in Tijuana, Lorenzo Antonio De la Fuente Manríquez (2003–2006) in Nogales, Jesús Delgado Muñoz (2002–2004) in Ciudad Juárez, and José Manuel Suárez López (2001–2004) in Nuevo Laredo; the state administrations of Eugenio Elorduy Walther (2000–2006) in Baja California, Eduardo Bours Castelo (2003–2009) in Sonora; Patricio Martínez García (1998–2004) in Chihuahua, and Tomás Yarrington Ruvalcaba (1998–2004) in Tamaulipas; and the federal administration of Vicente Fox (2000–2006).

15. Research participants were interviewed for approximately one hour and asked about their organization, its activities, and its interaction with Mexican nonprofit organizations.

Throughout the text, specific primary resources are not typically cited to comply with rules for the protection of human subjects. In some cases, the names of interviewees are offered, with the express consent of the study participants. Some proper names have been changed.

Chapter 3. Nuevo Laredo

1. Similar powerful labor leaders emerged in other Tamaulipas cities including Agapito González Cavazos in Matamoros, Reynaldo Garza Cantú in Reynosa, and Joaquín Hernández Galicia in Tampico-Madero.

2. All translations of Spanish-language quotations are mine unless otherwise noted.

Chapter 5. Binational Collaboration

1. As discussed in chapter 3, a project promoted by the Comisión Municipal de Agua Potable y Alcantarillado (COMAPA) of Nuevo Laredo and approved in 2004 by the Border Environment Cooperation Commission is designed to rehabilitate the sewer infrastructure in the city center and to halt the flow of untreated sewage into the Río Bravo / Rio Grande.

2. It should be mentioned that, according to the early literature on U.S.–Mexico binational collaboration, the NAFTA brought together a number of groups in their joint *opposition* to the agreement (Brooks and Fox 2002; Thorup 1991; 1993). Another government agency not discussed here is the International Boundary and Water Commission (IBWC). Despite its name, the IBWC is actually two separate government agencies organized under the U.S. and Mexican foreign ministries. Given this division, and the organizations' preference for formal diplomatic protocol, the IBWC does not offer binational political opportunities for non-state actors.

3. It should also be mentioned, however, that both the Laredo-based Frank M. Tejeda Center and the San Marcos–based Texas Watch have worked with Nuevo Laredo's municipal government.

4. The term "Minute" is given to agreements between the U.S. and Mexican sections of the IBWC.

5. See *People of the State of California v. Arturo Duran*, U.S. District Court for the Southern District of California, case no. 01-CV-0270-BTM(JFS), December 6, 2004.

6. This conclusion might be surprising given Kay's finding (2005) that a similar labor institution created under the side agreements to the NAFTA, the North American Agreement on Labor Cooperation (NAALC), does in fact produce binational cooperation. Although both institutions lack teeth, the NAALC differs from the CEC in that it requires that labor complaints be filed in a NAFTA country *other* than the one where the alleged violation occurred. This rule forces labor unions to develop cross-border ties to file submissions. Binational collaboration is an unintended consequence.

7. In fact, the Mexican and U.S. public representatives on the BECC's old board of directors often found themselves on opposing sides of disputes. In 2004, the BECC board of directors was merged with the NADB board, and new public representatives were not appointed until 2006.

8. BECCnet can be accessed at http://udallcenter.Arizona.edu/ programs/usmex/beccnet/index.html. Lara (1999) has argued that the impact of the BECC, NADB, and the CEC on cross-border civil society cooperation has been profound, albeit indirect. He suggests institutional reforms have created a climate that encourages binational thinking.

9. EPA funding rules would later be amended, allowing the agency to use the BECC as a pass-through to fund Mexican organizations without a U.S. partner.

10. In 2006, Rincon left Environmental Defense to work for the Environmental Protection Agency.

Chapter 6. The Other Border

1. Combining for-profit corporations with the businessmen and -women who run them is potentially confusing: studies of the nonprofit sector in the United States often distinguish between individual and corporate philanthropy (Useem 1987). Both conceptualizations are potentially problematic because philanthropy includes much more than contributions from economic elites, but a contribution from a wealthy businesswoman, for example, is not necessarily analytically distinct from a contribution from her company. Although I am concerned with the issue of philanthropy more generally, focusing on the business community offers methodological advantages over examining the whole universe of philanthropic support, even as it avoids limiting the study to solely corporate philanthropy.

2. On the other hand, scandals have periodically damaged the legitimacy of the nonprofit sector in the United States as well. Recently, the United Way came under fire for paying exceedingly high salaries and retirement benefits to its leadership, and the Red Cross was criticized for its mismanagement of September 11 relief funds. Still the legitimacy of the sector stands high among the U.S. public (for a discussion, see Lenkowsky 2002, 54–57).

3. As can be seen in the study's tabulated data, not all fifty-seven study organizations responded to certain requests for information, and several participants could not be reached for a second interview. I was also unable to obtain accurate financial data about the organizations, and as a result no precise financial data are presented.

4. The distinction between *empresarios* (businesspeople) and *profesionistas* (professionals) is well accepted in Mexico and emerged through pilot surveys.

5. In the cities studied, of twelve civil society organizations having close ties to the for-profit sector, five are rooted in the business community: Fundación del Empresariado Chihuahuense (FECHAC) and Plan Estratégico de Juárez in Ciudad Juárez; Asociación de Profesionales de Seguridad Ambiental (APSA) and Fundación del Empresariado Sonorense (FESAC) in Nogales; and Consejo de Desarrollo Económico de Tijuana in Tijuana. The remaining seven serve in coalitions with the business community: Grupo Promotor Parque Río Bravo (GPPRP) and Paso del Norte Water Task Force in Ciudad Juárez; the Ambos Nogales Revegetation Partnership (ARAN) in Nogales; the Comité Regional de Vigilancia y Protección al Medio Ambiente, Consejo Coordinador Ciudadano (CCC), and Consejo de Institutiones de Nuevo Laredo in Nuevo Laredo; and the Tijuana River Watershed Binational Vision Project in Tijuana.

6. Among 41 respondents asked whether they strongly agreed, agreed, disagreed, or strongly disagreed that the private sector had interests in common with organizations like theirs, the association between those disagreeing or strongly disagreeing and those working for an environmental organization or directly on an environmental contamination issue is statistically significant: .543 (p < .001), as measured using a Kendall's Tau-c.

7. Nonetheless, it should be noted that greenwashing is present in the region. Low-

intensity activities in the policy arena without nonprofit partnerships appear more likely to be motivated by greenwashing. For example, many maquiladoras and domestic businesses participate in government-initiated environmental education fairs. These businesses pay to set up booths at environmental fairs and hire young personable staff to conduct environmental activities with students; the fairs allow them to associate their names with an environmental cause through low-intensity, low-impact activities.

8. Of 44 respondents asked whether foreign businesses such as maquiladoras or Mexican businesses are more supportive of civil society organizations, 19 (43 percent) said Mexican; 14 (32 percent) said foreign; 7 (16 percent) said both equally; and 4 (9 percent) said neither.

9. Some respondents argued, however, that even though domestic businesses may have more ties to nonprofits, the *amount* that maquiladoras give them in donations is actually greater. For these respondents, maquiladoras support civil society continuously, as a matter of company policy, whereas domestic businesses do so only occasionally and unreliably. Thus FESAC, though started by Mexican businesspeople in Nogales, draws a majority of its financial support from maquiladoras.

10. Among 59 respondents, the association between organizations with DA status and financial or in-kind support from the business community is statistically significant: .401 (p = .001), as measured using a Kendall's Tau-b.

11. It was not until 2003 that most environmental organizations were eligible for authorized donee (DA) status (for a discussion, see Castro Salinas 2001).

12. Established after the bulk of research in Tijuana, CIGA was not included in the main portion of this study.

Chapter 7. Continuity and Change

1. Tamaulipas eventually did pass an access-to-information law in late 2004.

2. The data for chapter 7 are drawn from interviews with government officials from these agencies, totaling 57, and with representatives of the study's 72 nonprofit organizations. They are also supplemented by archival research and observation at public meetings. Although my focus is on relations between government officials and nonprofit organizations, most political opportunities are available to any Mexican resident. I therefore will often use the term "civil society" rather than "civil society organizations" to refer both to the formal organizations and to concerned citizens who make use of such opportunities. Several questions explored in the study are limited to only 48 of the interviewed organizations and exclude nonrespondents, several participants who could not be reached for a second interview, and many of the professional organizations. Additional fieldwork on the persistence of clientelism in low-income communities, discussed in chapter 2, was conducted at the colonia level and includes interviews with 11 of Asociación de Colonias Populares (ACOPO; Association of Popular Colonias) neighborhood presidents in Nuevo Laredo and with 25 neighborhood committee leaders in Ciudad Juárez. It also benefits from an unpublished survey of 127 Tijuana

neighborhood committee leaders administered by the Comisión de Planeación y Desarrollo Municipal (COPLADEM; Municipal Commission for Planning and Development) and my interviews with 24 of these respondents.

As also discussed in chapter 2, the COPLADEM survey has methodological limitations that warrant repeating. The main concern is that the survey was not anonymous. Given that it was administered by the municipality, on which the neighborhood committees were dependent, there were incentives to manipulate responses. Moreover, survey questionnaires were filled out by those committee leaders who attended meetings convened by COPLADEM and therefore are not a random sample of the existing committees. Nonetheless there are still insights to be gleaned from the survey. The specific questions used in this study are less apt to have been affected by the survey's methodological flaws; respondents faced reduced incentives to falsely report their opinions in the one-on-one interviews I conducted.

3. Some evidence from the twenty-five Ciudad Juárez neighborhood committees examined in this study also supports this claim.

4. Unfortunately, the Nogales street-paving project would later run into serious financing and implementation problems.

5. In fact, Articles 6 and 8 of the Mexican constitution had already guaranteed the public the right to government information, although, absent implementing legislation, they had never been enforced.

6. As for the sites themselves, only Nuevo Laredo had taken a significant step toward greater transparency (as noted in section 7.2): it made detailed financial information available on the city's Web site. Moreover, many of the state and municipal transparency laws enacted since the research period have not passed critical muster (McVea 2005). And enactment of even a well-drafted law is not, in itself, enough; only eleven states have enacted implementing legislation (IFAI 2006).

7. Recognizing the potential of Tijuana's growing nonprofit sector, the city's social development agency maintained a directory of nonprofit organizations and regularly referred citizens to these civil society initiatives.

8. Unfortunately, the Strategic Plan of Juárez has encountered some difficulties in actually obtaining the full amount of committed support.

9. Ciudad Juárez's IMIP would later become severely marginalized by future municipal administrations.

10. Although new to Chihuahua, such a governing council would not be new to Mexico. Essentially, the legislation sought to institutionalize institutions of private assistance (IAPs), which are under the strict control of the Private Assistance Board (JAP), making them mandatory. As discussed in chapter 1, the IAP system, created in 1899 by the government of Porfirio Díaz, allows for the creation of a philanthropic sector while maintaining control over private philanthropic initiatives. Interview respondents in civil society viewed the proposed legislation as a blatant attempt to rein in the sector.

11. CONAGUA convened watershed councils (consejos de cuenca) throughout Mexico. Public participation in these has, however, been plagued by jurisdictional

conflict between CONAGUA and the CILA (the Mexican section of the International Boundary and Water Commission; Brown and Mumme 2000). Although a Rio Grande/ Río Bravo watershed council was formally convened in 1999, no members of civil society interviewed for this study participated on the council. After publicly committing itself to creating public participation committees in 2003, CILA backed away from its commitment.

Chapter 8. Networks and the Art of Association

1. Victor Lichtinger Waisman's admission was made at an informal lecture at the Center for U.S.–Mexican Studies of the University of California, San Diego, on October 25, 2004.

References

Abramson, Alan J., and Rachel McCarthy. 2002. Infrastructure Organizations. In *The State of Nonprofit America*, edited by L. M. Salamon. Washington, DC: Brookings Institution Press.

Adler, Glenn, and Jonny Steinberg, eds. 2000. *From Comrades to Citizens: The South African Civics Movement and the Transition to Democracy.* New York: St. Martin's Press; Albert Einstein Institution.

Alegría O., Tito, and Gerardo Ordóñez B. 2002. *Regularización de la tenencia de la tierra y consolidación urbana en Tijuana, B.C.* Tijuana: Tijuana Trabaja, Consejo de Desarrollo Economico de Tijuana A.C., El Colegio de la Frontera Norte.

Alfie Cohen, Miriam. 2002. Imágenes de ONG ambientalistas en la frontera México-Estados Unidos. *Frontera Norte* 14 (27): 83–122.

Almond, Gabriel A., and Sidney Verba. 1963. *The Civic Culture: Political Attitudes and Democracy in Five Nations.* Princeton, NJ: Princeton University Press.

Alvarez, Sonia E., Dagnino Evelina, and Arturo Escobar. 1998. Introduction: The Cultural and the Political in Latin American Social Movements. In *Cultures of Politics, Politics of Cultures: Re-Visioning Latin American Social Movements*, edited by Sonia E. Alvarez, Dagnino Evelina, and Arturo Escobar. Boulder, CO: Westview Press.

Angulo, Cesar. 2004. Crossborder Organizing to Save the Colorado River Delta. Interhemispheric Resource Center.

Arato, Andrew. 1981. Civil Society against the State. *Telos* 47:23–47.

Austin, James, Ezequiel Reficco, and SEKN Research Team. 2004a. The Key Collaboration Questions. In *Social Partnering in Latin America: Lessons Drawn from Collaboration of Business and Civil Society Organizations*, edited by James Austin et al. Cambridge, MA: David Rockefeller Center for Latin American Studies, Harvard University.

———. 2004b. Building Cross-Sector Bridges. In *Social Partnering in Latin America: Lessons Drawn from Collaborations of Businesses and Civil Society Organizations*, edited by James Austin et al. Cambridge, MA: David Rockefeller Center Series on Latin American Studies, Harvard University.

Axelrod, Robert. 1986. An Evolutionary Approach to Norms. *American Political Science Review* 80 (4): 1095–1111.

Aziz, Alberto. 1987. Electoral Practices and Democracy in Chihuahua. In *Electoral Patterns and Perspectives in Mexico*, edited by A. Alvarado. La Jolla, CA: Center for U.S.–Mexican Studies.

Bailey, Michael. 1999. Fundraising in Brazil: The Major Implications for Civil Society Organisations and International NGO's. *Development in Practice* 9 (1–2): 103–117.

Bandow, Doug. 1993. Environmentalists: The New Nattering Nabobs of Negativism. *Business and Society Review* 84:24–28.

Bandy, Joe. 2004. Paradoxes of Transnational Civil Societies under Neoliberalism: The Coalition for Justice in the Maquiladoras. *Social Problems* 51 (3): 410–431.

Barber, Benjamin. 1996. Strengthening Democracy by Creating Civil Society. Paper read at the Independent Sector Conference on Civil Society, Washington, D.C., September 5.

Barkin, David. 1998. *Wealth, Poverty and Sustainable Development*. Mexico City: Editorial Jus, Centro de Ecología y Desarrollo.

———. 1999. *The Greening of Business in Mexico*. Geneva: United Nations Research Institute for Social Development.

Bejarano, Fernando. 2002. Mexico–U.S. Environmental Partnerships. In *Cross Border Dialogues: U.S.–Mexico Social Movement Networking*, edited by J. Fox and D. Brooks. La Jolla, CA: Center for U.S.–Mexican Studies.

Ben-Ner, A., and T. Van Hoomissen. 1992. An Empirical Investigation of the Joint Determination of the Size of the For-Profit, Nonprofit and Voluntary Sectors. *Annals of Public and Cooperative Economics* 63:391–413.

Bennett, Vivienne. 1995. *The Politics of Water: Urban Protest, Gender, and Power in Monterrey, Mexico*. Pittsburgh: University of Pittsburgh Press.

Bernhard, Michael. 1993. Civil Society and Democratic Transition in East Central Europe. *Political Science Quarterly* 108 (2): 307–326.

Biekart, Kees. 2004. The Reality of Sustainability: The Survival of Civil Society Organisations in Latin America after the Withdrawal of International Aid. Paper read at ISTR (International Society for Third-Sector Research) Sixth International Conference, Toronto, July 11–14.

Birdsall, Nancy, and David Wheeler. 1993. Trade Policy and Industrial Pollution in Latin America: Where Are the Pollution Havens? *Journal of Environment and Development* 2 (1): 137.

Bizberg, Ilán. 2003. Transition or Restructuring Society. In *Mexico's Politics and Society in Transition*, edited by J. S. Tulchin and A. D. Selee. Boulder, CO: Lynne Rienner Publishers.

Blau, Peter Michael. 1964. *Exchange and Power in Social Life*. New York: Wiley.

Border Environment Cooperation Commission (BECC). n.d. *Project Certification Criteria*. http://www.cocef.org/Certification—criteria.pdf (accessed January 16, 2005).

———. 2004. *Mejoras al Sistema de Agua Potable y Alcantarillado de Nuevo Laredo, Tamaulipas*. http://www.cocef.org/aproyectos/ExcomNuevoLaredo2004—07esp.pdf (accessed February 13, 2007).

Brooks, David, and Jonathan Fox, eds. 2002. Cross-Border Dialogues: U.S.–Mexico Social Movement *Networking*. La Jolla, CA: Center for U.S.–Mexican Studies.

Brown, Christopher, José Luis Castro Ruiz, Nancy Lowery, and Richard Wright. 2003. Comparative Analysis of Transborder Water Management Strategies: Case Studies on the U.S.–Mexico Border. In *The U.S.–Mexico Border Environment: Binational Water Management Planning*, edited by S. Michel. San Diego: San Diego State University Press.

Brown, Christopher, and Stephen P. Mumme. 2000. Applied and Theoretical Aspects of Binational Watershed Councils (Consejos de Cuencas) in the U.S.–Mexico Borderlands. *Natural Resources Journal* 40 (2): 895–929.

Browning-Aiken, Anne, Holly Richter, David Goodrich, Bob Strain, and Robert Varady. 2004. Upper San Pedro Basin: Fostering Collaborative Binational Watershed Management. *Water Resources Development* 20 (3): 353–367.

Burdick, John. 2004. *Legacies of Liberation: The Progressive Catholic Church in Brazil at the Start of the New Milennium*. Burlington, VT: Ashgate.

Burt, Ronald S. 1990. Kinds of Relations in American Discussion Networks. In *Structures of Power and Constraint*, edited by C. Calhoun, M. W. Meyer and W. R. Scott. New York: Cambridge University Press.

———. 1992. *Structural Holes: The Social Structure of Competition*: Harvard University Press.

Camp Dresser & McKee Inc. 2003. *Plan Maestro de Agua Potable y Saneamiento en los Municipios de Tijuana y Playas de Rosarito*. Carlsbad, CA: Camp Dresser & McKee Inc.

Cardoso, Fernando, and Enzo Faletto. 1979. *Dependency and Development in Latin America*. Berkeley: University of California Press.

Carillo Gamboa, Emilio. 1997. Mexico. In *The International Guide to Nonprofit Law*, edited by L. M. Salamon. New York: Wiley.

Carothers, Thomas, and William Barndt. 2000. Civil Society. *Foreign Policy* 117:18–29.

Castleman, Barry. 1987. Workplace Health in Developing Countries. In *Multinational Corporations, Environment, and Third World: Business Matters*, edited by C. S. Pearson. Dirham, NC: Duke University Press.

Castro Salinas, Consuelo. 2001. Mexico. In *El tercer sector Iberoamericano: Fundaciones, asociaciones, y ONG's*, edited by J. L. Piñar Mañas and R. Sánchez Rivera. Valencia: Tirant lo Blanch.

Centro Mexicano para la Filantropía (CEMEFI). 1996. Understanding Mexican Philanthropy. In *Changing Structure of Mexico: Political, Social and Economic Prospects*, edited by L. Randall. Armonia, New York: M. E. Sharpe.

Chalmers, Douglas A., and Kerianne Piester. 1995. NGO's and the Changing Structure of Mexican Politics. In *Changing Structure of Mexico: Political, Social, and Economic Prospects*, edited by L. Randall. Armonk, NY: M. E. Sharpe.

Chand, Vikram. 2001. *Mexico's Political Awakening*. Notre Dame, IN: University of Notre Dame Press.

Clark, Dana, Jonathan Fox, and Kay Treakle, eds. 2003. *Demanding Accountability: Civil society Claims and the World Bank Inspection Panel*. Lanham, MD: Rowman and Littlefield.

Claudio, Javier. 2004. Aseguran Lluvias Agua por 5 Años. *El Mañana*, April 13, 2B.

Clement, Norris C. 2002. *The U.S.–Mexican Border Environment: U.S.–Mexican Border Communities in the NAFTA Era*. Vol. 4. SCERP Monograph Series. San Diego: San Diego State University Press.

Coleman, James. 1988. Social Capital in the Creation of Human Capital. *American Journal of Sociology* 94:95–120.

Commission for Environmental Cooperation (CEC). 2002. *Metales y Derivados Final Factual Record*. SEM-98-007. Montreal.

———. 2003. *Public Access to Government-Held Environmental Information*. Quebec: Editions Yvon Blais.

Cook, Karen S. 1977. Exchange and Power in Networks of Interorganizational Relations. *Sociological Quarterly* 18:62–81.

Cook, María Lorena, Kevin J. Middlebrook, and Juan Molinar Horcasitas. 1994. The Politics of Economic Restructuring in Mexico: Actors, Sequencing, and Coalition Change. In *The Politics of Economic Restructuring: State-Society Relations and Regime Change in Mexico*, edited by M. L. Cook, K. J. Middlebrook, and J. Molinar Horcasitas. La Jolla, CA: Center for U.S.–Mexican Studies.

Corbin, John Joseph. 1999. A Study of Factors Influencing the Growth of Nonprofits in Social Services. *Nonprofit and Voluntary Sector Quarterly* 28 (3): 296–314.

Córdova Bojórquez, Gustavo. 2003a. La gobernación del agua en Ciudad Juárez. Paper read at Congreso de la Red Nacional de Investigación Urbana, Puebla, September 22–26.

———. 2003b. Proyecto de tesis: Aqua y participación social en Ciudad Juárez. Ciudad Juárez.

Corliss, Donovan. 2000. Regulating the Border Environment: Toxics, Maquiladoras, and the Public Right to Know. In *Shared Spaces: Rethinking the U.S.–Mexico Border Environment*, edited by L. Herzog. La Jolla, CA: Center for U.S.–Mexican Studies.

Cornelius, Wayne A. 1975. *Politics and the Migrant Poor in Mexico City*. Stanford, CA: Stanford University Press.

Cornelius, Wayne A., Ann L. Craig, and Jonathan Fox, eds. 1994. *Transforming State-Society Relations: The National Solidarity Strategy, U.S.–Mexico Contemporary Perspectives Series 6*. La Jolla, CA: Center for U.S.–Mexican Studies.

CorpWatch. 2001. *Greenwash Fact Sheet*. http://www.corpwatch.org/article.php?id=242 (accessed December 16, 2004).

Craig, Ann L., and Wayne A. Cornelius. 1980. Political Culture in Mexico: Continuities and Revisionist Interpretations. In *The Civic Culture Revisited*, edited by G. A. Almond and S. Verba. Boston: Little, Brown.

Crawford, Sue E. S., and Elinor Ostrom. 1995. A Grammar of Institutions. *The American Political Science Review* 89 (3): 582–600.

Davis, Gina, and Elinor Ostrom. 1991. A Public Economy Approach to Education: Choice and Coproduction. *International Political Science Review* 12 (4): 313–335.

Delgado, Hector. 2000. Democracia y gobernabilidad en una experiencia local: El caso de Ciudad Juárez visto desde la perspectiva de la clase política. In *Transición democrática y gobernabilidad: México y America Latina*, edited by J. Labatista, M. del Campo, A. Camou, and N. Lujan Ponce. Mexico City: Plaza y Vades, Facultad Latinoamericano de Ciuencias Sociales, Instituto de Investigación Social UNAM.

de Mello Lemos, María Carmen, and Antonio Luna. 1999. Public Participation in the BECC: Lessons from the Acuaférico Project, Nogales, Sonora. *Journal of Borderlands Studies* 14 (1): 43–64.

Desarrollo Social Municipal. 2003. *Directorio de organismos de la sociedad civil*. Tijuana: H. Ayuntamiento de Tijuana.

Dewey, John. 1927. *The Public and Its Problems*. Athens: Swallow Press, Ohio University Press.

Diamond, Larry. 1999. *Developing Democracy: Toward Consolidation*. Baltimore: John Hopkins University Press.

El Diario. 1984a. No Me Han Destituido Aún: PPI. February 23.

———. 1984b. Primero Lider Sindical; Ahora Prospero Empresario. February 24.

Douglas, James. 1983. *Why Charity?* Beverly Hills, CA: Sage.

Duenas, Ruben. 1984. Pedro Pretende Paralizar Tamaulipas. *El Diario*, February 24.

Eckstein, Harry. 1988. A Culturalist Theory of Political Change. *American Political Science Review* 82 (3): 789–804.

Eckstein, Susan. 1990. Formal vs. Substantive Democracy. *Mexican Studies / Estudios Mexicanos* 6:213–234.

———. 2001. Poor People Versus the State and Capital: Anatomy of a Successful Community Mobilization for Housing in Mexico City. In *Power and Popular Protest: Latin American Social Movements*, edited by S. Eckstein. Berkeley: University of California Press.

Ellickson, Robert C. 1998. Law and Economics Discovers Social Norms. *Journal of Legal Studies* 27 (2): 537–552.

Environmental Education Exchange. 2000. *Border Environmental Education Resource Guide*. Tucson, AZ: Environmental Education Exchange.

Environmental Protection Agency (EPA) and Secretaría de Medio Ambiente y Recursos Naturales (SEMARNAT). 2003. *Border 2012: U.S.–Mexico Environmental Program*. Washington, DC: Environmental Protection Agency.

Esman, Milton, J., and Norman Thomas Uphoff. 1984. *Local Organizations: Intermediaries in Rural Development*. Ithaca, NY: Cornell University Press.

Espinoza Valle, Víctor Alejandro. 2000. *Alternancia política y gestión pública: El Partido Acción Nacional en el gobierno de Baja California*. Tijuana: El Colegio de la Frontera Norte and Plaza y Valdes Editores.

Ewig, Christina. 1999. The Strengths and Limits of the NGO Women's Movement Model: Shaping Nicaragua's Democratic Insitutions. *Latin American Research Review* 34 (3): 75–102.

Fehrenbach, T. R. 1995. *Fire and Blood: A History of Mexico*. Reprint, New York: Da Capo Press.

Finnemore, Martha, and Kathryn Sikkink. 1998. International Norm Dynamics and Political Change. *International Organization* 52 (4): 887–917.

Fischer, Claude S. 1982. *To Dwell among Friends: Personal Networks in Town and City*. Chicago: University of Chicago Press.

Flores, Ricardo. 2004. Llaman a Rechazar el Aumento al Agua. *El Mañana*, May 23, 7B.

Foley, Michael W., and Bob Edwards. 1996. The Paradox of Civil Society. *Journal of Democracy* 7 (3): 38–52.

Foley, Michael W., and Virginia A. Hodgkinson. 2003. Introduction. In *The Civil Society Reader*, edited by V. A. Hodgkinson and M. W. Foley. Lebanon, NH: University Press of New England.

Forment, Carlos. 2003. *Democracy in Latin America, 1760–1900*. Vol. 1: *Civic Selfhood and Public Life in Mexico and Peru*. Chicago: University of Chicago Press.

Foster, Vivien. 1996. *Policy Issues for the Water and Sanitation Sectors*. Washington, DC: Inter-American Development Bank.

Fox, Claire F. 1999. *The Fence and the River: Culture and Politics and the U.S.–Mexico Border*. Minneapolis: University of Minnesota Press.

Fox, Jonathan. 1994. The Difficult Transition from Clientelism to Citizenship: Lessons from Mexico. *World Politics* 46 (2).

———. 2002. Lessons from Civil Society Coalitions. In *Cross-Border Dialogues: U.S.–Mexico Social Movement Networking*, edited by D. Brooks and J. Fox. La Jolla, CA: Center for U.S.–Mexican Studies.

Frank, Andre Gunder. 1967. *Capitalism and Underdevelopment in Latin America*. New York: Monthly Review Press.

Fry, Louis W., Gerald D. Keim, and Roger E. Meiners. 1982. Corporate Contributions: Altruistic of For-Profit? *Academy of Management Journal* 25 (1): 94–106.

Fundación del Empresariado Chihuahuense A.C. (FECHAC). 2000. *Directorio de las organizaciones de la sociedad civil de Chihuahua*. Chihuahua City.

———. 2002. *Ver con nuestros ojos: Informe de actividades 2001–2002*. http://www .fundacion.org.mx/pdf/informe2002.pdf (accessed April 18, 2005).

———. 2006. Juntos haciendo caminos: Informe de actividades 2005. Chihuahua City: Fundación del Empresariado Chihuahuense A.C.

Fundación del Empresariado Sonorense A.C. (FESAC). 2003. *FESAC–Nogales Directorio de las organizaciones de la sociedad, 2003–2004*. Nogales, Sonora: Fundación del Empresariado Sonorense A.C.

Gaberman, Barry. 2003. Building the Global Infrastructure for Philanthropy. Paper read at Waldemar A. Nielsen Issues in Philanthropy Seminar Series, Washington, D.C., April 11.

Galaskiewicz, Joseph. 1979. *Exchange Networks and Community Politics*: Sage.

———. 1985. Interorganizational Relations. *Annual Review of Sociology* 11:281–304.

Galaskiewicz, Joseph, and D. Shatin. 1981. Leadership and Networking among Neighborhood Human Service Organization. *Administrative Science Quarterly* 26:434–448.

García, Connie, and Amelia Simpson. 2004. *Globalization at the Crossroads: Ten Years of NAFTA in the San Diego / Tijuana Border.* San Diego: Environmental Health Coalition.

García, Jesús. 1984. La Iglesia mexicana desde 1962. In *Historia general de la Iglesia en America Latina.* Vol. 5. Mexico City: CEHILA/Sigueme/Paulinas.

García Mata, Víctor. 2005. La planeación urbana en Ciudad Juárez. Paper read at XXVIII Encuentro Red Nacional de Investigación Urbana, Ciudad Juárez, September 22–23.

Garza, Enrique, and José Luis Pariente Fregosa. 2000. La organización estatal y municipal. In *Tamaulipas y los retos del desarrollo,* edited by M. A. Navarro and J. L. Pariente Fregosa. Ciudad Victoria: Universidad Autónoma de Tamaulipas.

Gay, Robert. 1994. *Popular Organization and Democracy in Rio de Janeiro: A Tale of Two Favelas.* Philadelphia: Temple University Press.

Gill, Graeme. 2000. *The Dynamics of Democratization: Elites, Civil Society, and the Transition Process.* New York: St. Martin's Press.

Glenn, John K., III. 2001. *Framing Democracy: Civil Society and Civic Movements in Eastern Europe.* Stanford, CA: Stanford University Press.

Good Neighbor Environmental Board (GNEB). 2005. *Water Resources Management on the U.S.–Mexico Border: Eighth Report to the President and the Congress of the United States.* Washington, DC.

Gould, Roger. 1993. Collective Action and Network Structure. *American Sociological Review* 58 (2): 182–196.

Granovetter, Mark. 1973. The Strength of Weak Ties. *American Journal of Sociology* 78:1360–1390.

———. 1985. Economic Action and Social Structure: The Problem of Embeddedness. *American Journal of Sociology* 91 (3): 481–510.

Grønbjerg, Kirsten. 1993. *Understanding Nonprofit Funding: Managing Revenues in Social Services and Community Development Organizations.* San Francisco: Jossey-Bass.

Grønbjerg, Kirsten, and Laurie Paarlberg. 2001. Community Variations in the Size and Scope of the Nonprofit Sector: Theory and Preliminary Findings. *Nonprofit and Voluntary Sector Quarterly* 30 (4): 684–706.

Groundwater Users' Advisory Council (GUAC). 1996. Letter to Roger Frauenfelder, Border Environment Cooperation Commission, General Manager. Nogales, February 28.

Guillén López, Tonatiuh. 1996. *Gobiernos municipales en México: Entre la modernización y la tradición política.* Mexico City: El Colegio de la Frontera Norte, Miguel Angel Porrua Grupo Editorial.

———. 2001. Democratic Transition in Baja California: Stages and Actors. In *Party*

Politics and the Struggle for Democracy in Mexico: National and State-Level Analyses of the Partido Acción Nacional, edited by K. J. Middlebrook. La Jolla, CA: Center for U.S.–Mexican Studies.

Gulati, Ranjay, and Martin Gargiulo. 1999. Where Do Interorganizational Networks Come From? *American Journal of Sociology* 104 (5): 1439–1493.

Gutiérrez, Gustavo. 2001. *A Theology of Liberation History, Politics, and Salvation.* New York: SCM Press.

Hall, Peter. 1975. The Model of Boston Charity: A Theory of Charitable Benevolence and Class Development. *Science and Society* 38 (4): 464–477.

———. 2001. Historical Perspectives on the Nonprofit Sector. In *The Nonprofit Sector: A Research Handbook*, edited by Walter W. Powell. New Haven, CT: Yale University Press.

Hall, Robert E., and Charles I. Jones. 1999. Why Do Some Countries Produce So Much More Output per Worker than Others? *Quarterly Journal of Economics* 114 (1): 83–116.

Hansmann, H. 1987. Economic Theories of Nonprofit Organizations. In *The Nonprofit Sector: A Research Handbook*, edited by Walter W. Powell. New Haven, CT: Yale University Press.

Hardin, Garrett. 1968. The Tragedy of the Commons. *Science* 162:1243–1248.

H. Ayuntamiento de Ciudad Juárez. 1994. Reglamento de los Comités de Vecinos del Municipio de Juárez. Ciudad Juárez: Dirección General de Desarrollo Social.

Heckathorn, Douglas D. 1988. Collective Sanctions and the Creation of Prisoner's Dilemma Norms. *American Journal of Sociology* 94(3): 535–562.

Hernández, Luis, and Jonathan Fox. 1995. Mexico's Difficult Democracy: Grassroots Movements, NGOs and Local Government. In *New Paths to Democratic Development in Latin America: The Rise of NGO Municipal Collaboration*, edited by Charles A. Reilly. Boulder, CO: Lynne Rienner.

Herrera, Octavio. 1999. *Breve historia de Tamaulipas.* Mexico City: El Colegio de México.

Herzog, Lawrence A. 1990. *Where North Meets South: Cities, Space, and Politics on the U.S.–Mexico Border.* Austin, TX: Center for Mexican American Studies.

Herzog, Lawrence, ed. 2000. *Shared Space: Rethining the U.S.–Mexico Border Environment.* La Jolla, CA: Center for U.S.–Mexican Studies.

Hill, Sarah. 2000. The Political Ecology of Environmental Learning in Ciudad Juárez and El Paso County. In *Shared Space: Rethinking the U.S.–Mexico Border Environment*, edited by L. Herzog. La Jolla, CA: Center for U.S.–Mexican Studies.

Hodgkinson, Virginia A., and Michael W. Foley, eds. 2003. *The Civil Society Reader.* Lebanon, NH: University Press of New England.

Holzner, Claudio. 2004. The End of Clientelism? Strong and Weak Networks in a Mexican Squatter Movement. *Mobilization: An International Journal* 9 (3): 223–240.

Inglehart, Ronald. 1987. *Culture Shift in Advanced Industrial Society.* Princeton, NJ: Princeton University Press.

Ingram, Helen. 2000. Transboundary Groundwater on the U.S.–Mexico Border: Is the Glass Half Full, Half Empty, or Even on the Table? *Natural Resources Journal* 4 (2): 185–188.

Ingram, Helen, Nancy K. Laney, and David M. Gillilan. 1995. *Divided Waters: Bridging the U.S.–Mexico Border*. Tucson: University of Arizona Press.

Innovative Mexican Regulations for Right to Know about Industrial Pollutants: Challenges and Opportunities for Social Binational Participation. 2003. Paper read at IV Encuentro Fronterizo, Tijuana, May 15–17.

Institute for Regional Studies of the Californias (IRSC) and Department of Geography of San Diego State University (SDSU). 2005. *A Binational Vision for the Tijuana River Watershed*. http://trw.sdsu.edu/English/Publications/draft/Final—ENG—9–16–05—press—4—BODY—APP.pdf.

Instituto Federal de Acceso a la Información Pública (IFAI). 2004. *Transparencia, acceso a la información y datos personales*. Mexico City: Instituto Federal de Acceso a la Información Pública.

———. 2006. *Estudio comparativo de leyes de acceso a la información pública*. http://www.ifai.org.mx/test/eym/Estudio—Comparativo.pdf (accessed February 23, 2007).

Instituto Municipal de Investigación y Planeación (IMPLAN). 2002. *Plan de desarrollo urbano de Ciudad Juárez*. Ciudad Juárez: Instituto Municipal de Investigación y Planeación.

Instituto Nacional de Estadística, Geografía e Informatica (INEGI). 2005. *II Conteo de Población y Vivenda*. http://www.inegi.gob.mx/est/contenidos/espanol/proyectos/conteos/conteo2005/default.asp?c=10215 (accessed November 20, 2007).

International Boundary and Water Commission (IBWC). 2002. *Binational Study Regarding the Intensive Monitoring of the Rio Grande Waters in the Vicinity of Laredo, Texas and Nuevo Laredo, Tamaulipas between the United States and Mexico, November 6–16, 2000*. El Paso.

———. 2004. *Third Phase of the Binational Study Regarding the Presence of Toxic Substances in the Upper Portion of the Rio Grande/Río Bravo between the United States and Mexico*. El Paso.

International Boundary and Water Commission and Texas Clean Rivers Program. 2004. *The Rio Grande Basin Highlights Report*. El Paso.

International Community Foundation (ICF). 2003. *Survey of Baja California Nonprofit Organizations*. San Diego: International Community Foundation.

———. 2006. *Fact Sheet*. http://www.icfdn.org/aboutus/factsheet.htm (accessed February 14, 2006).

Jackman, Robert, and Ross Miller. 2004. *Before Norms: Institutions and Civic Culture*. Ann Arbor: University of Michigan Press.

James, Kellee. 2002. *How CSR and an Entrepreneurial Business Culture Go Hand-in-Hand*. Inter-American Foundation. http://www.iaf.gov/grants/downloads/fechac—eng.pdf (accessed June 12, 2006).

Kay, Tamara. 2005. Labor Transnationalism and Global Goverance: The Impact of NAFTA on Transnational Labor Relationships in North America. *American Journal of Sociology* 111 (3): 715–756.

Keck, Margaret E., and Kathryn Sikkink. 1998. *Activists beyond Borders: Advocacy Networks in International Politics.* Ithaca, NY: Cornell University Press.

Kelly, Mary E. 2002. Cross-Border Work on the Environment: Evolution, Successes, Problems, and Future Outlook. In *Cross-Border Dialogues: U.S.–Mexico Social Movement Networking*, edited by D. Brooks and J. Fox. La Jolla, CA: Center for U.S.–Mexican Studies.

Ketter, Robert. 1998. *Paso del Norte Air Quality Task Force: A Case Study.* El Paso: Environmental Defense Fund, Ford Foundation.

Khalid, Sulaiman. 2004. Donor–NGO Relationship in Northern Nigeria. Paper read at ISTR (International Society for Third-Sector Research) Sixth International Conference, Toronto, July 11–14.

Kiy, Richard, Julieta Mendez, Kenn Morris, Javier H. Valdés, and Rafael Valdez Mingramm. 2005. *Corporate Giving Trends in the U.S.–Mexico Border Region.* San Diego: US-Mexico Border Philanthropy Partnership.

Kollock, Peter. 1994. The Emergence of Exchange Structures: An Experimental Study of Uncertaintly, Commitment, and Trust. *American Journal of Sociology* 100 (313–45).

Kopinak, Kathryn M., and Rocio Barajas. 2002. Too Close for Comfort? The Proximity of Industrial Hazardous Wastes to Local Populations in Tijuana, Baja California. *Journal of Environment and Development* 11 (3): 215–246.

Kotler, Philip, and Nancy Lee. 2004. *Corporate Social Responsibility: Doing the Most Good for Your Company and Cause.* Hoboken, NJ: Wiley.

Krauze, Enrique. 1998. *Mexico: Biography of Power.* New York: Perennial.

Lara, Francisco. 1999. Transboundary Networks for Environmental Management in the San Diego-Tijuana Border Region. In *Shared Space: Rethinking the U.S.–Mexico Border Environment*, edited by L. Herzog. La Jolla, CA: Center for U.S.–Mexican Studies.

———. 2000. Transboundary Networks for Environmental Management in the San Diego-Tijuana Border Region. In *Shared Space: Rethinking the U.S.–Mexico Border Environment*, edited by L. Herzog. La Jolla, CA: Center for U.S.–Mexican Studies.

Lara, María Luisa. 2000. *Filantropía empresarial: Convicción y estrategia.* Mexico City: Editorial Pax Mexico.

Lara Valencia, Francisco, and Roberto Sánchez. 1994. Servicios públicos y movilización social en las ciudades de la frontera: El caso de Nogales, Sonora. *Revista de El Colegio de Sonora* 8:9–30.

Lau, Ruben, and Victor M. Quintana Silveyra. 1991. *Movimientos populares en Chihuahua.* Ciudad Juárez: Universidad Autonoma de Ciudad Juárez.

Layton, Michael. 2004. Funding Sources for Civil Society in Mexico: Constructing a Matrix of Funders and Organizational Typology. Paper read at ISTR (International

Society for Third-Sector Research) Sixth International Conference. Toronto, July 11–14.

——. 2006. ¿Como se paga el capital social? *Foreign Affairs en Español* 6 (2).

Lenkowsky, Leslie. 2002. Foundations and Corporate Philanthropy. In *The State of the Nonprofit America*, edited by L. M. Salamon. Washington, DC: Brookings Institution Press.

Levi, Margaret. 1988. *Of Rule and Revenue*. Berkeley: University of California Press.

Levine, S., and F. P. White. 1961. Exchange as a Conceptual Framework for the Study of Interorganizational Relationships. *Administrative Science Quarterly* 5:583–601.

Lindquist, Diane. 2004. Mexican Agency Warns of Potential for LNG Disaster. *San Diego Union Tribune*, January 23, 1.

Linz, Juan J., and Alfred Stepan. 1996. *Problems of Democratic Transition and Consolidation: Southern Europe, South America, and Post-Communist Europe*. Baltimore: Johns Hopkins University Press.

Liverman, Diana M., Robert G. Varady, Octavio Chávez, and Roberto Sánchez. 1999. Environmental Issues along the United States-Mexico Border: Drivers of Change and Responses of Citizens and Institutions. *Annual Review of Energy and the Environment* 24:607–43.

Loaeza, Soledad. 1985. La Iglesia y la democracia en México. *Revista Mexicana de Sociología* 47 (1): 161–168.

Lohmann, Roger A. 2001. And Lettuce Is Nonanimal: Toward a Positive Economics of Voluntary Action. In *The Nature of the Nonprofit Sector*, edited by J. S. Ott. Boulder, CO: Westview Press.

López González, José Luis. 1998. *Sinopsis del movimiento obrero en Nuevo Laredo: FTNL-CTM*. Nuevo Laredo: Talleres del RO-AL Impresores.

Lowi, Theodore. 1964. American Business, Public Policy, Case-Studies, and Political Theory. *World Politics* July:677–715.

Lozano Fernandez, Norma Yadira. 2001. La participación ciudadana en el proceso de planeación urbana: El caso de las colonias López Mateos y Díaz Ordaz en Ciudad Juárez, Chihuahua. Master's thesis, Instituto de Ciencias Sociales y Administración, Universidad Autónoma de Ciudad Juárez.

Mabry, Donald. 1982. *The Mexican University and State-Student Conflicts: 1910–1971*. College Station: Texas A&M University Press.

El Mañana. 2004. Cisterna Eterna. January 16, 1B.

Marsden, Peter V. 1987. Core Discussion Networks of Americans. *American Sociological Review* 52(1): 122–131.

Marsh, F. K. 1995. *The State of Nonprofit Deteroit: Facts, Figures, and Agendas*. Detroit: Wayne State University.

Martínez, Marcos. 2004. Alza, Fuera de Realidad. *El Mañana*, May 14, 1B.

Martínez, Oscar J. 1994. *Border People: Life and Society in the U.S.–Mexico Borderlands*. Tucson: University of Arizona Press.

——. 1997. Border People and Their Cultural Roles: The Case of the U.S.–Mexican

Borderlands. In *Borders and Border Regions in Europe and North America*, edited by P. Ganster, A. Sweedler, J. Scott, and W. Dieter-Eberwein. San Diego: San Diego State University.

McCarthy, John D., and Mayer N. Zald. 1973. *The Trend of Social Movements in America: Professionalization and Resource Mobilization*. Morristown, NJ: General Learning Press.

———. 1977. Resource Mobilization and Social Movements: A Partial Theory. *American Journal of Sociology* 82 (6): 1212–1241.

McVea, Denise. 2005. Local Transparency Still Opaque for Many Mexican Communities. Silver City, NM: International Relations Center.

Medina, Martin. 2000. Low-Tech Option for Wastewater. *BioCycle International* October:66–69.

Michel, Suzanne. 2000. Place and Water Quality Politics. In *Shared Spaces: Rethinking the US-Meixco Border Environment*, edited by L. Herzog. La Jolla, CA: Center for U.S.–Mexican Studies.

———, ed. 2003. *The U.S.–Mexican Border Environment: Binational Water Planning*. San Diego: San Diego State University Press.

Middleton, Melissa. 1987. Nonprofit Boards of Directors: Beyond the Governance Function. In *The Nonprofit Sector: A Research Handbook*, edited by Walter W. Powell. New Haven, CT: Yale University Press.

Mitchell, Kenneth Edward. 2001. *State-Society Relations in Mexico: Clientelism, Neoliberal State Reform, and the Case of CONASUPO*. Burlington, VT: Ashgate.

Mizrahi, Yemile. 2003. *From Martyrdom to Power*. Notre Dame, IN: University of Notre Dame Press.

Montero, Alfred P., and David J. Samuels. 2004. The Political Determinants of Decentralization in Latin America: Causes and Consequences. In *Decentralization and Democracy in Latin America*, edited by A. P. Montero and D. J. Samuels. Notre Dame, IN: University of Notre Dame Press.

Moreno, Alejandro. 2002. Corruption and Democracy: A Cultural Assessment. *Comparative Sociology* 1 (3–4): 495–507.

Morris, Aldon. 1981. Black Southern Student Sit-In Movement: An Analyis of Internal Organization. *American Sociological Review* 46 (6): 744–767.

Mumme, Stephen P. 2000a. Sustainable Development and Environmental Decentralization on the Border: Insights from Sonora. In *Shared Spaces: Rethinking the U.S.–Mexico Border Environment*, edited by L. Herzog. La Jolla, CA: Center for U.S.–Mexican Studies.

———. 2000b. Minute 242 and Beyond: Challenges and Opportunities for Managing Transboundary Groundwater on the Mexico–U.S. Border. *Natural Resources Journal* 40 (2): 341–378.

———. 2004. El 60 aniversario del Tratado de Aguas de 1944: Logros y reformas requeridas. *Boletín del Archivo Histórico del Agua* 9 (May–August).

Mumme, Stephen P., and Christopher Brown. 2002. Decentralizing Water Policy on the

Border. In *Protecting a Sacred Gift: Water and Social Change in Mexico*, edited by S. Whiteford and R. Melville. La Jolla, CA: Center for U.S.–Mexican Studies.

Muro González, Víctor Gabriel. 1994. *Iglesia y movimientos sociales en México, 1972–1987: Los casos de Ciudad Juárez y el Istmo de Tehuantepec.* Mexico City: Red Nacional de Investigación Urbana; El Colegio de Michoacán.

Mutz, Diana. 2002. Cross-Cutting Social Networks: Testing Democratic Theory in Practice. *American Political Science Review* 96 (1): 111–126.

Natal, Alejandro. 2002. *Recursos privados para fines públicos: Las instituciones donantes mexicanas.* Mexico City: Synergos Institute, el Centro Mexicano para la Filantropia y el Colegio Mexiquense.

Nogales–Santa Cruz County Chamber of Commerce. 2002. *Nogales.* Nogales, AZ.

North, Douglass. 1990. *Institutions, Institutional Change and Economic Performance.* New York: Cambridge University Press.

Núñez González, Oscar. 1990. *Innovaciones democrático-culturales del movimiento urbano popular: ¿Hacia nuevas culturas locales?* Mexico City: Universidad Autonoma Metropolitana.

Oakerson, Ronald J., and Roger B. Parks. 1988. Citizen Voice and Public Entrepreneurship: The Organization Dynamic of a Complex Metropolitan County. *Publius: Journal of Federalism* 18 (4): 91–112.

Oberschall, A. 1973. *Social Conflict and Social Movement.* Englewood Cliffs, NJ: Prentice-Hall.

O'Connell, Brian. 2000. Civil Society: Definitions and Descriptions. *Nonprofit and Voluntary Sector Quarterly* 29 (3): 471–478.

Olson, Mancur. 1965. *The Logic of Collective Action.* Cambridge, MA: Harvard University Press.

Olvera Rivera, Alberto. 2001. *Movimientos sociales pro-democráticos, democratización y esfera pública en México: El caso de Alianza Civica, sociedad civil y gobernabilidad en México.* Mexico City: Universidad Veracruzana.

———. 2004. Civil Society in Mexico at Century's End. In *Dilemmas of Political Change in Mexico*, edited by K. J. Middlebrook. London: Institute of Latin American Studies; La Jolla, CA: Center for U.S.–Mexican Studies.

Ostrom, Elinor. 1965. Public Entrepreneurship: A Case Study in Groundwater Basin Management. Ph.D. diss., University of California, Los Angeles.

———. 1990. *Governing the Commons.* New York: Cambridge University Press.

———. 1996. Crossing the Great Divide: Coproduction, Synergy, and Development. *World Development* 24 (6): 1073–87.

———. 1999. Institutional Rational Choice: An Assessment of the Institutional Analysis and Development Framework. In *Theories of the Policy Process*, edited by P. Sabatier. Boulder, CO: Westview Press.

Ostrom, Elinor, Roy Gardner, and James Walker. 1994. *Rules, Games, and Common-Pool Resources.* Ann Arbor: University of Michigan Press.

Ostrom, Elinor, Roger B. Parks, and Gordon P. Whitaker. 1973. Do We Really Want to

Consolidate Urban Police Forces? A Reappraisal of Some Old Assertions. *Public Administration Review* 33 (5): 423–432.

Ostrom, Elinor, Larry Schroeder, and Susan Wynne. 1993. *Institutional Incentives and Sustainable Development: Infrastructure Policies in Perspective*. Boulder, CO: Westview Press.

Ozuna, Teofila, Jr., and Irma Adriana Gomez. 1998. *Regulation, Organization, and Incentives: The Political Economy of Potable Water Services in Mexico*. Washington, DC: Banco Interamericano de Desarrollo.

Padilla Delgado, Hector. 2000. Democracia y gobernabilidad en una experiencia local: El caso de Ciudad Juárez visto desde la perspectiva de la clase política. In *Transición democrática y gobernabilidad: México y America Latina*, edited by J. Labatista, M. del Campo, A. Camou, and N. Lujan Ponce. Mexico City: Plaza y Vades, Facultad Latinoamericano de Ciuencias Sociales, Instituto de Investigación Social UNAM.

Parsons Engineering. 2002. *Sistema de agua potable de Nuevo Laredo, Tamaulipas: Informe de diagnóstico, modelaje, y expansión: Preparado para United States Section, IBWC*.

———. 2004. *Draft Supplemental Environmental Impact Statement: Clean Water Act Compliance at the South Bay International Wastewater Treatment Plant*. Pasadena, CA: Parsons Engineering.

Paz, Octavio. 1979. *El ogro filantropico: Historia y política (1971–1978)*. Mexico City: Joaquín Mortiz.

Peña, Devon Gerardo. 1997. *The Terror of the Machine: Technology, Work, Gender, and Ecology on the U.S.–Mexico Border*. Austin, TX: CMAS Books.

Percy, Stephen. 1981. Citizen Participation in Coproduction of Urban Services. *Urban Affairs Quarterly* 19 (4): 431–446.

Pesenti, Chris, and Kama S. Dean. 2003. Development Challenges on the Baja California Peninsula: The Escalera Náutica. *Journal of Environment and Development* 12 (4): 445–454.

Peterson, George. 1997. *Decentralization in Latin America: Learning through Experience*. Washington, DC: World Bank.

Pezzoli, Keith. 2000. From Pollution Prevention to Industrial Ecology: An Agenda for Research and Practice. In *Shared Spaces: Rethinking the U.S.–Mexico Border Environment*, edited by L. Herzog. La Jolla, CA: Center for U.S.–Mexican Studies.

Pfeffer, Jeffrey. 1973. Size, Composition, and Function of Hospital Boards of Directors: A Study of Organization-Environment Linkages. *Administrative Science Quarterly* 18:349–364.

Pfeffer, Jeffrey, and Gerald R. Salancik. 1978. *The External Control of Organizations: A Resource Dependence Perspective*. New York: Harper and Row.

Popielarz, Pamela A., and J. Miller McPherson. 1995. On the Edge or In Between: Niche Position, Niche Overlap, and the Duration of Voluntary Association Membership. *American Journal of Sociology* 101 (3): 698–720.

Pressman, Jeffrey L., and Aaron Wildavsky. 1984. *Implementation: How Greater Ex-*

pectations in Washington Are Dashed in Oakland. 3rd ed. Berkeley: University of California Press.

Proyecto sobre filantropía y sociedad civil. 2005. *Encuesta nacional sobre filantropía y sociedad civil*. Instituto Tecnológico Autónoma de México. http://www.filantropia .itam.mx/docs/ENAFI—2005.pdf (accessed January 16, 2007).

Putnam, Robert. 1993. *Making Democracy Work: Civic Traditions in Modern Italy*. Princeton, NJ: Princeton University Press.

———. 2000. *Bowling Along: The Collapse and Revival of American Community*: Simon and Schuster.

R. Ayuntamiento de Nuevo Laredo. 2006. *Nuevo Laredo: Una ciudad con visión de inversión*. Nuevo Laredo.

La Reforma. 2004. Gana Limosna al Altruismo. May 23, 4B.

Rico Valera, Gabriel. 2002. La Junta de Asistencia Privada. *La Filantropía en México*, no. 10.

Rodríguez, Victoria E. 1997. *Decentralization in Mexico: From Reforma Municipal to Solidaridad to Nuevo Federalismo*. Boulder, CO: Westview Press.

Rubio, Luis, and Roberto Newell. 1984. *Mexico's Dilemma: The Political Origins of Economic Crisis*. Boulder, CO: Westview Press.

Safa Barraza, Patricia. 1997. *Experiencias de Colaboración Binacional en la Frontera México-Estados Unidos*.Mexico City: DEMOS, A.C. / Inter-American Foundation.

Salamon, Lester M. 1987. Of Market Failure, Voluntary Failure, and Third-Party Government: Toward a Theory of Government-Nonprofit Relations in the Modern Welfare State. *Nonprofit and Voluntary Sector Quarterly* 16 (1–2): 29–49.

Salamon, Lester M., Helmut K. Anheire, and Associates. 1999. Civil Society in Comparative Perspective. In *Global Civil Society: Dimensions of the Nonprofit Sector*, edited by L. M. Salamon et al. Baltimore: Center for Civil Society Studies.

Salamon, Lester M., S. Wojciech Sokolowski, and Helmut K. Anheire. 2000. Social Origins of Civil Society: An Overview. Working Papers of the John Hopkins Comparative Nonprofit Sector Project.

Salazar, Joanna. 1999. Sustainable Development in San Diego-Tijuana? The Case of the International Wastewater Plant. In *Sustainable Development in San Diego-Tijuana: Environmental, Social, and Economic Implications of Interdependence*, edited by M. Spalding. La Jolla, CA: Center for U.S.–Mexican Studies.

Salzman, Harold, and G. William Domhoff. 1983. Nonprofit Organization and the Corporate Community. *Social Science History* 7:205–216.

Sánchez, Roberto. 1990. Health and Environmental Risks of the Maquiladoras in Mexicali. *Natural Resources Journal* 30 (1): 163–186.

Sánchez Munguía, Vicente. 2004. *El revestimiento del Canal Todo Americano: ¿Competencia o cooperación por el agua en la frontera México-Estados Unidos?* Tijuana: El Colegio de la Frontera Norte, Plaza y Valdes Editores.

Savas, E. S. 1977. *The Organization and Efficiency of Solid Waste Collection*. Lexington, MA: D.C. Health.

Schmidt, Samuel. 1997. Stereotypes, Culture, and cooperation in the U.S.–Mexican Borderlands. In *Borders and Border Regions in Europe and North America*, edited by P. Ganster, A. Sweedler, J. Scott, and W. Dieter-Eberwein. San Diego: San Diego State University Press.

Scholte, Jan Aart. 2004. Civil Society and Democratically Accountable Governance. *Government and Opposition* 39 (2): 211.

Schumpeter, Joseph. 1942. *Capitalism, Socialism, and Democracy*. New York: Harper and Row.

Scrivner, Gary N. 2001. A Brief History of Tax Policy Changes Affecting Charitable Organizations. In *The Nature of the Nonprofit Sector*, edited by J. S. Ott. Boulder, CO: Westview Press.

Secretaría de Gobernación. 2003. *Encuesta nacional sobre cultura política y prácticas ciudadanas: Resumen de resultados*. Mexico City: Secretaría de Gobernación.

Secretaría de Infraestructura Urbana y Ecología (SIUE). 1995. *Proyecto Integral de Agua Potable: Resumen Ejecutivo*. Hermosillo, Sonora: Secretaría de Infraestructura Urbana y Ecología.

Selee, Andrew D. 2006. *The Paradox of Local Empowerment: Decentralization and Democratic Governance in Mexico*. College Park: University of Maryland.

Selznick, Philip. 1966. *TVA and the Grass Roots: A Study in the Sociology of Formal Organization*. New York: Harper and Row.

Shaw, Bill, and Frederick R. Post. 1993. A Moral Basis for Corporate Philanthropy. *Business Ethics* 12 (10): 745–751.

Siddiquee, Noore Alam. 2005. Public Accountability in Malaysia: Challenges and Critical Concerns. *International Journal of Public Administration* 28 (2): 107.

Sinclair, Michelle, and Joseph Galaskiewicz. 1997. Corporate-Nonprofit Partnerships: Varieties and Covariates. *New York Law School Law Review* 41:1059–1090.

Sistema de Solicitudes de Información (SISI). 2006. *Estadísticas del SISI*. Instituto Federal de Acceso a la Información Pública. http://www.ifai.org.mx/textos/stats.xls (accessed August 14, 2006).

Sklair, Leslie. 2000. Global Capitalism and Sustainable Development: Exploring the Contradictions. In *Shared Spaces: Rethinking the U.S.–Mexico Border Environment*, edited by L. Herzog. La Jolla, CA: Center for U.S.–Mexican Studies.

Skocpol, Theda, and Morris P. Fiorina. 1999. *Civic Engagement in American Democracy*. Washington, DC: Brookings Institution Press; Russell Sage Foundation.

Spalding, Mark J., and John J. Audley. 1997. *Promising Potential for the U.S.–Mexico Border and the for the Future: An Assessment of the BECC / NADBank Institutions*. Washington, DC: National Wildlife Federation.

Spalding, Ruth J. 1981. State Power and its Limits: Corporatism in Mexico. *Comparative Political Studies* 14 (2): 139–161.

Sprouse, Terry, Dennis Cory, and Robert Varady. 1996. Aquifer Contamination and Safe Drinking Water: The Recent Santa Cruz County Experience. In *Hydrology and Water Resources in Arizona and the Southwest*, vol. 26. Proceedings of the 1996

Meeting of the Arizona Section, American Water Resource Association and Hydrology Section, Arizona-Nevada Academy of Science.

Stauber, John, and Sheldon Rampton. 1995. *Toxic Sludge is Good for You: Lies, Damn Lies and the Public Relations Industry*. Monroe, ME: Common Courage Press.

Staudt, Kathleen, and Irasema Coronado. 2002. *Fronteras No Más: Toward Social Justice at the U.S.–Mexico Border*. New York: Palgrave Macmillan.

Stendardi, Edward J. 1992. Corporate Philanthropy: The Redefinition of Enlightened Self-Interest. *Social Science Journal* 29 (1): 21–30.

Stepan, Alfred. 1978. *The State and Society: Peru in Comparative Perspective*. Princeton, NJ: Princeton University Press.

Stevens, Evelyn P. 1974. *Protest and Response in Mexico*. Cambridge, MA: MIT Press.

Stokes, Susan C. 1995. Politics and Latin America's Urban Poor: Reflections from a Lima Shantytown. *Latin American Research Review* 26 (2): 75–101.

Sunstein, Cass R. 1996. Social Norms and Social Roles. *Columbia Law Review* 96 (4): 903–968.

Tarrow, Sidney. 1994. *Power in Movement: Social Movement, Collective Action, and Politics*. New York: Cambridge University Press.

———. 2000. *Beyond Globalization: Why Creating Transnational Social Movements Is So Hard and When It Is Most Likely to Happen*. Global Solidarity Dialogue. http://www.antenna.nl/waterman/tarrow.html (accessed October 21, 2004).

Teichman, Judith A. 1988. *Policymaking in Mexico: From Boom to Crisis*. Boston: Allen and Unwin.

Texas Agricultural Experiment Station. 2005. Drought Watch on the Rio Grande. El Paso: Texas A&M University System: Agricultural Research and Extension Center, El Paso.

Texas Center for Policy Studies (TCPS). 2002. *The Dispute over Shared Waters of the Rio Grande/Río Bravo: A Primer*. http://www.environmentaldefense.org/documents/2874—RioGrande—waterdispute.pdf (accessed October 15, 2006).

Thompson, Michael, Richard Ellis, and Aaron Wildavsky. 1990. *Cultural Theory*. Boulder, CO: Westview Press.

Thorup, Cathryn L. 1991. The Politics of Free Trade and the Dynamics of Cross-Border Coalitions in U.S.–Mexico Relations. *Columbia Journal of World Business* 26 (11): 12–26.

———. 1993. Redefining Governance in North America: Citizeen Diplomacy and Cross-Border Coalitions. *Enfoque* (Spring). La Jolla: Center for U.S.–Mexican Studies.

Tilly, Charles. 1978. *From Mobilization to Revolution*. Reading, MA: Addison-Wesley.

Tocqueville, Alexis de. 1969. *Democracy in America*. Translated by G. Lawrence. Edited by J. P. Mayer. New York: Harper Perennial.

Turner, Charles, Edwin Hamlyn, and Oscar Ibáñez Hernández. 2003. The Challenge of Balancing Water Supply and Demand in Paso del Norte. In *The U.S.–Mexican Border Environment: Binational Water Management Planning*, edited by S. Michel. San Diego: San Diego State University Press.

United States Customs and Border Patrol. 2006. *Performance and Accountability Report: Fiscal Year 2006*. Washington, DC.

Useem, Michael. 1987. Corporate Philanthropy. In *The Nonprofit Sector: A Research Handbook*, edited by Walter W. Powell. New Haven, CT: Yale University Press.

Varady, Robert, and Maura Mack. 1995. Transboundary Water Resources and Public Health. *Journal of Environmental Health* 57 (8): 8–14.

Verduzco, Gustavo. 2003. *Organizaciones no lucrativas: Visión de su trayectoria en México*. Mexico City: El Colegio de México, Centro Mexicano para la Filantropía.

Verduzco, Gustavo, Regina List, and Lester M. Salamon. 1999. Mexico. In *Global Civil Society: Dimensions of the Nonprofit Sector*, edited by L. M. Salamon et al. Baltimore: Center for Civil Society Studies.

Verduzco Chávez, Basilio. 2001. Contribuciones del ambientalismo a la movilización de la sociedad civil: Un model interpretativo de la experiencia en la frontera México-Estados Unidos. *Región y Sociedad* 8 (22): 3–48.

Villacorta, Claudia, and Ricardo Martínez. 2005. Dispelling a Myth of Industrial Wastewater Pollution in Tijuana. *Southwest Hydrology* 4 (5): 30–31.

Wakida, Fernando, and Karen Riveles. 1997. *The Tijuana River Basin: Basic Environmental and Socioeconomic Data*. San Diego: Institute for Regional Studies of the Californias.

Walzer, Michael. 2003. A Better Vision: The Idea of Civil Society. In *The Civil Society Reader*, edited by V. A. Hodgkinson and M. W. Foley. Hanover: Tufts University, University Press of New England.

Ward, Peter. 1986. *Welfare Politics in Mexico: Papering over the Cracks*. London: Allen and Unwin.

Ward, Peter, and Victoria E. Rodríguez. 1999. *New Federalism and State Government in Mexico: Bringing the States Back In*. Austin: LBJ School of Public Affairs at the University of Texas.

Weisbrod, Burton. 1988. *The Nonprofit Economy*. Cambridge, MA: Harvard University Press.

Weyland, Kurt. 1996. *Democracy without Equity: Failures of Reform in Brazil*. Pittsburgh: University of Pittsburgh Press.

Wiarda, Howard J. 1973. Toward a Framework for the Study of Political Change in the Iberic-Latin World: The Corporative Model. *World Politics* 25 (January): 206–235.

Wiarda, Howard J., and Carlos Guajardo. 1988. Mexico: The Unravelling of a Corporatist Regime. *Journal of Interamerican Studies and World Affairs* 30 (4): 1–28.

William and Flora Hewlett Foundation. 2001. *Annual Report 2000*. http://www.hewlett.org/AboutUs/AnnualReports/2000AnnualReport.htm (accessed June 2, 2006).

Willis, Eliza, Christopher da C. B. Garman, and Stephan Haggard. 1999. The Politics of Decentralization in Latin America. *Latin American Research Review* 34 (1): 7–55.

Winder, David. 2004. *Innovations in Strategic Philanthropy: Comparative Lessons from Asia, Africa, Latin America, and Central and Eastern Europe: The Case of Mexico*. New York: Synergos Institute.

Wolpert, Julian, and Thomas Reiner. 1980. *The Metropolitan Philadelphia Philanthropy Study*. Philadelphia: School of Public and Urban Policy, University of Pennsylvania.

Woodhouse, Betsy. 2005. An End to Mexico's Rio Grande Deficit? *Southwest Hydrology* 4(5): 19–20.

Yang, Tseming. 2004. *The Effectiveness of the NAFTA Environmental Side Agreement's Citizen Submission Process*. http://www.vermontlaw.edu/faculty/faclibrary/tyang/CECMetales1.pdf (accessed September 2006).

Yashar, Deborah. 1999. Democracy, Indigenous Movements, and the Postliberal Challenge in Latin America. *World Politics* 52 (1): 76–104.

Zabin, Carol. 1997. Nongovernmental Organizations in Mexico's Northern Border. *Journal of Borderlands Studies* 7 (1): 41–67.

Zakour, M. J., and D. F. Gilespie. 1969. The Power and Functions of Boards of Directors: A Theoretical Synthesis. *American Journal of Sociology* 75 (1): 97–111.

———. 1998. Effects of Organizational Type and Localism on Volunteerism and Resource Sharing During Disasters. *Nonprofit and Voluntary Sector Quarterly* 27:49–65.

Zald, Mayer N. 1969. The Power and Functions of Boards of Directors: A Theoretical Synthesis. *American Journal of Sociology* 75 (1): 97–111.

Index

About the Author

Daniel M. Sabet is currently a visiting professor at Georgetown University. A former Fulbright-García Robles fellow in Mexico, Sabet holds a PhD in political science from Indiana University. While conducting research for this book, Sabet was affiliated with the Colegio de la Frontera Norte (COLEF) and the University of California, San Diego, where he helped coordinate the Border Water Project. Although he continues to focus on civil society in the border region, his most recent research and policy work explores the role of civil society in improving public security and holding police agencies accountable.